My Date with Cancer

Dr. Moitreyee Saha

PARTRIDGE

A Penguin Random House Company

ISBN: Softcover   978-1-4828-2099-7
                 eBook   978-1-4828-2098-0

To order additional copies of this book, contact
Partridge India
000 800 10062 62
orders.india@partridgepublishing.com

www.partridgepublishing.com/india

"WITHOUT YOU,
IT WOULD NOT BE POSSIBLE"

Dedicated to Sqd. Ldr. Chitta Ranjan Saha and
Mrs. Chitra Saha (Parents), Dr. Benu Gopal
Saha (Husband) and Daughters, Gargi and
Gauravi (Nini).

"A mother is the truest friend we have, when trials heavy and sudden fall upon us; when adversity takes the place of prosperity; when friends desert us; when trouble thickens around us, still will she cling to us, and endeavor with her kind precepts and counsels to dissipate the cloud of darkness, and cause peace to return to our hearts."

– Washington Irving

This sketch depicts strength that my mother possesses and her struggle coupled with pains and tribulations, to achieve the sweet secret of life; filled with happiness, beauty and joy.

– Gauravi Saha (Nini)

CONTENTS

FOREWORD

It is indeed my pleasure to write a foreword, for the book "My date with Cancer" authored by Dr. Moitreyee Saha. I have known Dr. Moitreyee Saha for more than two decades and seen her grow from a young teacher and researcher to a very mature and empowered woman, full of enthusiasm and optimism. Her passion and involvement for anything she takes up is highly appreciable.

Dr. Moitreyee is one of my favourite research students. She has worked under my guidance for her Ph.D. She is sincere, warm, dynamic and a caring teacher. On a personal level, I know her to be a caring mother of two intelligent and cultured daughters, Gargi and Gauravi. Both have studied in Birla College Kalyan, when I was the Principal there.

I appreciate the remarkable efforts taken by Dr. Moitreyee to participate in number of programs by Cenray Mahila Pragati. A dedicated teacher, talented singer and a proficient dancer, she is an enthusiastic researcher who spends time and takes pain by continuing to gain new knowledge in her field—Botany and Biotechnology. She has won accolades for her research papers, in national and international conferences. We have worked jointly on a major research project from University Grants commission (UGC), New Delhi and have co-authored a number of scientific papers published in national and international journals.

Life was bliss for her until the sudden confrontation with one of the most deadly disease . . . Cancer! She accepted doctor's verdict and instead of bowing down, took the challenge head on and started her fight with cancer.

This book, "My date with Cancer" is a memoir, of Dr. Moitreyee Saha's two years struggle with cancer and a true story of how she fought cancer and survived Ovarian Cancer stage IV, underwent six cycles of chemotherapy and a surgery. She underwent "pan-hysterectomy, appendectomy and 4 layer of complete Omentectomy."

Dr. Moitreyee stands for "Making things possible from impossible". She wrote this book to share the agony she experienced, dealt with and learnt to share with all cancer patients, their family members and friends. In her own words there were days when holding a pen was painful, but she overcame her physical disability. Though traumatic, it was cathartic for her to write this book and as she started to write she could not stop, time passed by and it gradually developed into a worth reading memoir.

To all intents and purpose, this book came from Dr. Moitreyee's desire to bare the minute details of her struggle as she fought cancer; her descriptions are honest and at times bleak. Several thoughts must have come to her mind but through it all she shows herself to be a strong, resilient woman determined to tackle the disease head-on while firmly refusing to get bogged down by the disease. The dialogues with her daughters, her involvement with them even when she struggled to survive shows her grit and determination.

It was her strong will power and a positive attitude which helped her to adapt to life changes and crisis as they arose. Her parents, her husband (Dr. Saha), daughters (Gargi and Gauravi), relatives, friends, students and colleagues were deeply concerned as to why, she was passing through this traumatic experience, but Dr. Moitreyee's energy and enthusiasm has brought hope and strength to others who have endured the desperation and horror of living with cancer as she started counseling other patients.

It shows her unflappable outlook on life which distinguishes her as she undergoes two more surgeries and treatment with nuclear medicines. A winner all the way, she writes, "My fight with cancer . . . which now . . . has taken a new turn as . . . Cancer revisits," but tells her husband, "Together we crossed the hurdle once and together will cross it again." She set an example when she was driven into the realities of her existence. The way she handled adversity is admirable, especially given some of the tribulations she experienced.

I extend my greetings and felicitations to the author of this precious book. I highly appreciate the commendable efforts and labour put in by Dr. Moitreyee Saha for writing this truly inspiring story of her journey against cancer.

I am sure the book will become a learning experience for cancer patients, their family and friends. I recommend this book to all those who want a deep insight into the struggle of a cancer patient and her family. Something as destructive and life threatening as cancer can be catalyst for a positive change . . . A must read.

Dr. Naresh Chandra
M.Sc., M.Phil., Ph.D
Pro-Vice Chancellor
University of Mumbai

AUTHORS PREFACE

This book is a memoir. It is about my life journey, which suddenly took an ugly turn and I stood stunned, not knowing what to do. "My date with cancer" is a true story . . . my story, which I want to share. The story begins with the diagnosis of cancer and stresses on the need for emotional calmness and mental well-being in addition to physical healing. In my cancer journey, having faced the dreaded disease twice, I familiarized myself with every nuance of my personality. I learnt that though life was messed up, to run away from the bitter truth was not the solution. And yes! The story ends with an important lesson that grit and determination conquers all.

The book was conceived, after I met Dr. Indu Nair (Counselor). She convinced me to fulfill my dream to write a book. A seed of thought was nurtured and it grew into a full-fledged memoir. While writing this book, I tried to produce a narrative in the same sequence as it happened. This book is the story of my life for the two years when I stayed positive, strong willed and welcomed the changes in me and my life. My spiritual growth was amazing and my faith in human relationship was reaffirmed. I realized that no one fights cancer alone. Family, friends and colleagues play a positive role in one's cancer journey.

This momentous episode in my life might have some relevance with the life of cancer patients, their family and friends. If yes! Then one can find little things, thoughts and gestures which go a long way towards holistic healing. This was my cancer journey . . . I am not a medical doctor and it is said that, every cancer patient have their own set of problems and a different approach. However what every cancer patient should do, is to immediately consult a doctor, keep the doors of communication open, be positive and get well. Holistic healing of cancer is the healing of mind, body and soul. It is a lifestyle approach . . . a wholesome approach where everyone can contribute.

As I am ready to embark on another leg of my life's journey . . . I pray for my near and dear, friends, and colleagues and for those who won't quit the fight . . . "Cancer is curable" . . . believe it.

OM SĀI RAM

ACKNOWLEDGMENT

I would like to take this opportunity to offer my heartfelt gratitude to all those, who have helped me to understand that, "Cancer is curable," and have stood by me, when two years ago my life almost collapsed.

My prayers and thanks to Late Gurudas Saha (father-in-law) and Late Amiyabala Saha (mother-in-law) for igniting the fire to fight. Sometimes the things we feel deepest are the most difficult to express. There seems to be no words that say, how thankful I am to Retd. Sqd. Ldr. C. R. Saha (father), Mrs. Chitra Saha (mother) and Dr. B.G Saha (husband). In my cancer journey, they stood by me, comforted me and helped me to remain calm and collected. How can I forget my beautiful daughters, my heart and my soul, Gargi and Gauravi, their mischief and laughter, kept me in high spirits, I am thankful to them for encouraging me for every little thing. I thank my family members Ashish-Da, Bipasha, Natasha, Ankan, Ujjal-Da, Sonali, Anjan, Arun-Da, Anu-Di and Ashrut for silently and patiently extending their support during this grueling journey.

My deepest gratitude is towards my doctors, Dr. P.G. Joshi, Dr. Leena Sonekar, Dr. Atul Mokashi, Dr. Meghana Bhalerao, Dr. Pratima B. Chipalkatti, Dr. Prakash Patil, Dr. B.K. Smruti, Dr. Mannan K. Jadliwala, Dr. B.A. Krishna, Dr. Nupur, Dr. Priyanka, Dr. Shefali Gokhale, Dr. Satya Prakash Bhattacherjee and Dr. Indu Nair as they inspired me to stay positive during my cancer journey.

I extend sincere thanks to my guide Dr. Naresh Chandra for his unceasing words of encouragement. I thank Dr. M. K. Pejaver (Principal) from the bottom of my heart for her guidance, love and cooperation. I am thankful to Dr. M. S. Mulgaonkar for her wholehearted support and cooperation. I thank my colleague Dr. V.M. Jamdhade, for his caring concern and moral support. I thank Dr. Kalpana Phal and Prof. Francena Luis for their warm friendship.

I also wish to express sincere thanks to my dear friends Babji and Alka, Sarita and Manjul, Anil and Sudha, Gargi's friends, Prerana, Sāi Neelesh, Shreyas and Aaron for lending their support during this journey and sharing my laughter, pain and tears.

With deepest gratitude I wish to thank my father, Ashish-Da, Gargi, Nini (Gauravi) and Mr. B.C. Mishra for their help in editing the book. Thanks from the bottom of my heart to Benu for helping me in everyway while I was writing the book and special thanks to Gargi for the cover page painting which beautifully depicts the inspiration I derived from nature during my cancer journey. Heartfelt thanks to Nini for her creative visualization of my triumph over cancer through her sketch. Thanks to Supreet Sahoo, for his artistic inputs. Thanks to my doctors, colleagues, friends and my family members for contributing to the chapter Reflections and Impressions. A special thank goes to my publisher Partridge India, a Penguine Random house company 1663 Liberty Drive, Bloomington, IN and also to Farrina Gailey, Senior Publishing Consultant and Gemma Ramos, Publishing Services Associate of Partridge Company.

Finally I would like to pay my obeisance to God almighty for his blessings.

RELATIONSHIPS IN SAHA CLAN WITH SELF

Self: Moitreyee Saha (Rina)
Husband: Benugopal Saha (Benu)
Daughter: Gargi
Daughter: Gauravi (Nini)

Father-in-law: (Late) Gurudas Saha
Mother-in-law: (Late) Amiyabala Saha
Father: Chitta Ranjan Saha
Mother: Chitra Saha

Brother: Ashish Kumar Saha (Ashish-Da)
Sister-in-law: Bipasha Saha
Niece: Natasha (Mimi)
Nephew: Ankan

Brother: Ujjal Kumar Saha (Ujjal-Da)
Sister-in-law: Sonali Saha
Nephew: Anjan

Sister-in-law: Anupama Saha (Anu-Di)
Brother-in-law: Arun Saha (Arun-Da)
Nephew: Ashrut

DOCTORS AT CENTURY RAYON HOSPITAL (SHAHAD)

Dr. P.G. Joshi M.B.B.S., A.F.I.H. Industrial Physician.
Dr. Leena Sonekar M.D., Medicine.
Dr. Meghana Bhalerao M.B.B.S., DGO.

DOCTORS AT BOMBAY HOSPITAL AND MEDICAL CENTRE, 12 NEW MARINE LINES MUMBAI

Dr. Pratima B. Chipalkatti M.D., DGO, Consultant Obstetrician and Gynecologist
Dr. Prakash Patil M.S. (Bom), D.N.B. (All India), F.I.C.S. (Oncology) Cancer Surgeon, Specialist in Thoracic Oncosurgery
Dr. B.K, Smruti Medical and Hemato-oncologist
Dr. Mannan K Jadliwala M.N.A.M.S. (Gen Surgery) Hon. Surgeon
Dr. Krishna MBBS, DRM (Bom), MNAMS, Consultant and Head Dept. of Nuclear Medicine & PET Imaging
Dr. Nupur M.D. students working under Dr. Pratima B. Chipalkatti
Dr. Priyanka M.D. students working under Dr. Pratima B. Chipalkatti
Dr. Indu Nair (Counselor)

INLAKS AND BUDHRANI HOSPITAL, KOREGOAN PARK PUNE

Dr. Shefali Gokhale DNB (Nuclear medicine), D.I.P.C.B. (Nuclear cardiology USA), Consultant, Nuclear medicine

<u>DR. BHATTACHERJEE CLINIC</u>
<u>& PATHOLOGY LAB, NASIK</u>

Dr. Satya Prakash Bhattacherjee D.M.S., B.M.S., M.D. (E.H.) D.M.L.T., D.E.C.T. (Calcutta), P.E.T., F.H.W.T. (Red Cross Society) Homeopathy

Chapter 1

My early years . . .

Our family, a typical Bengali household had five members—my father, mother, two elder brothers and self. My father, an officer in the *Indian Air Force*, was a disciplined military man who believed in the motto, *"Service before Self."* My mother, an intelligent and loving home maker, was a role model for us. My elder brothers—*Ashish-Da* and *Ujjal-Da* (*"Da or dada" is a respectful suffix added to the name of elder brothers in Bengali language*) were four and two years my senior respectively. I was the youngest of the lot and my father's darling daughter. My father called me *"Maitreyee" (Moitreyee in Bengali)* inspired by a woman seer and a philosopher mentioned in the ancient scriptures of the *Rig Veda. Maitreyee* was a learned lady from the, *golden age of women* and my father wanted that his daughter should study and be an educated independent lady, like *Maitreyee.* He filled our house with books and said, *"Education is priceless and it is something that will shape the rest of your life."* My mother called me *"Rina"* (*pet name*) and *Ujjal-Da* affectionately called me *"Rinki."*

As far as my early years goes, it was filled with warmth, love, fun and frolic. There was plenty of adventure as every two to three year my father was posted to different *Air force stations* throughout *India*. Every time he was posted out, we would pack our luggage and move to a new destination. We loved travelling and because of our nomadic life style, we could stay in different cities in East, West, North and South of *India*. Exploring new places, meeting people and understanding their beliefs, cuisine and culture was our passion. We made new friends and tried to learn different languages. The sheer diversity was staggering and a learning process for us. My passion for gardening, singing, dancing, painting and reading was nurtured by some great teachers I met in different states. I learnt *Bharatanatyam* and *Manipuri* (*dance form*) in *Bangalore* and *Chandigarh*, *Hindustani classical* (*vocals*) and *oil painting* in *Chandigarh* and *Kanpur*. My schooling was from "*Kendriya Vidyalaya*" in different states of *India* and higher studies from *Bangalore* and *Kanpur*. The frequent change of schools and colleges however, never hampered my grades.

Beautiful memories of time spent with loving parents, simple sheltered existence with devoted and adventurous brothers and a childhood which was immensely secure emotionally, pre-dominates my childhood memories.

I hero-worshipped *Ashish-Da* and was overjoyed to see him receiving his Engineering Degree. His campus placement was with "*Universal Electricals*," *Faridabad* and then he switched to "*Escorts Ltd.*," *Faridabad* (*Haryana*). In 1982, he joined "*VIP Industries*" at *Nasik* (*Maharashtra*).

When my father was posted to *Kanpur*, *Ujjal-Da* completed Masters and I did B.Sc., from *Christ Church College* (*Kanpur University*). As a teenager, college was all about making and meeting friends. It was time spent in exploring new ideas, discovering new career options, attending lectures and missing some. If college was about discussing professors and their notes, then it was also about movies, storybooks and cloths.

Ujjal-Da joined the *"Indian Army"* as an officer (*short service commission*) and was posted first to *Jhansi* (*Uttar Pradesh*) and then to *Kashmir*. While I was studying in M.Sc. Part II (*Christ Church College, Kanpur*), my father was posted to *Air O.P. Nasik* (*choice posting*). Mother stayed back with me in *Kanpur*, till my examination was over. After exams, it was time to say goodbye to all my college friends as I was now ready to explore a new city . . . *Nasik* (*Maharashtra)*.

In *Nasik*, I remained unhinged as it was nerve wracking to wait for my results. I could not decide whether to study further (*Ph.D.*) or accept the job of a lecturer. My indecisiveness frustrated me and I sorely missed my friends. My parents told me to relax, forget about my impending results and start exploring the city. *Nasik,* a beautiful old city had history attached to it. This city of temples was one of the holiest places in *India*, with many ancient Hindu temples dotting the banks of the holy river, *Godavari*. The area around *Artillery Centre, Deolali* and *Air O.P.* was breathtaking. My favorite was the open fields, gliders club and paragliding facility in *Artillery Centre*. I was enjoying discovering the city with my brothers when *out of the blue* my marriage was arranged by my parents (*Indian custom*).

I married a wonderful young man, *Dr. Benu Gopal Saha* (*Benu*), on *29th May 1985*. *Benu* was doctorate (*Ph.D.*) from BITS *Pilani*, recently transferred from "*Grasim Industries Ltd.*," *Nagda* (*Madhya Pradesh*) to "*Century Rayon Ltd.*" *Shahad* (*Mumbai*). *Benu's* parents came from *West Bengal* to get him married. His father (*businessman*) was a great sportsperson having played football for various clubs in *Bengal*. *Benu's* mother was a home maker. His sister "*Anupama,*" in short *Anu-Di* ("*Di or didi" is a suffix in Bengali language denoting elder sister*) and brother-in-law "*Arun-Da*" lived in *Powai* (*Mumbai*).

Arun-Da and my parents set the foundation, after taking our consent and then blessed this holy union and marriage. It was a traditional Indian Hindu wedding. Before marriage, I lived a checkered life of moving to different places in *India* however, we settled in *Shahad* (*Maharashtra*), after marriage. *Benu* was a brilliant sports person like his father. He played football as a kid but later, he concentrated on indoor games. He played badminton, table tennis, billiards and snooker. He was good in carrom and an excellent swimmer. He won most of the tournaments he participated in and received championship award quite often.

I was his opposite as my interest in sports was almost nil. I preferred spending my time in reading, gardening or listening to music. *Benu* was a talkative person and I was a good listener. It is said that opposites attract and the same happened here, with my love for books, music etc. and his passion for sports, we started sharing and enjoying each other's hobbies immensely.

After my M.Sc. result was declared, *Benu* encouraged me to put my education to good use and motivated me to study further. Soon I was working as a lecturer at "*B.N. Bandodkar College of Science, Thane.*" I also took admission for *M. Phil.* and received the degree from *University of Mumbai* in *May 1989*.

The year *1989* was auspicious for us because, after five blissful years of marriage, we were blessed with my elder daughter '*Gargi*' on *18*th *November 1989*. My father who was well versed in ancient literatures, named her "*Gargi.*" Gargi was the name of a *Vedic prophetess* from *Rig Veda,* a great natural philosopher who questioned the origin of all existence. After four years, on *29*th *October 1993*, my younger daughter was born. *Benu* named her "*Gauravi*" and *Anjan*, my nephew named his doll-like cousin, "*Nini*" which became her pet name.

Benu and I decided that we would try to do all the right things to secure our future. We brought home decent salaries and made proper savings. We invested in shares and fixed deposits in each member's name. Life insurances and other investments were done for tax benefits. Our bank balance seemed reasonably healthy. Our major assets were a scooter, car and a flat purchased in a prestigious locality. *Yes!* We were progressing towards building a comfortable niche for ourselves.

Well, look into the lifestyle of any Indian middle class family, it is the same story everywhere and we were not, in any way different.

I was a happily married young mother, who was complacent that life was on the right track, everything seemed to be in place. *Yes*, there were some ups and downs; however, whenever some major crisis cropped up, they were always solved with the help of our family and friends.

Benu was a pious person and a staunch devotee of *Śrī Sāi Bābā of Shirdi*. He believed that his rise from his humble beginning to the current stature was *Sāi Bābā's* blessings. He looked upon *Śrī Sāi* as his *God*. Every year we religiously visited *Shirdi (a small village in Kopargaon Taluka, in Ahmednagar district, Maharashtra)* for his benediction and also to thank *Sāi Bābā* for his blessings and the strength of mind he bestowed on us to face life. Like my father, I was neither really a religious person nor an atheist; but *Benu's* unfathomable devotion and faith in *Sāi Bābā*, slowly converted me. Initially for me, these trips were mere outings for enjoyment but when they changed to spiritual journey, I don't know.

Life was a mixture of success and failure, pleasure and pain, ups and downs.

Though contented with my personal life, I was not exactly happy with my professional life. I was a Senior lecturer with *M.Sc.* and *M.Phil.* Degrees, but these degrees did not satisfy me. There was something, which was urging me to study further, do some research work and join for *Ph.D.* This was an important but a difficult decision to make as I was a working mother with two hyperactive daughters.

Research work called for commitment and hard work. It was challenging and time consuming but I was prepared for it because *Benu* encouraged me to study further and get a doctorate degree like him. My guide *Dr. Naresh Chandra, Pro-Vice Chancellor, University of Mumbai,* inspired me to work hard and strive for the best. I was awarded doctorate degree from *University of Mumbai* after five years of research work. Our family rejoiced when the prefix "*Dr.*" was added to my name. My family and friends called me *Rina* and I was addressed as *Dr. Moitreyee Saha* in my professional world.

Time passed and slowly I realized that I remained extremely busy and my responsibilities grew every day. Balancing my personal and professional life required good managerial skill.

Somewhere down the line, I also realized that my carefree and daredevil attitude was lost forever. My life was a roller coaster ride; the routine was almost same for many years with few minor changes as my daughters grew up. Every morning, I got up early to study and the same habit was inculcated by my daughters. Getting my daughters ready for school was a race against time.

After sending them to school, *did I relax?*

Yes! You guessed right.

Where was the time to relax?

We stayed in *Shahad* and my college was in *Thane,* which meant commuting. I relied on *auto-rickshaws* and *local trains.*

Need I say more?

True, every working mother goes through this grind for few years.

As a lecturer, I had to be well prepared with my lectures and stay abreast with my knowledge. Working in a college gave me the opportunity to be surrounded by talented young minds who kept me charged. Being involved in research work, the day to day challenges in the lab, experiments, students, work-shops and conferences kept me extremely busy.

My dream to write books on *Genetics or Biotechnology* remained a dream.

Why?

Well, with my busy schedule, where was the time?

Reaching home during rush hour was an ordeal, something that any *Mumbaikar* can vouch for. Home sweet home was always filled with music, dance, laughter and my husband being a sportsperson, lots of sports events to attend. I was a member of '*Cenray Mahila Pragati*', a ladies club of *Century Rayon Company*. I had the opportunity to take active part in various programs organized by the club. There were friends, outings and get-togethers. Evenings also meant homework, studies and dinner.

My life was all about completing a task in hand and then immediately moving on to the next task without a pause. In fact, I was like any other multitasking working mother who wanted to excel in both her personal and professional life and was always of the opinion that twenty four hours in a day was less for fulfilling all our commitments.

Our little angels were growing up and they made us so proud. *Gargi* and *Nini* studied in *Holy Cross Convent School*, *Kalyan* and were proficient in academics. They were busy pursuing their hobbies which included dancing, singing, painting, sketching and self-defense (*black belt in karate*). *Gargi* grew up into a beautiful talented young girl. She received the best student award and stood second in her school for SSC examination. She joined *Birla College, Kalyan*, where she participated in various co-curricular activities and played badminton (*district level*). The feather in her cap was when she was crowned "*Miss Birla, 2005*" in a personality contest organized by the college. She did well in *HSC Board examinations* and *BITSAT entrance test* (*Birla Institute of Technology and Science Aptitude test*). She left home to study in "*BITS Pilani*" (*Birla Institute of Technology and Science Pilani, Rajasthan*) in 2007.

Nini was such a contrast to *Gargi*. She was attractive in a charming way. Her smile was her best feature. We often admired her extreme meticulousness and punctuality, her perfectly combed hair, neat and tidy uniform. We believed she inherited these qualities from her maternal grandfather (*Defense officer*). She was a talented dancer who kept the audience enthralled. In 2009, *Nini* did well in *SSC examination* and was felicitated by different institutions in *Kalyan* as she topped in two subjects. Like *Gargi*, she joined *Birla College, Kalyan* and was doing well in academics.

Our total involvement with each other made the journey of our life so blissful.

All my family members are well placed, each one prospering in his or her respective spheres. Presently, *Anu-Di, Arun-Da* and their son, *Ashrut* are doing great. *Ashrut* is in *Glasgow* (*Scotland*) for higher studies. My father is working as *General Manager of B.I.S. India* Ltd. *Ashish-Da*, wife *Bipasha*, my niece *Natasha* and nephew *Ankan* are well placed. *Ashish-Da* is now the *Director of VIP Industries, Nasik*. *Ujjal-Da* is working abroad; his wife *Sonali* is a "*Colonel*" in the *Indian Army* and my nephew *Anjan* is working in *Accenture* (*Mumbai*).

However, our life was not always rosy. My mother, *Ashish-Da, Sonali* and I suffered from high B.P., high cholesterol. Later *Bipasha* and I were diagnosed with hypothyroidism. So all of us remain under continuous medical supervision and have to take medicines lifelong. *Bipasha* suffered from brain hemorrhage and survived. *Arun-Da, Bipasha* and *Sonali* underwent major operations. I lost my father-in-law. My mother-in-law was diagnosed with cervical cancer. She was treated at *Nanavati hospital, Mumbai.* This was my life for the last few years but we were a close knit family and we kept in touch with each other sharing our joys and sorrows.

> *The Saha family of five now consisted of many new members and the family as a whole was growing . . . consisting of three generations.*

Though busy, we were enjoying every moment of our life together, as we believed in simple living. *We always felt that the simplest thing in this world is life itself . . . and the most complicated thing . . . is the way we live it.* We were a happy fun loving family, very proud of our achievements.

Life was going at a very fast pace, from a young girl I was now, a mother of two teenaged daughters. I liked to do too many things together, always multitasking and frequently running from one place to another to meet set targets.

Though life was hectic, it was also gratifying . . . it was a blissful journey filled with love and compassion. I was contented in the niche that we created for ourselves . . . and then, what happened in *August 2010* completely shook my family out of our complacency. I call it destiny . . . strange but true . . . I dreamt of writing a book on *Genetics* or *Biotechnology* . . . but never got the time . . . and today . . . here I am . . . writing a book . . . a memoir . . . on two years of my journey . . . *My Cancer Journey.*

Chapter 2

The year that was not meant to be . . .

December 2009; *Gargi* was with us for the semester break. She and *Nini* were busy making plans for the New Year Eve party. We always celebrate the occasion with family and friends at *Century Rayon Club, Shahad*. This year, as usual, there were games, dancing, singing, good food and fireworks to welcome the *New Year, 2010*.

Gargi left for *Pilani*, on *4th January* for her fifth semester. After she left, *Nini* started studying seriously. She finished her XI examination by *March* and after that was busy preparing for her boards and entrance examinations. *February* to *April* I was busy completing syllabus, conducting examinations and correcting papers in college.

By *May*, *Gargi* was home for the semester break. As it was summer holidays, we decided to go for our yearly spiritual journey to *Shirdi*. It was a ritual in our family to visit "*Sāi Mandir*" every year. We thanked *Sadguru Śrī Sāi Mahārāja* for his blessings and humbly surrendered all our desires and worries in his holy feet.

After returning from *Shirdi*, *Gargi* and *Nini* started making arrangements for my wedding anniversary (*29th*

May). This year was special for us as it was our silver wedding anniversary. The entire *Saha clan* turned up to celebrate. It was a joyous occasion spent with my dear relatives and close friends. They made the occasion special and full of happy remembrance. We made a promise, "*The Saha clan will gather again to celebrate our golden wedding anniversary.*"

The new session in college, started in the month of *June* and as always, life was hectic. The demands made in my professional and personal life kept me on my toes. In same month, I lost my mother-in-law. She had led a peaceful life for the last fifteen years as a cancer survivor. She was a gritty old lady of eighty nine years of age and we felt abandoned when she left us.

We realized, it was not often that life turns out
as per our expectations so we must face our fear
and pain, and find a way as life goes on.

Nini was appearing for *HSC* board examination in *February 2011*. She was busy juggling between coaching classes and college as she was also preparing for *IIT-JEE* and *BITSAT entrance examinations* to be held in *April 2011*. She was over-worked, stressed and we were concerned about her erratic, busy time table and the extensive travelling she did to reach her coaching classes. As parents, the year was turning out to be very hectic for us. We looked into the situation realistically and decided to reorganize our schedule. *Benu* would look into her day to day timetable and I planned to take a month leave to be with *Nini* during her board examination.

However, during this period, I felt stressed out, overwhelmed and often wondered whether my hectic schedule was harming me. I started losing my temper on very small issues, was cranky with huge mood swings and was experiencing some kind of physical discomfort like hot flushes, abnormal menstruation cycle, heavy bleeding etc.

I was married at the age of twenty one and had just celebrated my silver wedding anniversary. Now, at forty seven years of age, I was probably entering a new phase of my life—"*Menopause*." This was a troublesome phase but there was no reason to get scared. Thus, lots of advice from elderly people, doctor friends and information from internet and books were gathered. Mindful of the hormonal changes taking place in my body, my mantra was to stay calm because all that registered was that I could not afford to be sick and disturb *Nini's* schedule.

One day, while returning from work, I met *Dr. Leena Sonekar*. We stayed in the same building, so we walked down the lane together. We discussed about her work, my research work etc. Then I told her about the mood swings and the physical discomforts I was facing. We spoke at length about menopause and we discussed about the healing effect of *yoga*.

Dr. Leena asked me for how long I have been suffering from these symptoms. When I told her that they had started recently, she asked me to focus and try to remember if the excessive bleeding with blood clots, that is the abnormal menstruation cycle had indeed started recently or it has been there for a long time. This made me uncomfortable. *I tried to recollect . . . When? When did all this start?*

Dr. Leena then asserted, "*Yoga and exercise is good but everything kept aside, you should go for a routine check-up immediately*".

I agreed, "*Yes doctor, I will come for a check-up, soon.*"

I however, completely forgot about our conversation due to my busy schedule at home and college. *Gargi* was allotted her *PS II* (*Practice school for industrial training*) in *Hyderabad* (*Andhra Pradesh*) for five months. By *July* end, I accompanied *Gargi* to *Hyderabad* as *Benu* was not free to escort her. I decided to turn this trip into a study trip and asked *Snehal Phirke* (*my research student*), to join us. I advised *Snehal* to conduct the literature survey, required for her research work at *IICT* (*Indian institute of chemical technology*), *CCMB* (*Centre for Cellular and Molecular Biology*) and *Hyderabad University*. It was chaotic but a good seven days spent settling *Gargi* as a *PG* (*paying guest*) and also spending some quality time with *Snehal* at various research institutes.

After returning from *Hyderabad*, the pain in my lower back started troubling me again. I felt hassled, tired and worn out. It was *August* . . . monsoon . . . there was continuous heavy rain and *Mumbai* was water-logged. Train services were hampered, *auto-rickshaws* were playing truant, sewage water and rain water filled the roads, drains were overflowing. It was pouring down heavily and umbrellas were merely for show as they hardly kept anyone dry.

On one such rainy day, I was teaching my first year B.Sc. class (*Under-graduates*) when there was dull ache, cramps in my lower abdomen.

What did it indicate? Dysentery! Probably Loose motion!

However as it was an interactive lecture, I soon forgot about the cramps. For rest of the day, there was a bloating sensation in the lower abdomen and a severe backache. Though aware of the serious repercussions of self-medication, I took some medicines and soon enough, the cramps subsided and the pain was bearable.

Second day, it was raining again and as usual *auto-rickshaws* were not available. The relentless monsoon rains had beaten down the people to a very slow pace life. It gave no pleasure to wade through the slush and knee deep puddles. I was drenched walking down from *Thane* station to the college. Blinking my way through the curtain of rain, I reached college just in time. It was a busy day in college and surprisingly I could again feel the cramps in my lower abdomen. I hesitated to pop pills without a doctor's prescription and thought that it was better to go to the hospital that evening and meet *Dr. Joshi* or *Dr. Leena*. As the day proceeded there was non-stop heavy rain, local train services were totally disrupted; reaching home was a problem.

After reaching home, I felt lethargic. Though worried about the cramps, I was too lazy to do anything about it. Hospital was only a five minute walk from my house but heavy rains stopped me from venturing out. My guilt for not heeding *Dr. Leena's* advice, to go for a check-up, troubled me. My excuse that I was busy, seem flimsy and this made me restless.

Nini realized that the abdominal pains, back ache and the cramps were troubling me. She hugged me and asked, *"Why are you not going to the hospital? I feel something is wrong."*

I cuddled her, *"Tomorrow . . . Nini, definitely."*

She pushed me back and scoffed, *"Tomorrow will never come. You will make some excuse, tomorrow."*

I said, *"Promise, I will go for a check-up, tomorrow."*

Still worried she enquired, *"Why don't you take leave, mummy?"*

"I have some important work, don't worry, I will come home early." I assured her.

She warned, *"Don't make any excuses tomorrow."*

On the third day it was cloudy but not raining. I could feel dull ache in my lower abdomen and was feverish. However, by evening, thunder rumbled on the horizon and later torrential rains again disrupted the train service. Again I reached home very late.

Nini was upset, she criticized, *"You promised, mummy!"*

I felt ashamed but by 9:00 p.m. all the doctors must have left, so there was no point going to the hospital.

Hands on her hips she stood in front of me and roared, *"Mummy you always say, promises made is not to be broken!"*

Ashamed, I said, *"Sorry dear."*

Nini asked, *"Can you take leave tomorrow?"*

I explained, *"No, we have a team visiting our department tomorrow. I have to be there but I promise not be late and will definitely consult a doctor tomorrow."*

"Promises are made to be broken!" She shouted trying to make me feel guilty.

The next day in college I developed high fever and a mouth ulcer, which was quiet painful. There was intense pain in my lower abdomen and this frightened me. So after work I went straight to *Century Rayon hospital.* Some kind of fear prompted me to call *Benu* and ask him to be with me.

I wondered if menopause was so painful or was it something worse. I repented to have not heeded *Dr. Leena's* advice. She had asked me to get a routine check-up done.

Oh God! Why did I ignore her advice?

Anyway, *what was done was done*, now we reported to *Dr. P.G. Joshi* the *C.M.O.* (*Chief medical officer*) of *Century Rayon hospital*. *Dr. Joshi* was also our family doctor as he has been treating my family members since the last twenty five years or more. He heard about the symptoms and referred me to a gynecologist. Since the gynecologist was not available immediately, he asked me to meet *Dr. Leena Sonekar*.

After examination, *Dr. Leena* told me softly, "*I can feel something, would like to get a proper picture.*"

She told me, "*Immediately get blood test done for CA125 and also get the ultra-sonography (USG) for abdomen-pelvis done, tomorrow.*"

This was the first time we heard about CA125 test, we wondered what was it?

After the blood test we went home. *Benu* left for club (*to play badminton*) and I sat surfing the internet, I found that *CA125* was *cancer antigen 125* (*tumour marker*). *CA125 test* was done to assess the concentration of *CA125* in blood and it's an accurate method for detecting the presence of ovarian cancer.

Test for Ovarian Cancer! I was stunned.

I immediately called *Sonali* and told her about my suspicion but she asked me to wait for the reports. I then called my College Principal, *Dr. Madhuri Pejaver* and asked her about *CA125*.

She said, "*It is a tumour detection test, but it does not mean that you are suffering from cancer.*"

After that, I buried my suspicions and did not discuss about it any further.

*I however, had an inkling that something
dreadful was going to unfold.*

USG was done on the next day and *Dr. Leena* saw the *USG* report on the third day. It showed, "*The presence of multiple cystic heterogeneous lesion measuring 136x110 mm and moderate free fluid in abdomen and pelvis.*"

Dr. Leena looked hassled after seeing the report. She avoided looking at me and started talking to *Benu*. She made an appointment for a *CT* scan of abdomen and pelvis at *Ajit Scan and Diagnostic Centre, Kalyan* and asked *Benu* to take me there the next day. *Benu* was unaware of the biological terms being used; he felt there was some gynecological complication.

I still remember that evening, *2nd September 2010*, it was *Dahi-Handi* (*Dahi-Handi is a joyous occasion in which youngsters make a human pyramid to reach an earthen pot containing butter, dry fruits and milk hung at a height and breaks it. There is music, dance and prize money for the enthusiastic youngsters. Later the ingredients in the pot are distributed as prasad*). The atmosphere was festive and I wanted to join my friends for the celebration. From my doctors expression however, I could conclude that things were not looking good.

When *Benu* was not present in her chamber, I gently asked *Dr. Leena*, "*Is it cancer, doctor?*"

She was pale and at pains to avoid uttering the "*C*" word. She said softly, "*Get the CT scan done, we will get a clear picture.*"

With all this running around in hospital, getting the tests done, I almost forgot that 2nd *September* was *Sonali's* birthday. She had joined her unit *INHS ASVINI*, (*Colaba Mumbai*) on the same day. When I called to wish her, she wanted to know about the *USG* reports. I told her about the report and said that *Dr. Leena* wanted me to go for a *CT* scan.

She told me, "*When in doubt, it's always better to go for a CT scan.*"

She then said, "*Get the scan done and wait for the reports, don't worry unnecessarily.*"

Not to worry is easy said than done.

The uncertainty was quite stressful so I called my mother. My mother could immediately make out something was wrong. She asked, "*What is the matter? Why do you sound so low? Is everything alright?*"

I cried out, "*No Mā, things are not looking good.*"

I then told her about the blood tests, *USG* and *CT* scan being done and about my fears but she asked me to have patience and not panic.

I warned her, *"Be prepared Mā, we may require your presence here."*

She assured me, *"We will be there, but have faith in God to make things bette*r.*"*

I called *Dr. Pejaver* again, thinking that since she taught Zoology in College, she might be familiar with some of the new medical terms, I was coming across. We spoke at length. She started explaining the terms one by one but insisted that I should wait for the *CT* scan report. She tried to instill confidence and encourage me to think positive.

She told me, *"Moitreyee, cysts can be benign so don't take unwanted tension."*

Everything was new to me, first the medical terminology, then various tests, *USG* (*got it done for the first time*) and now *CT* scan. I was 47 years old and this was my first *CT* scan. For the *CT* scan I was asked to fast for the procedure and report by 9:00 a.m. to the Scan Centre. The nurse asked if I was allergic to any medicine and by 9:30 a.m. she gave me a bottle filled with a blue coloured fluid and a glass. She asked me to drink the fluid in three hours. I was asked to wear a loose fitting cotton uniform, remove my jewelry and other metal accessories like pins, metal clips etc. After three hours I was sent to a room housing the *CT* scan machine. It was really cold in there.

A different nurse this time asked me to lie on the bed of the scan machine and covered me with a blanket. Intravenous line was started to inject a contrast medium. There was a warm feeling throughout my body about which the technician had pre-warned me. After the scan machine started everyone left the room and the technician guided me through the microphone. I was asked to breathe in, hold and then breathe out. The procedure took almost an hour.

The day spent waiting for the *CT* scan report was long and dark. The *CT* scan report on *3*rd September *2010* showed, *"Hepatomegaly with 2.3x3.0 cm sized hypodense area in the VI right lobe of the liver, a large solid cystic lesion in the pelvis, possibility of ovarian neoplasm and moderate amount of free fluid in abdomen and pelvis."*

In these few days, the entire scenario of my house changed. My whole world was up-side down but I tried to stay unperturbed. *Benu* was constantly by my side, sensing a major upheaval. Words like *cystic mass, peritoneal fluid, neoplasm, etc.* was frightening me. I was relentlessly searching the web to get some clarity and more information on the medical terms we were coming across.

> *I knew that our life was taking an ugly turn. It was hard to focus on the positive, stay unruffled when I felt my little world tumbling . . . like a*

pack of cards . . . I call it kismat . . . Bhāgya . . .
I could see the darkness engulfing me . . . I
didn't know what had hit me . . . I felt like
crying . . . but I kept quiet.

On 4ᵗʰ *September 2010*, we received the report for *CA125* which was "*394.0 U/ml, normal was between 2.0-35.0 U/ml*."

The CA125 report . . . nailed it.

Life is full of decisions, making the right call, at the right time was important. I told *Benu*, "*Let us take all the reports to Dr. Joshi immediately*."

We showed all the reports to *Dr. Joshi*. He took his time going through the reports and after some deliberation told us, "*The reports indicated that it is a suspected case of ovarian cancer*."

Benu was stunned, he felt as if someone struck a blow on his head. He was searching for words . . . then he shouted . . .

Cancer! Ovarian cancer!

He was staggered . . . with tears in his eyes *Benu* said, "*I did not expect this, I thought it was some gynecological problem*."

I already knew that he had not realized the implications of the reports. *Dr. Joshi* also realized it. So to give him time to accept the prognosis, the doctor started discussing the reports with him in detail. *Benu* however, was finding it extremely difficult to accept that I was suffering from ovarian cancer. He kept repeating, **Ovarian Cancer! Cancer! Cancer!**

Usually sentiments are, "Cancer always happened to others" . . . it will knock at our doors, is something, we find very hard to accept.

Dr. Joshi wanted to pacify *Benu* so he started discussing about the facilities available in different hospitals. He said, "*Let me think, which will be the best hospital for her.*"

He made enquiries in different hospitals and found that immediate treatment was not available in some of the hospitals because of long queue. *Dr. Joshi* felt that I required immediate treatment, so he referred my case to *Dr. Pratima Chipalkatti*, gynecologist in *Bombay hospital, Mumbai.*

As *Dr. Joshi* and *Benu* were making enquiries with *Bombay Hospital* regarding the admission procedure, I sat with them in silence, focusing on what was happening with me. I saw my present crumbling and taking a turn for the worse. My stomach began to twist and turn. A shudder ran through my body.

*I felt sick . . . scared . . . in a state of shock . . .
I tried to control my wayward emotions . . . I
sat there alone in my thoughts . . . as I found my
world falling apart.*

My inside started churning as realization hit me that our little world, our dreams and our life was tumbling down and was in ruins.

I did not know how to put my life back together again. I was trying to plan for the future but not knowing, what the future had in store for me, was the toughest part.

My achievements in life called for dedication, patience and lot of sacrifice. My life, as a daughter of a defense officer, taught me the real values that I wanted to live my own life by. I learnt early in my life that discipline, hard work and perseverance are the qualities which help to achieve goals.

I schooled myself to change my attitude towards cancer, as only a change in attitude could make a big difference in its acceptance.

It was only courage, strong will power and positive attitude that mattered now. I immediately controlled my feelings and tried to make a conscious choice that I would change the stumbling blocks into stepping stones.

I looked at Dr. Joshi and told him simply, "I will fight it out, Doctor."

Chapter 3

Living in denial . . .

Living in denial is an extremely difficult situation to be in and it was evident that *Benu* was "*living in a state of denial*" about my condition. He repeatedly went through the reports and was annoyed with what they showed. He was short tempered, irritated and at his wits end.

The worst lies are the lies we tell ourselves and we do this because we are scared.

I tried discussing the reports with him. I wanted to make it easier for him to accept the findings, but I found a barrier and realized that he could not accept the fact that *the cyst in ovary was malignant.*

I sat down with him and asked, "*What happened?*"

He said, "*Fifteen years back, we saw my mother suffering from cervical cancer, didn't we? You remember—she showed plenty of symptoms.*"

I agreed, "*Yes.*"

He asked me, "*Don't you feel, in your case, there should have been some indication because other than general weakness, you were fit and fine.*"

"*Hmmm,*" I murmured.

He kept repeating, "*I find it hard to believe that you are suffering from cancer . . . No, it can't be . . . How it can be so?*"

Finally I said, "*Even I find it difficult to believe, but . . . you know what the reports say?*"

He whispered, "*There is some mistake somewhere . . . Wrong prognosis . . . There is a mistake.*"

"*Facts are facts and will not disappear on account of your likes.*"

Jawaharlal Nehru (1889-1964)
Political leader, Freedom fighter and First Prime Minister
of India

Benu strongly believed that there was some mistake in the reports so he rang our close friends (*Alka, Babji, Sarita and Manjul*), to get them at our place and plan the future course of action.

"*A trouble shared is a trouble halved.*"

Early 20ᵗʰ century proverb

Our dear friends who always surrounded us with unconditional love and laughter were speechless, stunned to silence to hear what *Benu* told them.

Rina, suffering from cancer! Cancer!

They couldn't believe, what they were hearing from other sources, was indeed true. They wanted to help, so we sat and did some introspection. It was proposed that all the tests could be repeated in another clinic. They also suggested that a second opinion was definitely required.

I knew, my journey had started and I had to take the first firm step, which was to accept the fact that I was suffering from cancer. To run away from the fact was not the solution as only with acceptance can there be recovery.

I told my friends that the gravity of the situation demanded that we did not waste any time. I wanted to have the courage to follow my intuition and get immediate treatment. Second opinion needed could be obtained from *Bombay Hospital*. They agreed and encouraged us to be positive. In the midst of challenges, trauma and grief, their smiles, genuine help and cheer, warmed our hearts.

After our friends left, it was time to sit down and deal with the situation firmly. I sat down with *Benu* and *Nini* and to turn their denial into acceptance, I emphasized sternly, **"The reports suggest Ovarian Cancer—accept it."**

I told this once and I told this thousand times but it was only when I shouted the dreaded sentence; it was loud and clear to me. I prayed that they understood it too. There was pin drop silence. It was as though they had turned into stones. There was an eerie silence for few minutes. I broke the silence as I reiterated, **"It is time . . . . you accept the fact."**

This opened the floodgate, *Benu* and *Nini* could no longer hold back their tears. Firm in my mind to see my family sail through this . . . I let them cry. I wanted to join them and but willed myself to stay unruffled.

Later I told *Benu*, "*It is very important not to waste time and energy in procrastination, as cancer is curable, if detected and treated early.*"

Nini was disconsolate; she was finding it very hard to believe that her mother was suffering from the dreaded disease. I cuddled *Nini* and asked her gently, "*The diagnosis of cancer causes panic, doesn't it?*

She nodded and said, "*Yes.*"

I told her, "*Don't be scared, trust God, to make things better.*"

She did not respond so I asked her, "*Do you have faith in God?*"

She barely nodded her head. I then asked, "*Do you have faith in modern medicines?*"

Again she nodded and then nestled herself in my arms, crying softly. I hugged her, stroking her hair and kissing her forehead, gently told her, "*Good, if one has faith, one has everything. Cancer is curable, believe it.*"

I held her, looked straight in her eyes and said, *"Will you trust me, if I say that cancer did not always mean death?"*

I repeated, *"Nini, Cancer does not mean death."*

She nodded and bent her head, weeping silently. This was an important year for *Nini* and I wanted her to be strong and steady. I realized for that, she required some pep talk so I advised—

> *"This is a real test; you can either make or break your career. If you get disturbed by the changes that are going to take place in our life then it will be a big loss for us however, if you fight all odds, then you will come out of it as a better person."*

I knew she was mentally exhausted but I asked her, *"Do you understand?"*

She nodded, I was happy that she was responding so I said, *"It is just a low phase in our lives; we will fight back, won't we?"*

> *Setbacks and adjustments are part and parcel of life but what we learn from them is the most important part.*

I don't know if she followed what I said, but she nodded her head again, wiped her tears, gave me a kiss, then hugged me tight and sat quietly with me.

"Let us not pray to be sheltered from dangers but to be fearless when facing them."

Rabindranath Tagore (1861-1941)
Indian Poet, Writer, Composer, Essayist, Playwright,
Painter and Nobel laureate

It was a difficult period for us but here we three were, at least together and were the support system for each other. *Gargi* however was away, staying all alone in *Hyderabad*. When she was informed, she could not believe that this could be happening to us.

She cried, *"Mā, how could you be diagnosed with cancer? You were with me in Hyderabad, just twenty days back."*

She was sobbing, her voice cracking into a barely audible whisper, *"How is it possible?"*

"Where did you get the tests done?"

"Are the reports correct?"

I told her, *"Shhh . . . Gargi, the reports are reliable and it suggests that, I am suffering from ovarian cancer."*

Gargi was inconsolable and her being so far away from us, was painful. I swallowed hard, determined not to breakdown; she would fall apart if she heard me crying.

I reminded her, *"Have you forgotten Gargi . . . we have three cancer survivors in the family."*

Benu, joined the conversation and told her about his aunt and late mother, how both suffered from cervical cancer and were cancer survivors. *Gargi* had seen my cousin sister fighting leukemia. She is a cancer survivor, leading a normal healthy life.

I asked her, *"Don't you think we should draw inspiration from them?"*

Gargi was stable after that and we promised to keep her informed about the developments.

I believed—

- *It is difficult to decide when and what to disclose to children.*

- *It is best to be honest with them.*

- *It will be heartbreaking, but it is better to tell them.*

- *You are tempted to avoid the word 'Cancer', but being specific reduces confusion and misunderstanding.*

- *Let them know the facts.*

- *Reassure them, listen to their queries and answer them. It will make them feel less anxious and more secure.*

- *Let them express their fears.*

- *Explain that cancer is not contagious.*

- *Reassure them that it is safe for them to be with you.*

- *If you don't tell or discuss with them, they will eventually know and may come to wrong conclusion and they may have the feelings of guilt, fear, sadness, frustration or anger.*

Our next step was to inform my parents and our relatives. I called my mother, "*Mā . . . Dr. Joshi has confirmed that I am suffering from ovarian cancer.*"

My mother told me, "*Don't panic, we are coming, immediately . . . Rina, don't panic.*"

After my parents arrived, we sat together and decided our next course of action. Hospitalization meant re-arrangements of finances, rescheduling and reorganizing home-affairs. We realized that cancer treatment was costly and would dig into our savings. We found to our surprise that though we had invested in few policies, none of them covered for cancer. All the policies were very good as an investment. We would receive a huge amount on maturity or my family would receive the amount after my sudden death. *Well what use was it for me now?*

Medical emergencies arise all of a sudden. It really hits you hard.

We wondered at our carelessness, "*Why did we not read the fine print or go deep into the details.*"

We had invested in a policy two years back which promised good returns. In spite of paying a huge premium every year, we now realized that it did not cover for the dreaded disease. Four policies on my name and what did all of them promise? *Oh God!*

Benu however reassured us, "*Don't worry, I have the facility for medical reimbursement.*"

So what medical facilities did a college professor get? I drew blank . . . just blank . . . in simple words, I did not know.

My carelessness was that I was not aware of what medical facilities I was entitled to. Though I was working as a professor for last twenty five years, to my chagrin I was totally blank on what medical cover I possessed.

The lesson we learnt—

- *It is essential to have a medical insurance.*

- *Be aware of your rights and medical facilities available at your workplace beforehand because emergencies can knock your door uninvited.*

- *Investment in various policies should be done only after reading their clauses and the fine prints meticulously.*

- *Financially, be prepared for every emergency.*

Hospitalization meant, leaving *Nini* alone at home. We did not know for how long . . . *Benu*, my parents and my brothers sat down to decide as to how things could be worked out, during my treatment.

It was a relief that *Nini* was safe with my parents. I thanked *God* for making me a part of such a wonderful family because, "*Fortunate are those, who in their life journey have their near and dear ones with them, in good times and bad times.*"

Arrangements made—

- *My father and Benu would accompany me to Bombay hospital, which was approximately two hour's drive from my home.*

- *We did not know anything about the treatment but it was decided that Benu would stay with me in the hospital.*

- *My father would be in the hospital from morning to evening.*

- *Sonali who was staying in Colaba (close to Bombay hospital) would join us, after her office hours.*

- *My mother would stay back to take care of Nini so that she could attend her lectures and coaching classes without any disturbance.*

- *My mother would visit the hospital occasionally.*

- *My brothers, if required would take leave from office.*

- *My brothers and sister-in-laws would help whenever required.*

I informed my Principal, *Dr. Pejaver* and the Head, Botany Department, *Dr. (Mrs.) M.S. Mulgaonkar*. They were in quandary, total disbelief and had lots of advice.

I remember the words of encouragement from *Pejaver* madam, *"The first thing you should remember is that cancer is curable, so don't get scared. Second, I have full faith Moitreyee, you will come through it."* Her conviction instilled a sense of confidence in me.

As we were getting ready for *Bombay Hospital*, *Alka*, *Babji*, *Sarita*, *Manjul*, *Prabha* and *B.C. Mishra* came to meet me. They were our friends with whom we shared scores of occasions filled with joy and sorrow. *Alka* knew, *Nini* was deeply attached to me and I would unnecessarily worry for her, so she hugged me tight and told me, "*Don't worry Rina, we will take care of Nini . . . go with a free mind . . . here everything will be fine . . . we will see to it.*"

Before starting my journey, I prostrated respectfully and surrendered before *Sāi Bābā* and *Bal-Gopāl* for their blessings. I touched my mother's feet, received a tight hug and kiss from *Nini*. As I looked back at my mother . . . my heart filled with a sense of peace . . . I drew positive vibes from her . . . I knew . . . she felt my fears but fortified my faith. She whispered softly, "*Have faith in God.*"

Yes, I had complete faith in God. But I had only one thought in my mind . . . why choose me?

"I know God will not give me anything I can't handle. I just wish, He didn't trust me so much."

Mother Teresa (1910-1997)
Sister, Social worker and Nobel Laureate.

Chapter 4

5ᵗʰ September 2010, the journey starts . . .

M_y *first impression of Bombay Hospital was that of an old fashioned multistoried building hidden in the densely populated, commercial area of Marine Lines, in South Mumbai.*

Babji had accompanied us to *Bombay Hospital. Benu* and *Babji* got busy with the admission procedure. My father was sitting with me in the car when *Benu* called and asked us to proceed to the 10ᵗʰ floor as we were allotted a room there. As we got down from the car a ward boy hurriedly brought a wheel chair.

I told the ward boy, "*I can walk, thank you.*"

My refusal to sit on the wheel chair was instantaneous . . . because something inside me prompted me, "*Rina, have the guts to walk and face your fears.*"

My father was happy, the smile on his lips, told me that he hailed my decision . . . the decision, to embark on this journey with confidence. He held my hand and I gripped it hard . . . we all have times . . . when the child in us would plead, "*Daddy, please hold my hand, I am scared.*"

In the non-descriptive lobby there was a magnificent idol of Lord Ganesha (Ganapati, Elephant God—God of good luck and dispeller of problems and obstacles) adorned with garlands of Marigold and Hibiscus flowers. I surrendered myself completely to him.

I prayed, "Take care Gannu (my pet name for Ganapati), take care."

We then took the lift for the 10th floor, I prayed silently to God almighty to show me the way to conquer the disease with dignity.

The view from the 10th floor was awesome, the majestic *"Wankhade Stadium (a dream place for a cricket crazy fan like Benu)"* was at one end of the corridor and the epitome of *Indian bazaar* . . . youngster's paradise, *"Fashion Street"* was at the other end. The nurse station was centrally located and this area was reserved for the sisters. There was nothing non-descriptive here; the interiors of the hospital looked grand.

One of the sisters showed us a room. There were some initial hiccups, as the room allotted to me was not to my father's liking. I was supposed to share the room with another patient (*twin bed*) and this was not acceptable to him. He also had issues regarding the room being far away from the nurse station. Soon we were allotted another room which was to our liking. *Benu* and *Babji* joined us after completing the formalities. *Benu* placed the *Śrī Sāi*'s *Udi* (*sacred ashes from the "Dhuni" which is kept burning in Dwarkamai, Shirdi*) by my bed side. Finally with all the formalities over, I was admitted under the care of *Dr. Pratima Chipalkatti*.

Bombay Hospital, 5ᵗʰ September, 2010 . . .
the journey towards progress . . .

Dr. Pratima and her students *Dr. Nupur* and *Dr. Priyanka* were there for the initial check-up. *Dr. Pratima* was smart, gracious and welcoming. We were impressed with her knack to include every member in the room, to be a part of the discussion.

Dr. Nupur and *Dr. Priyanka* were inquisitive, caring and endearing. They were two young, curious and very talkative doctors, who filled the room with cheers. *Dr. Pratima* started examining me, she kept pressing my lower abdomen to show the presence of the tumour to her students, both of them tried to locate the lump. Unable to suppress my curiosity, I tried to locate it and *Yes! I could feel the lump.*

Initially, the doctors were cautious about mentioning the "C" word in my presence. They discussed my case using only medical terminology. I listened for a while and then made it clear to the doctors that I not only knew about my cancer diagnosis, but by now also understood the medical terms they were using. They were pleasantly surprised but happy that they could talk freely.

Dr. Pratima told us, *"We rarely find patients who have accepted that they are suffering from cancer and are ready to fight it."*

Dr. Nupur found out that I was a professor and was starting my treatment on *"Teachers day"* so she wished me, *"A very happy teacher's day madam, a good day to start your journey."*

Soon other doctors, sisters and *ward-boys* followed suit and started wishing me for *teacher's day.*

I thought, *"Well! This made a good start."*

My room was buzzing with activity as *Dr. Pratima*, *Dr. Priyanka* and *Dr. Nupur* would walk in individually or sometimes together. Their only agenda was to collect as much information as they could.

Dr. Pratima asked my age. She then asked if we have any kids. When I told her about my daughters, she wanted to know about them, their age etc. *Dr. Priyanka* asked me if in the past I had any health issues. *Health issues! No!* Only that I was admitted in *Century Rayon Hospital* twice; during *Gargi's* and *Nini's* birth. So the doctor wanted to know if delivery was normal or caesarean.

The doctors also questioned my father and *Benu* about our family members (*both maternal and paternal*) and their medical history etc. They asked me about the symptoms which brought me to the hospital. They had taken all my reports with them and were studying it thoroughly.

Finally, *Dr. Pratima* decided that further consultation was required so she called *Dr. B.K. Smruti* (*Medical and hemato-oncologist*) and *Dr. Prakash Patil* (*Onco-surgeon*), both from *Bombay Hospital*.

Each doctor came with his or her own students, teaching them while examining me. I found this very interesting because it was a learning process for me too. My belief was, "*To become a good teacher, always remain a student.*"

Dr. Prakash Patil entered in my room and introduced himself, "*I am Dr. Prakash Patil.*"

Immediately it struck, "*Well! Here is a doctor who looks strict, stern and very serious.*"

I realized that he had already gone through my reports and had indeed done his home-work well because he started explaining his student, about my case.

He said, "*She has visible abdominal distention.*"

He pressed my abdomen and showed his student, how to judge that there was moderate amount of fluid in my abdomen.

Doctor told him, "*This is a matter of concern.*"

He tapped my abdomen listening with concentration to the sound . . . He tapped again and stood listening . . . I looked at him and was transported thirty years back . . . as a student of Biology class . . . standing with my classmates . . . over a dissected frog. Our professor gravely explaining the placement and function of various organs of a frog to us and frowning when we students, a bunch of giggly teenagers, looked at the poor frog which was cut open and pinned on a tray, with different expressions.

Our inquisitiveness, frown, indifference, disinterest or even revulsion could not price an expression out of him, the man never smiled. On the contrary, our staid professor, without any expression on his face would sternly ask us to observe carefully.

Today after thirty years, there was a major *role reversal.*

"I was the frog, here"

I lay on the hospital bed, looked at *Dr. Patil's* grave face and almost burst out laughing at my thoughts . . . but unaware of my wayward thoughts *Dr. Patil* flooded me with questions. His repeated cross questioning was mind boggling.

He told, *"You must have ignored the symptoms."*

Surprised, I asked, *"What symptoms? I did not have any symptoms."*

He told me, *"Symptoms were there, you were not aware of them."*

I told him, *"Doctor, every day I travel for three hours or more by local trains, auto-rickshaws etc . . .*

I teach in a college . . . do research work and am totally involved with my daughter's studies and other activities . . . except for eight hours sleep at night, I am active for most of the day."

Dr. Patil told me seriously, *"Your body must have given you signals but you were too busy to take notice."*

"When I noticed the symptoms doctor, I landed in the hospital," I sighed.

He gravely told me, *"Cancer is probably in fourth stage, symptoms existed and you have overlooked them."*

How did it feel to be interrogated? Bad, very bad! Having worked as a professor for a very long time, the experience of being interrogated was completely erased from my memory. I was never in the line of fire as I was always the one who fired. Now, I realized how my students felt, when cross examined and decided to stop doing that in future.

I told *Dr. Patil* rather crossly, **"Bloating, backache, vague pelvic and abdominal pain was too common a symptom for me to suspect cancer."**

This brought a hint of smile on his face so I told him quietly, *"I am on medication for high blood pressure, high cholesterol and hypothyroidism for the last few years."*

Dr. Patil was examining me again. While pressing my neck, searching for lumps he noticed something. He took out his pen and made a round mark on upper side of my right chest and told his student to see the slight difference in the colour of the skin.

Dr. Patil told him, "*We will get a mammography done.*"

When I asked what for? He said he wanted to rule out breast cancer.

Dr. Patil recommended few more tests. He wanted a mammography, *2-D echo* for heart and *T3*, *T4* and *TSH* for thyroid done before deciding my treatment schedule with other doctors.

After he left I immediately jumped out of the bed and rushed to the mirror to inspect the area on my chest which the doctor had marked. Yes, I could see the slight difference in the colour of the skin. I went back to my bed and found that *Sonali*, *Babji*, *Benu* and my father were back in the room and were discussing about the doctors whom *Dr. Pratima* had called.

When *Dr. Smruti* came and stood beside me, my first impression of her was that of a very smart lady with a pleasant and charismatic disposition. She enquired whether there was a history of cancer in the family.

I told her about my late mother-in-law and her sister who suffered from cervical cancer, but she informed me, "*Both are not your blood relative.*"

The third person was my cousin i.e. my maternal uncle's daughter, who suffered from blood cancer. She nodded and asked me if there was a history of ovarian cancer in my parent's families.

My father who was standing nearby said that as far as he could remember, none from our family had been diagnosed with ovarian cancer. My specialization being Cytogenetic, I asked the doctor if cancer was inherited. I also asked her about oncogenes and why there was an increased incidence of cancer now-a-days.

Doctor told me, "*Cancer was a life style disease. Urban multitasking women often ignore the symptoms till it was too late.*"

What we could gather was that cancer did not happen all of a sudden. First *Dr. Pratima* . . . then *Dr. Patil* . . . and now *Dr. Smruti* . . . each one of them was reiterating the same thing . . . echoing the same statement . . . "*You have ignored the symptoms.*"

> "*I wondered whether my ignorance would cost my life*"

And by now I felt like a foolish, illiterate and ignorant person, who had committed a major blunder. In distress . . . I cursed myself, "*Fool . . . fool . . . fool . . . . I consider myself smart . . . educated . . . well! I was a fool! The biggest fool ever!*"

We always try to justify the misdeed we committed. So it didn't surprise me when I tried arguing with myself, "*After college hours, if I can sit for hours with my research work, can look after my daughters need, study late in night completing notes or preparing for lectures, sleep only for eight hours and commute daily for three to four hours, then how can I be suffering from cancer?"*

I was a workaholic . . . yes. Busy . . . yes. But my hectic schedule never caused any problem for me. *What were the symptoms? Which symptom did I ignore? Let me think! Think? How could I think? Disturbing thoughts made me restless. It was disquieting. Was this an anxiety attack?*

Keep peace with your inner self in midst of the turmoil in your life.

I was stressed out, distraught and was feeling lost. I could do nothing to control my thoughts, it was like a nightmare. However, realizing the futility of getting tense and remembering the three cardinal principles of yoga, *"Relax the body, slow down the breath and calm down the mind,"* I started meditating and after some time was able to compose myself. Ignorance has no beginning but it certainly has an end . . . so I sat quietly to do some serious introspection . . . I made a mental note of all that happened in the past year . . . the important symptoms . . . which the doctors thought, I must have ignored.

I went back a year or so down the memory lane and remembered an important occasion in my college. *September 2009*, a Two Day National Seminar organized by Botany department. I was busy multitasking, running around and working overtime. I felt hassled and stressed out during that period and often could feel dull ache, cramps in my lower abdomen. Thinking it to be due to nervousness I ignored it. *Now I wondered about the cramps . . . Was it a symptom?*

I also remembered another isolated incident which now appeared relevant. In *February* 2010, I suffered from severe hair loss. I was always proud of my crowning glory, never having faced the problem of hair loss before. I consulted a doctor. Soon the hair fall stopped and the incident was forgotten. *Was hair loss a symptom?*

I was obese (*75 kg*) with a bloated tummy and abdominal distention. My weight increased by 10-12 kg in just a few years and this made me extremely conscious. I took efforts to reduce my weight by exercising and going for regular walks. I also took care of my diet as I was suffering from high blood pressure, high cholesterol and hypothyroidism. *Did obesity, abdominal distention indicate that I was suffering from cancer?*

As in every Bengali household having non-vegetarian food in breakfast, lunch and dinner was inevitable. I was also fond of Fast food. *Chicken burger, Chicken nuggets, French fries* and *Pizza's* oozing with *cheese* was my weakness. Yes, I binged on Fast food quite often. *Though it was pure joy . . . pure ecstasy to have them, I now wondered if in the long run it affected me!*

I had severe burning sensation in my eyes whenever I washed my face or had bath. I consulted an eye specialist but the sensation persisted. *Was this a symptom? Did I ignore it?*

I recollected about a security feature of face recognition in my new laptop. The laptop would start only when my face came in focus. However, I found that in the last few days, this option would not work as it could not recognize my face. *I wondered if this was significant.*

I did not suffer from any discomfort during menstruation but bleeding was excessive with few blood clots. There were no pre-menstruation symptoms like period pain, bloating, lack of concentration or clumsiness. Though there was heavy bleeding, the menstruation cycle was always on time every month, except for the last two months (*June and July, 2010*) before I landed in the hospital. *Was heavy bleeding a symptom?*

I also noticed that there was urinary discomfort, in terms of frequency and urgency. *Was this a symptom?* I was aware of changes such as mood swings, tiredness, hot flushes and severe back ache. I kept reading, talking and collecting information about menopause, but I did not follow the simple advice given by *Dr. Leena*, "*Go for a routine check-up.*" I was always too busy to go to the hospital. *What a shame!*

Then, I remembered the night I woke up suddenly from deep slumber because I felt shooting pain in my pelvis. I had almost doubled over the bed, pressing my belly, my face contorted in pain. After sometime when the pain subsided, I sat in silence wondering what was that all about . . . *I had completely ignored this incident, it was a symptom, wasn't it?*

My need for being perfect in my professional and personal life kept me on my toes. Trying to fulfil our needs or having wishes unfulfilled often led to stress, but did I pay heed to the repercussions of leading a stressful and tension filled life. *Did I slow down? Well you guessed right—No.*

The misconception was that I was indispensable both in personal and professional world.

However, common symptoms like vague pain in the abdomen and pelvis, cramps, backache, tiredness, later high fever and mouth ulcers forced me to report to the hospital.

"Coming events casts their shadow before."

Early 19ᵗʰ century proverb

Probably these were the symptoms . . . common unrelated symptoms . . . which the doctors insisted that I must have ignored . . . I realized my blunder . . . but did not lose hope.

> *Was on medication for high blood pressure, high cholesterol and hypothyroidism for last five years. But the symptoms I ignored—*
>
> - *Cramps in lower abdomen.*
>
> - *Obesity with abdominal distention.*
>
> - *Severe hair loss.*
>
> - *Heavy bleeding every month though the menstruation cycle was always on time except in the last two months.*
>
> - *Burning of eye when in contact with water.*
>
> - *Urinary discomfort.*
>
> - *Symptoms such as vague pain in the abdomen and pelvis, cramps, backache, tiredness and later high fever and mouth ulcer.*

When *Dr. Pratima* came for a visit I told her about the symptoms and then told her, "*I am smart, educated and knowledgeable but my present circumstance shows me to be just the opposite. I feel like an ignoramus person of mediocre intellect. How is it possible that I was unaware of these symptoms?*"

Was it was too late? Was my life was at risk?

Dr. Pratima sympathetically explained, "*Usually the symptoms are such common ones that you tend to go for self-medication or simply ignore them.*"

I told her, "*My education is of no use if I could not understand the changes taking place in my own body.*"

Dr. Pratima told me, "*Educated ladies tend to neglect their health and working ladies are worse*".

I agreed, but it still surprised me that there was not a single day during my stay in *Hyderabad*, when I felt indisposed.

Yes! I was tired and cranky but there were no symptoms to tell me that I was terribly sick and after twenty days, I would be detected with cancer.

I grumbled, "*It was absurd that these few unrelated symptoms over the past year indicate cancer!*"

Dr. Pratima said, "*In women, the tiny ovarian gland is a cause of major worry and amongst the ovarian, cervical and breast cancer, ovarian cancer is the worst. There are no effective methods to screen for ovarian cancer at initial stage and it remains silent until it is too late for a complete recovery.*"

She said, "*The cysts growing in the ovary of the patients has plenty of space to grow thus there is no pain initially.*"

She insisted that, "*Working ladies neglect their health, don't eat proper meals, are overworked and stressed.*"

She told me that in urban ladies, the incident of cancer was on rise and it was a worldwide trend. It was a lifestyle disease which was usually blamed on the rapid westernization, stress and hectic pace of urban life.

"Your body was giving signals but you were too busy to take notice of them."

My doctors had given me a lot food for thought. I was thinking about everything being told to me . . . I was in a pensive mood . . . it was very quiet . . . my father was holding my hands and whispering some words of encouragement.

There was heavy silence in the room as we were digesting the information given by the doctor. Silently relating to the cause or trying to find answers to the innumerable question coagulating our minds.

Babji smiled. The charming friend of mine told me, "*Rina, you are smart . . . your smile is as gorgeous as Shilpa Shetty (Hindi film actress). Be positive . . . and believe that you are worth it. Don't worry you will be fine.*"

I smiled back at *Babji*, "*A friend indeed . . . one in million . . . ever smiling . . . always positive . . . generous with complements . . . spreading love and cheer.*"

His smile was infectious and his complements were audacious, cheeky *Shilpa Shetty* indeed! When Shilpa Shetty comes to know about the comparison, she will first hunt for me, take a look and laugh at the joke. Perish the thought *Babji*, perish the thought! But suddenly the dynamics changed in the room. The absurd complement relaxed me and my smile was back.

It started raining heavily. My father kissed me and told me that he would come back early morning, the next day. *Babji* and my father left, as the return journey would take more than two hours. It was very quiet after they left, I felt queasy, lonely and nervous.

The same night around 11:00 p.m., I was taken from my 10th floor room to the ground floor for routine blood tests. This time the ward boy insisted that I use a wheel chair. A war of words struck between us but I conceded as he was adamant, almost mulish.

I was a determined lady with a very strong will power and a positive attitude. It appeared there was nothing to stop me . . . come what may . . . I was raring to start my cancer journey. However, what happened next is something we find hard to believe. Everything was fine till I was returning back to my room . . . when realization hit me . . .

"My life has suddenly taken an ugly turn and everything right is now horribly wrong"

Everything went blank . . . it was after some time . . . I realized that . . . people were trying to help me up from the floor, the doctors and nurses were around me and it was an emergency.

God! I was unconscious . . . I fainted. It was unbelievable!

Doctors told *Benu*, "*She has bottled up her feelings and it had to erupt sometime.*"

Dr. Nupur asked me, "*Are you scared*?"

I denied, "*Sorry I fainted . . . and . . . surprised that I did. But No, I am not scared.*"

She told me, "*Don't be scared, you are in good hands . . . in a very renowned hospital. There is nothing to worry. You are suffering from cancer but cancer is curable.*"

> ## "There is perhaps nothing so bad and so dangerous in life as fear."
>
> *Jawaharlal Nehru (1889-1964)*
> *Political leader, Freedom fighter and First Prime Minister of India*

It was nearing midnight, *Benu* and I sat in silence, holding hands. I was restless thinking about the past few days, how our life had completely changed.

> *Benu was the only one in front of whom I revealed my true self . . . my flaws . . . my weaknesses. It was only in front of him that I let my emotions surface. I was worried sick as I started doubting whether I would live through all this? Would I live to see my daughters achieving their goals? All that I had planned for in my life would now remain a big question mark.*

I became frantic sitting there and thinking of our future, the more I thought, the worse it seemed. I started sobbing, my shoulders shaking with my gasping sobs and for the first time I cried my heart out.

Tears spilled over my cheek. I covered my face with my hands but it could not mask my bleeding heart. I cried as though this was the end and there was possibly nothing I could do about it.

"We need never be ashamed of our tears."

Charles Dickens (1812-1870)
Writer

The flood gates had opened and I sobbed till there were no more tears left. Much later, I closed my eyes, trying to soothe my frayed nerves with slow and steady breathing. I felt exhausted, tired and ashamed of my emotional outbreak, but gradually, from all that weeping, a healing and peaceful aura settled into the room.

I sat quietly trying to control my emotions, I promised myself, *"This is the first and the last time . . . I have cried . . . no more tears Rina, no more tears."*

There is more to life than sorrow. My loving husband was still holding my hands, he looked disturbed, at loss of words but his eyes told me all. Realization struck, I was loved so why waste energy crying. Peace prevailed, now all I really wanted to do was to shift my attention and focus on the love around me.

"To weep is to make less the depth of grief."

William Shakespeare (1564-1616)
English Poet, Dramatist and Playwright

I remembered my late mother-in-law who was diagnosed with cervical cancer fifteen years ago. She had come from *West Bengal* to *Mumbai* for treatment at *Nanavati hospital*. She required thirty radiations.

She once saw me crying when I saw how repeated radiotherapy was affecting her. She asked me, "*Why are you crying?*"

She was suffering so much that I found it hard to deal with my sentiments. I could not reply as emotions blocked my throat and she, so simply asked me why I was crying.

She saw my inner struggle and comforted me, "*Don't worry, nothing will happen to me, I will be fine.*"

Surprisingly she was relaxed, without any trace of anxiety and stress on her face. She made me sit by her side and told me about her sister who suffered from cervical cancer twenty years ago.

She told me, "*Cancer medicines were not that advanced then, but my sister survived. Today with greater awareness and wider access to medical facilities things are much better than what they were earlier.*"

She then told me, "*I will be fine. I am in the best hospital and have the best doctors.*"

I admired her confidence and was pleased when she was cured. She was fine for the next fifteen years and now here I was, her daughter-in-law, diagnosed with cancer. *Oh God! I really missed her.* But then I drew strength from the words she had uttered fifteen years back.

"Nothing will happen to me, I will be fine."

Her words stayed with me, it overwhelmed me but remembering the blessings she bestowed on me, reduced my pain and healed my heart, putting things in proper perspective . . .

My pledge was that though I could not go back and make a brand new start, I could always start now and make a brand new ending.

Chapter 5

Ovarian cancer . . .

On my second day in *Bombay Hospital*, few more tests were done. We already had the blood reports with us. Good news was that the *2-D echo* report was normal in spite of the fact that my cholesterol, triglyceride and blood pressure was high. This made me happy but what really made me happy was the attitude of the doctor who did the *2-D echo*. He was an extremely good singer and during the entire procedure he was happily humming an old Hindi song. Realization struck that here was a person who surely enjoyed his work and the positivity in the room was contagious. I was positive that my *2-D echo* report would be normal.

For mammography, the ward-boy wheeled me downstairs on a wheelchair. The mammogram machine was kept in a small room with lot of privacy as the patient had to undress from waist up for the investigation. Mammography was taking time; there were butterfly in my stomach till I saw a small calendar with the photograph of *Sāi Bābā* in the room. Yes, *Dr. Patil's* doubts had made me a bit nervous but the mammography report fortunately showed no signs of breast cancer.

Blood test report for *T3*, *T4* and *TSH* showed discrepancy so *Dr. Amin* was called for consultation. *Dr. Amin* advised me to continue with my medicine for hypothyroidism.

After lunch a nurse entered in our room and started arranging all the reports carefully in different folders. She told us that the doctors were discussing my case and they had asked for the reports. We were waiting impatiently for the doctor's verdict regarding the course of my treatment, when *Benu* was called to *Dr. Pratima's* chamber.

Benu returned after an hour. My father enquired eagerly, *"What happened? What did the doctor say?"*

Benu described, what transpired in *Dr. Pratima's* chamber to us.

He said, *"As I entered the chamber I saw Dr. Pratima, Dr. Smruti and Dr. Patil seated there. It frightened me to see all the three doctors waiting for me."*

Dr. Pratima said, *"Sit down Dr. Saha. We would like to explain what the reports show and what we want to do for your wife."*

Benu quickly sat down as he felt that his legs would not support him. The air conditioner was working full blast but he was perspiring profusely.

Dr. Patil said, "Cancer of the ovary is probably in fourth stage."

Benu said that he started shivering and was at his wits end when he heard *Dr. Patil*. He could not digest the fact that his wife could be suffering from cancer which was in stage IV. *Hale and hearty person like Rina! Such an advanced stage! How could it happen?*

Dr. Pratima realized that *Benu* was finding it hard to grasp the facts. So she explained what she had told me before regarding ovarian cancer and why it was difficult to detect ovarian cancer at an early stage. *Dr. Patil* then made few diagrams to illustrate the exact position of the cysts on both right and left ovaries.

Benu was then told that the cyst on the fourth lobe of the liver was problematic. The position of this cyst was such that, the surgeon would find it difficult removing it without damaging the diaphragm. Again, some diagrams were made to show the position of the fourth lobe of the liver, cyst and the diaphragm.

Dr. Pratima told him, "***We cannot reach it without damaging the diaphragm***."

Dr. Smruti said that the only alternative was to administer chemotherapy to reduce the size of the cysts and then to go for surgery.

She told him that the doctors had decided, "***There will be three cycles of chemotherapy followed by a surgery. Post-surgery, three cycles of chemotherapy will be repeated.***"

Benu was totally dejected; he knew that everything was going horribly wrong and he felt helpless as he could not do anything to help his wife.

He completely broke down. In his despair, he heard *Dr. Patil*, speaking very softly, ***"Don't worry Dr. Saha, cancer is curable and your wife will pull through it."***

The impact of these simple words of encouragement from Dr. Patil was like a lifeline to a drowning man. Benu clutched them close to his heart and realized that all was not lost. He felt that there might still be a route out from this desperate situation.

> *"If it were not for hope, the heart would break."*
>
> *Mid 13th century proverb*

Dr. Smruti informed *Benu*, *"Your wife will be administered Taxol and it is a costly cancer drug."*

He told her, *"Save her doctor, we will think about the cost later."*

She asked him, *"Which manufacturer should we use, Indian or British, the Indian drug is cheaper."*

Benu responded, *"Use the one which will cure her, don't worry about the cost."*

Benu then told me, *"You will now be under the care of Dr. Smruti and from 7th September the first cycle of chemotherapy will start."*

My father told me, *"Mamoni (Darling), there will be changes . . . lots of changes . . . but we will face them together with courage and dignity."*

I looked at him and then at *Sonali*, both defense officers. They were strong, courageous and spirited. Next, I looked at *Benu*, humane and dignified. I thought of my mother, a lady with positive attitude and strong will power. My beautiful daughters . . . I was thankful to *God* that my family was with me in my cancer journey. Yes, the journey ahead would be filled with hurdles, my well organized life would turn topsy-turvy, but come what may I would face the changes with dignity.

> *"It is not the strongest of the species that survive or the most intelligent, but the one most responsive to change."*
>
> *Charles Darwin (1809-1882)*
> *English Naturalist and Geologist*

Dr. Smruti came for a visit, around 4:00 p.m. She explained the chemotherapy procedure and the schedule to us in detail. She informed, *"Initially, you will be given three cycles of chemotherapy."*

"There will be a gap of twenty one days between each cycle of chemotherapy," she explained.

After the third chemotherapy, if the *CA125* is within limits and the *CT* scan showed reduction in the size of the cysts then surgery. After surgery, one month to recuperate and then three more cycles of chemotherapy would be given. The entire procedure would take around 10 months or so, provided I did not delay the procedure by contracting other diseases.

She said, *"If by mistake you contract some other disease (communicable disease like cough, cold or viral fever etc.) and become sick, then your illness will assume gigantic proportion as your immune system will be weak and it will become increasingly difficult to cure you."*

She reiterated, *"Take care, if you contract a simple disease like cold or fever, it may have a cascading effect in your case. Chemotherapy will be delayed leading to unwanted complication in cancer cure."*

Routine suggested by the doctor—

- *Three cycles of chemotherapy*
- *Surgery*
- *Three cycles of chemotherapy*
- *There would be a gap of twenty one days between each chemo.*

She told that for chemotherapy, *Taxol (300 mg)* and *Carboplatin (700 mg)* would be administered. As a professor in Botany, I knew that *Taxol* was extracted from *Pacific or western yew* (*Taxus brevifolia*), a conifer, native to North America. Recently, *Taxol* was isolated from the endophytic bacteria growing on this plant. The anti-cancerous activity of *Taxol* and how it targeted not only the cancer cells but also the normal cells was known to me. I was aware of the side effects and discussed about them with the doctor.

She told us, *"At the time of chemotherapy avoid eating raw food like salads and eat only those fruits which can be peeled."*

We spoke about the persistent pesticide and their residue which remained on the agricultural products causing harm. After she left we started discussing about the beneficial effect of organic farming.

Dr. Patil was in my room around 5:00 p.m. He told my father, *"Three cycles of chemotherapy may not be sufficient."*

My father asked, *"Why not doctor?"*

He said, *"If the hypo-dense area in the liver does not disappear after third cycle of chemotherapy, then your daughter will have to take few more chemo and only after that she will be operated."*

Sonali asked, *"What about the peritoneal fluid, doctor?"*

Dr. Patil said, *"Let's wait and watch if required aspiration will be done."*

This worried me and it was reflected on my face. *Dr. Patil* at once told me, *"Don't worry you will be fine."*

After *Dr. Patil* left, a lady entered the room and introduced herself as the counselor, *Dr. Indu Nair*. She told me that she suffered from breast cancer, twenty years back and was a cancer survivor. She told me about her experience as a cancer patient and stressed on the power of positive thinking.

I was pleasantly surprised to see that my colleagues, *Dr. Mulgaonkar* and *Dr. Jamdhade* came to meet me in the hospital. They met my parents and were happy to see that we had full support from my family members, in this hour of crisis. I started discussing about the syllabus covered and the portion yet to be covered by me but *Mulgaonkar* madam stopped me and said, "*Don't worry about college; you first concentrate on getting well.*"

She also told me, "*Pejaver madam has sent the message that you can avail a special leave and she wants you to have strong will power and positive attitude to combat the disease.*"

Dr. Jamdhade sat talking with my father. Suddenly he got up and stood near me. He took my hands in his and told me with sincerity ringing in his voice, "*You will be fine, madam.*" There was something in his voice that touched my heart and offered me a sense of wellbeing.

My room was filled with my friends. Realization struck that I was loved not only as a wife, mother, daughter and sister but also as a friend, colleague and a teacher. I was receiving "*Get well*" wishes from students but what happened next left me speechless. Three persons entered my room, presented a basket filled with apples and enquired about my health. *They looked familiar . . . Who were they?* Then with a start I realized that they were the *auto-rickshaw* drivers whom I did not know by name, but had travelled with them regularly for years together, from home to *Shahad* station and return. Their presence was a pleasant surprise and I felt truly blessed.

I promised that I would rise above the obstacles taking one step at a time. I just needed to have the courage and sheer determination to succeed.

Chapter 6

A day of reckoning . . .

The morning of 7th *September, 2010* was hectic for *Benu* as he was running around to get everything ready for the first cycle of chemotherapy. A list of medicines to be brought from the pharmacy (*drug store*) of the hospital was handed over to him. A ward-boy was deployed but *Benu* decided to accompany him. After an hour when he returned, another list was handed over. This was a list for the other requirements like gloves, special mask, bottles for the intravenous injections etc. This time the ward-boy went but when he returned the nurse was unhappy.

She shouted, *"I told glass bottles for Taxol not plastic ones."*

The ward-boy shouted back, *"If it is not available, what should I do?"*

So, war of words ensued, finally *Benu* put an end to it by asking the nurse what did she want exactly?

The nurse explained, *"I want glass bottles and not plastic ones for the dilution of Taxol."*

Benu assured her that he will go and get them. After some time *Benu* called my dad and told him that the glass bottles were not available in the hospital drug store. He was going to search for it in other medical stores outside the hospital. *Benu* returned quite late as this took time however when everything required for the chemo was ready the nurse was still taking her own time to start the intravenous.

When she was asked about it she explained, "*Dr. Smruti has not yet given us instructions on the quantity of Taxol which will be used.*"

Benu jumped up, "*She is downstairs, I will get it from her. She had told us 300 mg Taxol will be administered. Anyway I will get the prescription from her.*"

The nurse stopped him, "*No-No! She will supervise, don't go now. Anyway a qualified nurse from onco-department will come here to start the drip.*"

Benu was not a person to sit quietly. He was trying his best to hasten things but was unsuccessful. I was irritated by the delay, my mind unmanageable and skittish. To soothe my frayed nerves and to reduce the accumulated stress, meditation was the only way out. Tranquility prevailed after some time. There was a strange calmness as I envisioned *Śrī Sāi* transforming in my mind . . . from the image of the photograph in my house . . . to an enlightening presence. Meditation revitalized my body, helped me to control my thoughts and restored my distracted mind. There was a strange peaceful satisfaction within me.

*My mother always says, "Whenever in dilemma,
seek the blessings of the God Almighty to give
direction to your troubled thoughts and lead you
towards the right path."*

My prayer was answered, as a nurse entered my room and gave me few anti-sickness pills as a precautionary measure against nausea and vomiting. *Dr. Nupur* came for a visit. She told us that most patients undergoing chemotherapy receive anti-emetic medicines before treatment begins.

By afternoon, my father and *Sonali* were with me and their presence relaxed me. *Sonali* was in conversation with the doctors about my treatment. We observed her and couldn't stop laughing because we found that she kept track of the medicines, controlled maids, helpers and the sisters on duty. She showed the trainee nurse how to make the bed properly. *Yes!* She kept every one busy and in high spirits. By late afternoon my mother, *Arun-Da*, *Anu-Di*, *Anjan* and our friends came to meet me.

We were keen for the treatment to start but it was only around 4:00 p.m. that two nurse from oncology department entered my room. They requested the visitors to leave the room. First they made a check list of the things required for chemotherapy and then gave me few pills to be swallowed with water. One of them started tapping my hand for a healthy vein to show up. Both consulted each other and selected a vein. One of them held my hand and the other gently pushed a small tube (*cannula*) into the vein. She then connected the drip bag with the cannula using a set of plastic tube. She started the drip. She told me that these were the medicines administered to avoid side effects of the chemo drugs. She then allowed my parents and family members to enter my room.

After seeking blessings of my parents, I surrendered myself to God Almighty so that my journey ahead would become much easier. Come what may, I was mentally prepared to overcome any physical discomfort I was going to encounter.

Yes, I was prepared for my cancer journey.

My father sat quietly, holding my hand. One look at him and I knew that he was crying his heart out and *yes! It reflected on his face.* He was a tough and hardened military solider but for his daughter, he was a softy at heart. I looked at my mother, a very beautiful, petite and strong willed lady. As our eyes met she smiled tranquilly and told me in Bengali, a proverb which meant, **"A storm has come; it will turn into a soft breeze, caress you and leave."**

Benu was looking pale and he was sweating profusely. There was a flicker of smile on his lips and an uncertain look on his face. We understood each other without having to speak . . . language had become redundant. Yes! You never know what *God* had in store for us . . . but *Benu's* smile was enough to strengthen my belief that cancer could not separate us.

After an hour the chemotherapy nurse started the intravenous drip for *Taxol.* Both of them kept a watch on the drip rate. They closely monitored the number of drop falling in the chamber. They wanted the drip to run for the right number of hours so that the chemotherapy was adjusted at the rate advised by the doctor.

I looked around and saw that my friends had quietly entered the room. *Alka, Babji, Sarita, Manjul, Anil, Sudha, Himanshu, Monica,* my neighbour *Bhatta-Ji (Ji is a respectful suffix added after the name for elderly persons)* and his wife had taken pains to be with me. Every one encouraged me to stay positive. I was getting sucked and rejuvenated by the flow of positive energy around me.

My thoughts were, *"I could not control the entry of this event in my life, Could I? But I could definitely control the result."*

We are the architect of our own fate. If the question was about Destiny, then the answer would be—we are the master of our own destiny.

> *"All that we are is the result of what we have thought. The mind is everything. What we think, we become."*
>
> *Gautama Buddha (CIRCA 563 BC-483 BC)*
> *Founder of Buddhism*

When the drip containing *Taxol (300 mg)* was started, it felt like any other, simple intravenous drip.

My thoughts were, *"Is there a lot of hype regarding chemotherapy being grueling? Was what we read about chemotherapy exaggerated? Didn't we read that chemotherapy can be as brutal on the patient as it is on cysts and cancer cells?"*

Ashish-Da was with me. He was talking quietly, encouraging me to be strong. We discussed about the information he could gather on ovarian cancer, from his doctor at *Nasik*. He made me very comfortable, so I was able to chat with everyone present in the room.

Then to my amazement, the situation changed drastically. All of a sudden, I felt hot and flustered. There was a feeling, as if my chest was being compressed with iron chains. The churning sensation in my stomach made me breathless and left me gasping for air. I felt suffocated.

My mouth was dry I croaked, "*Mā, getting choked . . . do something.*"

My parents, *Ashish-Da* and *Sonali* found it very difficult to hold me on to the bed. I could feel my pulse intensify. The forceful thumping of my heart was taking my breath away. My vision clouded, the churning sensation in my belly increased and I started uttering incoherently. I was soaked in perspiration, my hospital uniform almost wet. *Sonali* and *Benu* were shouting for the doctor. *Arun-Da* ran to the nurse station to apprise them about the emergency. The nurse had already informed the doctors and they were with me immediately. Doctors soon realized that it was a reaction that occurred in some patients. I was given an antidote and soon things normalized.

Everyone in the room looked tense. *Dr. Nupur* asked everyone to relax. My father was in a melancholy sort of mood, he was gently stroking my forehead.

I told him, "*Bābā, I am fine now, don't worry, I am just feeling sleepy*" (*Bābā means father*).

He did not utter a single word but started patting and pressing my forehead so that I could relax and sleep. A friendly voice announcing dinner woke me up. There were dim lights in the room. It was very quiet and serene. *Benu* was rubbing his fingers against my hand trying to pacify my frayed nerves. Though there was no pain due to the intravenous, it was soothing to feel the steady rhythm of his touch.

It was obvious that *Benu* was happy to see me awake. He waited for me to say something. *Well! I did not disappoint him.* I flooded him with questions. *Everyone left? When did they go? When did mom and dad leave? Ashish-Da left? Where did he go? How did our friends return by local train or by car? Did Gargi call? Did Nini come back from coaching class? Is it still raining? What happened after my reaction? I am hungry. Can I have my dinner?* I wanted to know everything.

His melting eyes and angelic smile was enchanting. He laughed and asked me, "*Do you recall anything after that?*" I shook my head so *Benu* filled in with whatever I missed out.

He told me that after sometime my friends left however it was rather difficult to send back my father. *Benu* requested dad to leave as he felt that due to heavy showers there were chances that several low lying areas would be flooded thereby restricting traffic movement. There was a high alert few days back and people had been asked to venture out only in emergency. But dad did not budge. He was just not ready to listen to anybody. It was only when mom reminded him that *Nini* had returned from her coaching class and was all alone at home, did he agree to leave.

Dinner was a simple fare provided by the hospital. *Dr. Nupur* and *Dr. Priyanka* visited several times in spite of their busy schedule. We found them energetic, friendly and informative.

Dr. Priyanka, who was Bengali, took interest and enquired about my family members. She told us, "*I find your family lively and well-informed. Talking to them is a refreshing change for me.*"

She told us that my family members discussed knowledgeably about each and every aspect of my treatment with the doctors. They also had a kind of hunger in them to know more and more about cancer and cancer cure.

Taxol (300 mg) was started in the evening but the intravenous drip would continue through the night so a helper informed *Benu* that though the nurses in the hospital were on duty it was better to stay alert or hire the services of a private night duty nurse.

It was impossible for *Benu* to stay awake through the night as he was dead tired. So we decided to hire a private night duty nurse to take care that the drip should run uninterrupted through the night.

Then the next day early morning *Carboplatin (700 mg)* was started. The private nurse left and my dad reached the hospital by 8:00 a.m. Sonali joined us just before lunch. *Dr. Patil, Dr. Smruti* and *Dr. Pratima* visited. Whenever any doctor entered the room after examining me they had to face a battery of questions from us. Sometimes we made a list of questions for the doctor. There were so many questions . . . there was so much to learn.

There were however, no more emergencies. After the initial hiccups, my response to the first cycle of chemotherapy was good but *Dr. Smruti* decided to keep me under observation till *10th September*.

Dr. Nupur was with us when a nurse returned all the reports. Doctor had asked *Benu* to photocopy all the reports to be on a safer side. Now, there were quite a number of reports which *Benu* had to arrange.

Dr. Nupur advised him, *"Keep all the reports according to date in separate folders."*

Benu asked, *"Why separate folders?"*

She explained, *"You never know when the doctor will ask for a particular report. They usually ask for some previous report out of the blue, so it is important that you have all the reports with you, arranged date wise, chemo-wise."*

When *Dr. Smruti* came for a visit she gave us some sound advice. She said, *"The most important effect of chemotherapy is that it kills cancer cells. However, chemotherapy also kills rapidly dividing normal cells and when normal cells are damaged, they cause severe side effects."*

> • *Chemotherapy kills rapidly dividing cancer cells.*
>
> • *Chemotherapy also kills rapidly dividing normal cells.*

She said, *"Taxol side effects are often predictable as to when they start and how long they remain."*

Side effects vary greatly, usually starting within a day or two after administration of chemo drugs. These side effects could however, be effectively managed with medicines. *Dr. Smruti* started explaining in detail about what to expect in the next few days and how to overcome the side effects.

She told me very softly, *"You will lose all your hair after two weeks."*

The very thought of going bald drove me into tears. On realizing this, doctor promptly asked me not to get disturbed because my hair would grow after my six cycles of chemo got over. In fact they would be better than what my hair was now.

She told, "*We find losing our hair very painful because hair is an important part of our personality. Losing our hair makes us feel unattractive.*"

She suggested, wearing a scarf or a wig would help.

The possible side effects observed when treated with Taxol and Carboplatin—

- *A low White blood cell (W.B.C.) count can be observed. Low W.B.C. count means prone to infection.*

- *It can reduce the production of blood platelets and can cause unexpected bleeding and blood spots or rashes on the skin.*

- *It can reduce the number of Red blood cells which causes anemia which makes the patient breathless and tired.*

- *Nausea and vomiting are two common side-effects. Doctors usually prescribe anti-emetic drugs to control both.*

- *Loss of appetite is common in chemotherapy treatment.*

- *Tiredness and insomnia are also common side-effects.*

- *Pain in the joints, backache and muscle pain is resolved within week or so.*

- *Numbness and tingling sensation in hands and feet (peripheral neuropathy) is observed in some patients.*

- *Mouth-sores, Diarrhea, constipation and darkening of skin, nail changing colour seen.*

- *Hair loss (alopecia) is one of the common symptoms seen when treated with Taxol.*

Dr. Smruti said that after each cycle of chemotherapy, the *W.B.C. count* would reduce drastically and this could not be prevented. However, what could be done is to take extra precautions to avoid any situation that might increase the risk of infection. As a general rule, she asked me to be very careful about meeting people because cancer patients when exposed to persons with contagious or any other communicable diseases tend to contract the same. The next cycle of chemotherapy, in that case gets delayed thereby disrupting the procedure which ultimately harms the cancer patient.

She told us, "*You both are highly educated I hope you understand what this means and how important this is?*"

Dr. Smruti noticed that my phone kept ringing so she told me that in today's world it would be difficult for me to stay away from the phone but to remain stable, in good mental health I should abstain from answering repeated queries by friends and acquaintances, about my illness.

She told that the side effects were different for every patient. It was important to know that there would be some physical discomforts but modern medicine had made vast improvement. With proper medication, care, rigidly followed diet schedule and light exercise, I could overcome the side effects.

She said, "*All the reports should be filed properly. Carry all the reports when you come back for consultation.*"

She advised, "*Two days after every chemo, get the blood tests done. If the White Blood Cell (W.B.C.) count is low then take one—one Grafeel or Neukine injections, in two days. Again two days later, get the blood test done, to check if the W.B.C. count is normal.*"

She then told me, "*Remember to get a fresh blood test done before you come back for the next chemo.*"

She gave us a printed list of medication to consult from, in case of emergency. She also assured us that she was available 24/7 and that we were free to call her.

Dr. Smruti advised me to have healthy, fresh, home cooked meals using less oil and spices. She asked me to drink plenty of water and stop drinking tea or coffee. She advised me to drink coconut water instead of cold drinks and avoid eating fast food or street food.

She told that one of the reasons for increased incidences of cancer in recent times was the use of excessive pesticides, while farming. She again advised me to avoid eating raw vegetables. I could boil vegetables and drink different types of nourishing soups. I could also have fruits that could be peeled like *oranges, banana, pomegranates* etc.

I was upset thinking that she was advising me to turn vegetarian. In a Bengali house-hold having *fish* every day, was a norm. *Chicken* and *mutton* was also prepared frequently so turning vegetarian was a daunting task for me. My eyes welled up with tears but *Dr. Smruti* took pity on me and told me to reduce the intake of *red meat* and *chicken* but to continue to have *fish*.

Her command was God's sermon for us. We knew that if we paid attention to the small things she was recommending, the larger ones would fall into place. So we decided to follow her instructions meticulously.

Doctor's instructions—

- *Two days after each cycle of chemotherapy, get the blood test done (CBC) for W.B.C., platelets and S. creatinine.*

- *If the White Blood Cell (W.B.C.) count is low then take, a Grafeel or Neukine injection on that day and another on the next day (one each in two days).*

- *Grafeel or Neukine injections are administered as a subcutaneous injection(below the skin)*

- *Again two days after taking the Grafeel injections, get the blood test (CBC) done for W.B.C., platelets and S. creatinine.*

- *If the White Blood Cell (W.B.C.) count is normal then no problem but if the White Blood Cell (W.B.C.) count is still low, then repeat step 2 and 4.*

- *Twenty one days gap between two cycles of chemotherapy.*

- *Two days before the next cycle of chemotherapy again get the blood test done for W.B.C., platelets and S. creatinine.*

- *Also get the CA125 done before reporting for the next chemo.*

- *Carry all the reports, properly filed and in order date wise and chemo-wise.*

- *Have healthy, fresh home cooked meals using very less oil and spices.*

- *Drink lot of water.*

- *Stop drinking tea and coffee.*

- *Drink coconut water instead of cold drinks.*

- *Avoid fast food.*

- *Avoid eating raw vegetables, salads etc.*

- *Drink different types of nourishing soups.*

- *I could also have fruits that could be peeled like oranges, banana, pomegranates etc.*

It is necessary here to fill in some details about the expenditure in critical care for the benefit of my readers. Critical care is often described as expensive care. The hospital bills were astronomical by any standard. We paid ₹ 19,970 for *Taxol* (*Paclitaxel 300 mg INJ*) of British Mfr., ₹ 7,630 for Carboplatin (*2 vials of 450mg/45 ml INJ*) of Pfizer Mfr. There were charges for other medicines, consultation charges of all the visiting doctors and an exorbitant room charge. *Yes, nothing is free!* You pay for doctor's consultancy just before the chemo starts, then you pay for each and every doctor who visits you during your stay in the hospital. Also you pay for every test done, equipment used, injections and medicines administered. You even pay for the mask and the gloves used by the nurse in your room.

At the time of discharge, we were busy in packing when we were surprised to see my father giving away ₹ 100-200 as tip to anyone and everyone who came and stood in front of him. When *Benu* asked dad, "*Do you know that hospital management has requested the patients and the family members to refrain from giving tips to the staff.*"

My father innocently replied, "*Why don't they educate their staff. Since morning each one of them are coming and listing what help they have given to my daughter. Even the person who distributes the newspaper wants a tip.*" But he did not argue further.

We spent a total sum of ₹ 50,000 and realized that chemotherapy was really expensive and this was just the first chemo. Five more cycles of chemotherapy and a surgery would follow. We calculated and the sum amount appeared to be huge. Though we were comfortable financially, this would empty our savings considerably and upset the comfortable niche we had made for ourselves.

"₹ *50,000 . . . ₹ 50,000 is huge!*" Staggered I asked, "*It is okay for us . . . though it pinches, we can somehow manage to pay this amount, but can everyone pay this amount for the treatment?*"

Benu told me that there were hospital beds which were costing less and based on room charges the cost of the doctor's consultation fee and other overheads also reduced. Thus a patient paid much less than what we paid. He also told me that if family income was less, there were welfare intuitions, charitable organizations which helped in the treatment. The patient should tell the authorities and produce a low income certificate.

Chapter 7

Savdhan . . . military rule in my house . . .

My journey back home was long and tedious. My father did not want *Benu* to drive in his present state of mind so he arranged for his chauffeur driven car from *Nasik. Mr. Pansare* (*chauffeur*) took utmost care while driving but to my dismay the smell of the leather seat covers was nauseating. I felt disoriented as dizziness and fatigue made the drive uncomfortable.

What kept us involved however was my father's *word to word* narration of *Dr. Smruti's* list of instructions to my mother, on phone. Each one of us tried to recollect the points and give some inputs. Time flew and soon we reached home.

"*Home sweet home*" was the most wonderful place to be in. I prayed and thanked "*Bal-Gopāl*" and "*Sāi Bābā*" for giving me the courage and strength to endure the first chemo. Later my mother ushered me to my room and told everyone to leave me alone. My room was fumigated and furniture rearranged.

My dear mother (*wife of a defense officer*) called for attention from all of us. Her voice was assertive, commanding as she set down some ground rules to be strictly followed by every member.

Savdhan . . . military rule in my house in my house . . .

Rules set down by my mother—

- *No one would enter my room in their outdoor clothes.*

- *No one would sit on my bed.*

- *Visitors were not allowed to enter my room.*

- *If someone did come, they would be entertained in the drawing room.*

- *I had to take my meals, water and medicines regularly.*

- *The bed cover would be washed daily.*

- *No one would use my washroom so that there would be less fear of infections.*

- *There was new loose cotton dresses washed and ironed for my use.*

- *There were water bottles kept near my bed, which I had to finish (four to five liters in a day).*

- *Our family member would refrain from coming to my room frequently.*

- *Nini would not cuddle me or sit on my bed.*

My mother would not have any problem with *Benu* and dad. They would follow all the stringent rules. Being a defense officer's daughter, I was used to discipline, tough schedules and authoritarian commands.

However, I wondered how she would manage Nini because I knew for sure that Nini would revolt . . . my little firecracker would go for it . . . if she was asked to stay away from me.

Predictably except *Nini*, everyone followed whatever my mother wanted. *Nini* refused to stay away from me. My mother highlighted the pros and cons, pleaded and scolded *Nini* but she found it very difficult to bar *Nini* from my room.

I sat on my bed and looked at them. They looked almost identical—round face, button like nose and straight haired beauties; one was seventy one years old and the other, sixteen. Both were strong willed, rigid and hot headed. They fought every now and then on this issue and temper tantrums were witnessed several times that day.

When admonished, *Nini* complained about the injustice of it all. She whispered, *"Tell Thamma (granny), I will enter this room as and when I wish! This is my house! You are my mom and nothing can keep me away from you! I will not stay away from you! No one can stop me from coming near you!"*

I teased, *"You tell her."*

Nini ran and gave me a tight hug which my mother saw and yelled, *"I have seen what you have done, Nini."*

I ganged up with *Nini* to trouble her. When I cuddled *Nini* my mom pointed her finger at us and sternly told us, *"Both of you . . . be careful!"*

Nini shouted defiantly, *"I won't! I won't stay away from mummy!"*

I reprimanded *Nini*, "*You know she does not want to keep you away from me, she is just following my doctor's advice.*"

Nini murmured insultingly, "*Like mother, like daughter!*"

She ran and gave me a hug before my mother could see and whispered in my ears, "*Don't listen to her.*"

This went on for two days, they argued, quarreled and complained about each other, so on the second day, a deal was struck. My mother gently asked *Nini*, "*Let's lay down the rules right at the beginning. You will follow them, won't you?*"

Tired of her persistence *Nini* agreed, "*Okay Thamma.*"

Rules for Nini—

- *She will always change her outdoor clothes before entering my room.*
- *She will not rush to my side, cuddle or hug me.*
- *She will not sit on my bed.*
- *She will use my study table for studies so that she can be near me when she was at home.*
- *She will not unnecessarily disturb me.*

Next few days were very difficult for me as there was severe weakness, shooting pain in my arms and legs. I felt weak and wretched because of vomiting sensation, aversion to strong smell, insomnia and slight bleeding. Untimely bleeding scared us however, when *Dr. Smruti* was informed, she asked me relax and prescribed some medicines which took care of these side effects.

Anyone from our colony who heard about my cancer diagnosis came to meet us. *Benu* and my parents were with them. Best wishes from our friends and colleagues filled our house with positive energy. Though I could not meet them personally, their positive vibes reached me and kept me motivated.

It was time for my first blood test. My mother panicked, dismayed she asked *Benu*, *"Rina has to go the hospital in this state."*

Benu comforted her, *"Mā, I will request the Path staff of Century Rayon Hospital, if they will come home to collect the blood samples."*

I told my mother, *"Mā, I can walk, don't worry, I will go to the hospital."*

> *One telling glance from her and I kept quiet.*
> *Perhaps, she was right . . . I did feel shaky.*

Benu took permission from *Dr. Joshi* of *Century Rayon Hospital*. *Ms. Alka Suryavanshi* from Pathlab (*Pathology laboratory*) and *Ms. Ratna Ningulkar* (*assistant*) came home to collect the blood samples. This eased my problem on two counts—one, I need not be exposed to other patients waiting for their turn in the pathlab and two, in my present state I need not climb stairs. Blood test was done on *14th September* and the report showed that the *W.B.C. count (Total leucocytes), S. creatinine* and *platelets (Total thrombocytes)* were low. *Dr. Smruti* was informed and she told *Benu* to purchase two *Grafeel* or *Neukine* injections.

Chemotherapy treatment is costly . . . we all know, but we found that the cost of various tests, medicines and the injections was also exorbitant. *Benu* paid ₹ 3000 for each injection.

A nurse had come from *Century Rayon hospital*, but unfortunately, she did not know how to administer a subcutaneous injection. *Dr. Smruti* explained the procedure to her on phone. After spending an hour with us, the nurse was finally ready to administer the injection in my tummy. The next day same time she returned and seemed much more confident. These injections were painful and the area around my navel was sore and tender. Two days later, *Ms. Jyoti Dhabak* from Pathlab and *Ms. Ratna Ningulkar (assistant)* came home to collect blood. This small gesture from their end made a huge difference in my cancer journey. The report showed that the *W.B.C. count, S. creatinine* and *blood platelets* were normal. *Dr. Smruti* was informed about it on phone.

Exactly after fifteen days, early morning while combing my hair, a lock of hair fell in my hand. Dismayed to see them, I ran to the dressing table to see what had happened? I stood staring at my reflection with great concentration. There was a bald patch on one side of my head.

*Alas! The first major side effect . . . I had just
entered a very difficult phase because physical
pain was bearable but losing one's hair was
unbearable.*

*My education . . . my intelligence . . . my over active
mind . . . told me . . . you know about Taxol! You know
how it works! You know about its side effects! You know
that your hair will grow back but . . . my heart did not
listen . . . and I somehow could not hold back my tears.*

Most of my hair (*black ones*) were gone within
the next few days. Don't know why . . . but I started
collecting and preserving them.

My experience said, "*It is the mental agony which
is more painful than all the physical discomforts after
chemotherapy.*"

Being bald was painful in the sense that it lowered
my self-confidence and hurt my ego. *It was tragic! My
new image broke my heart! It scared me! Where was
this journey taking me? I brooded over my looks! It was
bereavement! I grieved for my beautiful hair.*

My family members were with me as they shared
my sorrow and comforted me. I was embarrassed to
look into the mirror and my family knew how I felt.
However, their positive outlook towards life did not
allow me to lose my self-confidence.

*"Everything in life is temporary, if things are
going bad it can't last forever."*

> *My feelings regarding hair loss—*
>
> - *Hair loss (alopecia) is the most distressing side effect of chemotherapy.*
>
> - *If you have to undergo chemotherapy, going bald is a reality and the very thought of going bald appalled me. I was always proud of my thick, black and silky mane—my crowning glory. I was frequently complimented for my hair and it was an integral part of my identity.*
>
> - *When I started losing my hair, my already fragile self-esteem broke apart. My hair was the first thing on my mind when I woke up and the last thing when I went to sleep.*
>
> - *Losing my hair depressed me. It made me feel unattractive and less feminine.*
>
> - *I felt ashamed of myself, a reaction resulting from the loss of control over the image I desired others to see.*
>
> - *I did every possible thing to conceal the visible changes in me.*

It became a tradition in our family that everyone dropped a kiss on my bald head at least once a day. They often told me how beautiful I looked with my bald head, chubby cheeks and huge lovely liquid black eyes.

Nini was almost inseparable from me. She was reprimanded frequently but she always made some excuse to be with me, to hug me and cuddle me. She covered all the mirrors in our house with curtains and would not allow me to look in the mirror. *But then who wanted a mirror? The love reflected in her eyes conquered all my misgivings.*

*Yes! Accepting my baldness was a learning
process. I never really accepted it or felt
comfortable being bald. But slowly with lot of
encouragement from my family, I learnt that
being bald did not rob my femininity.*

Nini started calling me with all sort of funny and loveable nick names like *"Gulli (as my face was round, pronounced as Gool-lee), Gullu, Gullad (variations of the same), Choogli-Poogli (yet to know what it means), Chaman lal bebo (babe with bald head), Baby—baybu etc."*

*Cancer is not funny but love and laughter are the
best medicine.*

These names made me laugh. It was like going back to being a child again. *Nini's* cheerful slightly teasing manner suited me perfectly. She was vibrant, her style was expansive and her very presence healed me. She became my life line and the joy of my life.

*They say that love is a great healer. I became more
open to receiving love, basking in the love, care
and support of my family.*

In the meantime *Gargi*, who was staying in *Hyderabad*, was going through the worst period of her life. She was away from family and the assurance given on phone was not sufficient. She was lonely, scared and the turbulence in her life was something, she could not adjust. There was no one with whom she could share her sorrow so after work she started visiting *"Śrī Venkaṭēśwara Swami temple"* near her residence in Srinagar colony.

The priest of the temple was very observant. He felt if a young girl with tears in her eyes sat praying day after day, it meant that she must be going through a rough patch. One day he spoke to her and she told him about the turmoil in her life.

He blessed *Gargi* and said, "*Don't worry dear, Śrī Veṅkaṭēśwara Swami is kind and he will listen to your prayers. Faith in God can produce miracles.*"

Gargi believed that God is eternal. God brings goodness in our life and God Almighty knows everything about us; our present, past and future.

She trusted the Lord, to take care of her mother. It became a ritual for her-after office she would go to the temple, sit there praying for hours. *Gargi* was receiving day to day account of all that was happening here from *Benu* and *Nini*. Finally she could not bear to stay away any longer and after repeated requests, she managed to get a few days leave to be with us.

We immediately observed the change in *Gargi*. She had grown up in these few days and was no longer the "*vivacious, chirpy young madam*" that she always was. She kept quiet and had matured beyond her age. She would sit talking to me for hours, following all the rules laid down by her granny. She kept surfing the internet for information on best diet schedule for chemotherapy patients and also showing me photographs of beautiful bald ladies, cute bald babies etc. She kept updating us on alternatives available, other than medicines to overcome the corrosive side effects of chemotherapy.

Gargi was amused with the funny nick names *Nini* had given me, so she decided to call me, *baby panda and sunflower baby (whenever I used to smile).*

"The best doctors are Dr. Diet, Dr. Quiet, and Dr. Merryman."

Mid 16th century proverb

Next few days were good, there were no side effects so my parents left for *Nasik* and kept *Gargi* in charge for few days. My parents carried photocopies of all my reports to consult *Dr. Bhattacherjee*, a famous homeopathy doctor at *Nasik*. My parents had complete faith in him and wanted me to take homeopathy as an alternative form of treatment.

Confined within the four walls, side effects after chemo and restriction in diet started taking its toll on me. There were few occasions when I remained depressed. Such instances were rare but whenever they happened, my family made sure that I bounced back quickly. My daughters were amiable and their sweet spirit radiated sunshine, when they were around. I called it holistic healing as their mere presence healed me.

Nini and *Gargi* liked to click photographs and posing for photographs was something they enjoyed. Smart phones with a 5 to 8 megapixel camera always in hand, I called them trigger happy, always ready to shoot. They tried to include me in their photo sessions but I refused to be clicked. I would either turn my face or hide my face.

Nini told me after one such session, *"Don't hide your face Gullad . . . you are wearing a scarf . . . so why hide it?"*

I complained, *"But I still look taklu (bald)."*

Then she did something . . . so beautiful that it brought tears in my eyes . . . tears of joy . . . love and affection.

Nini suddenly pulled my scarf away and before I could react, she brought her head above mine and let her long tresses fall on either side of my face. I sat stunned, as she arranged her long hair, such that they looked as my own. She then asked *Gargi* to click our picture.

*A memorable instance . . . filled with sheer bliss
of being with my daughters.*

My daughters purchased some beautiful scarves for me because they knew that the sight of my bald head (*though, I was not completely bald*) troubled me. *Gargi* kept me engaged, forced me to eat healthy fresh food and kept the stress level low by singing, dancing and telling jokes. She discussed scientifically proven health diet with me as she knew that the researcher in me would look for proven fact. She encouraged me to be strong and stay positive. This was possible as I was surrounded with love and laughter.

*There was complete role reversal as my kids
started treating me as a child and were behaving
like my mother. I started enjoying this change, as
I was transported back to my childhood days.*

Holistic healing—

- *Hair loss (alopecia) wrecked my self-esteem. But positive approach of my family, to face life helped me to remain sane and to recover my self-confidence when I was in need of physical healing, emotional calm and mental well-being.*

- *A holistic healing of mind, body and soul was an ongoing journey, in which faith in God, modern medicines and doctors helped.*

- *Holistic healing is an overall healing process.*

- *It is a lifestyle approach in which my friends and family members helped me to recover my self-esteem.*

It was festive time. Heavy rains were playing havoc however it could not dampen the spirit of *Ganesh Chaturthi. Mr. Ranade*, our family friend had settled in *Kalyan*, after retiring from *Century Rayon*. He was our neighbour for ten years. It was a tradition in *Ranade* household to bring home *Ganapati* during *Ganesh Chaturthi*, for five days every year. During this period we would attend the *Puja* and *Ārati*.

They realized that something was wrong when we neither called them nor attended the puja. Our common friends informed them that I was diagnosed with cancer. This shocked *Mr. Ranade* to such an extent that he broke down in front of the Lord. *Meeta (his wife)* called *Benu* and told him that *Mr. Ranade* told *Ganapati*, "*Rina could not come this year, a tradition broken; I want a promise from you that she will be cured. When you return the next year, she should be here with us.*" *Shailesh*, their son came all the way from *Kalyan* with *kumkum* and *prasad (blessings from Ganapati)* for me.

With plenty of time in hand, it appeared to me that there were some loose ends in my life, which required my immediate attention. During one quite moment, I called *Dr. Pejaver* and told her that I wanted to get my papers in order so that under any adverse situation, my pension benefits would reach my benefactors (*Benu, Gargi and Nini*), without any hassles. I had to take precautions while talking to her, given the situation at home, with all of them on guard . . . 24/7.

Pejaver madam reassured me that she and her office staff would take care of everything and the relevant paper would be sent to me for signature. She further informed me that according to the Government regulations, I would have to first finish my sick leave which was available to me till *22nd December 2010* and then proceed for special medical leave for one year (*with pay*) followed by two years special medical leave without pay.

She was however, positive that I would get well much before that and then insisted, "*Meditate everyday Moitreyee, it helps.*"

There was a time when I felt twenty four hours, in a day was less for fulfilling all my commitments Well! Now…confined within four walls…It was a different scenario altogether. With so much time in hand, I thought to make the best of my time by revising the review article I wrote earlier for the scientific journal "*Bionano Frontiers*". After revising it was sent to the Editor.

Gargi's leave was expiring so she planned to leave for *Hyderabad* within a day or two. During her stay, we saw a marked change in *Benu*. He was more energetic and most importantly, he was smiling again. *Gargi* is her father's darling daughter; they would sit for hours talking. Her presence was healing not only for me but also for *Benu* and *Nini*.

I got the blood test done on *24*th *September* as per schedule. The report showed that the *W.B.C. count*, *blood platelets* and *S. creatinine* were normal. *CA125* was 315.5 U/ml slightly lower than the earlier report.

> *Yes, I was ready for my second cycle of*
> *chemotherapy.*

The good news from *Nasik* was that *Dr. Bhattacherjee* was positive after he saw my reports. He gave repeated assurance to my parents that I would be cured completely with his medicines. He was confident that the cyst on the liver and the peritoneal fluid would disappear with homeopathic medicines.

Homeopathy—

Homeopathy derives from two Greek words, homios-like and patheia-pain. It is a complementary or alternative medicine (CAM). It is based on a series of ideas developed in the 1790s by a German doctor called Samuel Hahnemann. There has been extensive investigation of the effectiveness of homeopathy. Homeopathy is based largely on the "law of similar," or the notion that "like cures like." It is a 'treatment' based on the use of highly diluted substances "law of infinitesimals," which states that the more a homeopathic solution is diluted, the more powerful it becomes.

He sent medicines for two months and told them that these medicines should be started immediately. He assured them that there would be no side effects in fact these medicines would reduce the side effects of chemotherapy.

After few days my parents returned with the homeopathy medicines. There were eleven medicines to be taken between 8:00 a.m. to 10:00 p.m. My schedule for homeopathy medicine was 8:00 a.m., 9:00 a.m., 10:00 a.m. 12.00 noon, 2:00 p.m., 3:00 p.m., 4:00 p.m., 6:00 p.m., 7:00 p.m., 8:00 p.m. and 10:00 p.m.

Instruction was not to drink water/ fluids or have food half an hour before and after taking the medicine. Stop drinking coffee; less oil while cooking, restrict eating raw onion, garlic, sour food and hot chilies and spices. Doctor's advice was to have fish regularly.

We were in a fix as there were medicines to be taken at 8:00 a.m., 9:00 a.m. and 10:00 a.m. This meant no water from 7:30 a.m. to 10:30 a.m. (three hours). Again medicines were to be taken from 6:00 p.m., 7:00 p.m. and 8:00 p.m. that is no water from 5:30 p.m. to 8:30 p.m. (three hours). This was not advisable as *Dr. Smruti's* recommendation was to drink plenty of water to flush out toxins from the body.

My schedule was totally in mess as I also had to take some allopathic medicine in between. There was total confusion, if there were so many medicines, then when to have food and when to have water.

So my father decided to explain the situation to *Dr. Bhattacherjee*, who immediately suggested some changes so that I could drink water in between and stay hydrated.

For a cancer patient these small issues often appear magnified and the same goes for the family members who are flummoxed as to what can be done? However it is always best to rely on your doctors to solve such issues as wisdom prevails.

During this period what helped me was the following-

- *Washed my hands frequently.*
- *Took care not cut or pick at cuticles in hands and feet.*
- *Did not squeeze or scratch pimples.*
- *Always wore shoe/slippers.*
- *Used unscented sunscreen to avoid sunburn.*
- *Did not receive any vaccinations.*
- *Did not have any dental work done.*
- *Stayed away from people who were sick.*
- *Avoided crowd and public transportation.*
- *Avoided anything that might have high concentrations of bacteria like still water, mobile phone etc.*
- *Did not do anything that could result in injury.*
- *Avoided eating raw fruits and vegetables and uncooked herbs.*
- *Wore a scarf or a monkey cap to bed to avoid cold and also to collect hair.*
- *Wore nonrestrictive clothing of cotton fabric.*
- *Had plenty of water to drink.*
- *Ate more high fiber food to avoid constipation.*

Chapter 8

*Second cycle of chemotherapy
and aftermath . . .*

It was time for my second cycle of chemotherapy. Concerned about my looks, I stood in front of the mirror and critically scrutinized myself.

What did I see?

Patch of grey hair, near my temples, some grey hair scattered on my bald pate. *Interesting!* All the black ones had disappeared. What still remained, were only the grey ones.

My impish daughter *Nini* stood by my side, gauging me with a naughty smile on her face.

Arching a perfect brow, she enquired, *"Gulli, what are you doing?"*

I pointed at my bald pate, *"Look, not all my hair is lost, if I bring these grey hair to the front and then tie the scarf, no one can make out that I am bald."*

I followed my words with action, tied my scarf and looked at her in anticipation.

Nini had a broad grin on her face and a twinkle in her eyes when she said, *"Gullad, you look so pretty with your chubby cheeks, big eyes and shiny round bald head, why do you want to hide behind a scarf?"*

I announced, *"My next visit to Bombay hospital, I will tie a scarf like this."*

Nini started singing, *"Gulli . . . you look so pretty . . . chubby cheeks . . . I will make a beautiful pony-tail."* Her singing made no sense but was entertaining.

I loved to sing the number *"You're My Heart, You're My Soul"* from the hit singles by *"Modern Talking"* for my daughters when they were little and I still sing it for them. Every time I sang the lyrics *"You're My Heart, You're My Soul, I keep it shining everywhere I go"* for them and they tried to figure out who is my heart and who is my soul?

So to tease her, I started singing and as expected she asked me, *"Mā, tell me who is your heart and who is your soul?"*

Just to tease her I gave her a mysterious smile and sat quietly.

On *28ᵗʰ September 2010*, twenty one days after my first chemo, *Nini* gently led me away from the mirror and made me sit on a chair. She then started experimenting with a scarf. She tied it fashionably and then ushered me to the mirror. Admiring her fashion sense but doubting its appropriateness, I told her, *"Nini,*

I look like a diva . . . this looks beautiful . . . and I am going to hospital, not to a fashion show."

"*But mummy, once a diva always a diva,*" She encouraged.

We were at *Bombay Hospital* by 8:00 a.m. *Ms. Malati* had informed *Benu* that we should come early. In the lobby, the beautiful idol of *Ganapati* looked majestic. I bowed in front of the Lord and prayed, "*Gannu, take care . . . only you can show me the way.*" *Benu* stood beside me with folded hands and surprisingly my father, who did not believe much in *God*, stood there praying.

The waiting area of *Dr. Smruti's* chamber was packed with cancer patients and their family members. We waited patiently for our turn. We found ways to keep ourselves busy. I sat quietly studying the body language of *Dr. Smruti's* personal assistant, *Ms. Malati*, other hospital staff, nurse, patients and their family members.

Benu was busy striking up conversation with almost everyone present in the waiting room. He did not sit at one place (*He would befriend people and go out of his way to help the relatives who came from faraway places. They usually felt lost in the hospital which was a crazy maze, with different floors, corridors and consultation rooms*).

I always sat quietly waiting for my turn. It could mean anything between two to five hours. I was never hurried or hassled and that was my nature. My father sat by my side reading a newspaper or talking to other patients. Being a defense officer, he was always smartly dressed *(habits die hard!)* and he always offered his seat to any lady looking for a place to sit. I was proud of my father who was chivalrous even at the age of seventy seven. However, whenever our eyes met, he would smile and talk to me softly in baby language *(a language only he can speak, but all of us in Saha clan can understand)* thereby completely negating the image of a tough military man.

In the waiting room we met children, teenagers, young and old suffering from cancer; we would interact with them and listen to their life-stories, as everyone had a story to tell. The waiting room appeared to be a place, where a range of human temperament was in display. There was an exhibition of diverse mentalities of people. There were patients who would try to jump the line or barge in. There were also people who would wait, but keep grumbling. There were few who were very serious and few on the mend. But no one could get past *Dr. Smruti's*, pragmatic and stern personal assistant, *Ms. Malati*.

For reasons unknown, *Ms. Malati* developed a liking for me and if any one complained or dared to rush in, she would point a pudgy finger at me and tell everyone, *"Look at her, she is a doctorate, a professor and she is waiting for her turn from morning, is she complaining?"*

Ms. Malati had a loud, booming voice so everyone would turn and look at me. First time I rather liked the way she said that, second time was tolerable but the third time I complain, "*My God Dad! Why is she doing that?*"

My Dad had the audacity to laugh at my predicament, "*Don't worry Mamoni (darling); she is admiring your guts. You should be happy.*"

Ms. Malati however, saw to it that we did not have to wait unnecessarily for my appointment. This was our second visit so she advised *Benu* about the admission procedure to be followed beforehand so that we could get a hospital bed in time.

In her chamber, Dr. Smruti was examining me. She was surprised that the fluid in my abdomen had disappeared completely.

She asked me, "*When was the aspiration done?*"

I was startled, "*You did not tell me to get it done.*"

She looked very happy, "*Good . . . Good.*"

She assured *Benu* and my father, "*She has responded well to the first chemotherapy, the peritoneal fluid has disappeared and it is a very good indication.*"

She then asked me to get admitted for the second cycle of chemotherapy.

I asked *Dr. Smruti*, "*Doctor, does Taxol spare grey hair?*"

Surprised, she asked me, "*Why, what happened?*"

I explained, "*Doctor, I have lost all my black hair, but the grey ones still remain.*"

She told me, "*No, nothing like that, eventually you will lose all of them. Why don't you cut them?*"

Cut them . . . well! How could I? They were my faithful ones! I thought.

Benu had gone to the administrative office to finish the admission procedure. It was after almost half an hour he called and told us to proceed to 7th floor as we had been allotted a room there. The room allotted was spacious and airy. I was called to the nurse station where my height, weight and other preliminary examinations were done. *Sonali* had an off-day so she was with us. The second chemo started with *Taxol* (*300 mg*) after all the preparatory medications were administered.

My father was again holding my hand and gently soothing my frayed nerves. I was slowly drifting off to sleep when I woke up with a start on hearing *Gargi's* voice. She was talking animatedly to *Sonali*, *Benu* and my father. She had left just a week ago, she was back, why? *Gargi* blew me a kiss and then told us enthusiastically that she wanted to be with me during my chemo.

After that, the room was filled with positive energy. *Gargi* talked about shop with *Sonali*, went down to fashion street market with *Benu* for shopping. She discovered the canteen, *"Paritrupti"* of *Bombay Hospital* and periodically went there with *Sonali*, *Benu* or her *Grandpa* for tea and snacks. She force fed me, when I refused to drink spinach soup. She was energetic, enthusiastic, brimming with positivity and she kept everyone busy. *Dr. Nupur* and *Dr. Priyanka* visited us often and were happy with my progress. They told my father that it was wonderful being with people who were optimistic and so full of life.

The next day early morning *Carboplatin* (*700 mg*) was administered. The drip continued. *Dr. Indu Nair* had come to meet me, she sat with me for nearly an hour, discussing about other cancer patients she met when she visited different hospitals. Her eyes were bright and her words were full of spirit. She encouraged me to live life with dignity and courage. Her dedication towards cancer patients and the difference she was making in the life of a cancer patient by counseling them, impressed me. *Mind you! She was not getting paid for it. She did this voluntary work for her own satisfaction.* I respected the good work she was doing and the next few hours was spent dreaming, thinking about the efforts I would make to tell cancer patients about my experience and in my dreams . . . imagined me as a counselor . . . doing the good work.

During our stay in the hospital, *Benu* disclosed to *Dr. Smruti, "Grafeel and Neukine injections were not available in Shahad. Hence, I had to purchase it from Kalyan."*

She smiled, *"But you could get Grafeel, isn't it?"*

Benu said, "*Yes doctor, I paid ₹ 3000, for each Grafeel injections.*"

Dr. Smruti was startled, "*₹ 3000!*" But she did not elaborate on it.

This bothered *Benu* so he started a survey. He discovered that the cost of one *Grafeel* injection was only ₹ 1500 in medical shops in front of *Bombay Hospital*.

"*Half the price . . . Half the price,*" He murmured, angry with himself.

He returned upset to have been fleeced, he muttered, "*Sala chor* (*** *thieves*), *they don't spare anyone.*"

He then told us about his discovery and wondered how could educated people like us be cheated so easily?

He again lost his temper, "*Sala chor.*"

Gargi consoled her father. Peace prevailed and soon the negativity disappeared. Dad, *Sonali* and I ganged up and started pulling *Benu's* leg and we all were laughing and smiling again. I was discharged from the hospital on *29*th *September*. The salesman of the medical shop packed two *Grafeel* injections in an icebox so that it would not spoil during the return journey. He asked us to store them properly in our refrigerator till required.

At home, we engaged a nurse (*Sheetal*) to take care of me. Her sole responsibility was to look after my needs. She was a jovial, talkative and amusing lady. She kept us busy with her non-stop gossips.

In the mean-time *Ujjal-Da* had received a mail intimating him of my condition. He immediately called Mom from *Johannesburg (S.A.)* and cried, "*Ma, Rinki is diagnosed with cancer, I can't believe it.*

They spoke for some time and then he asked mom to hand over the phone to me. Mom put the speakers on and we three spoke for an hour and then he suddenly announced, "*I am booking my tickets I will come to meet you, Rinki.*"

The last time we met was in *July 2006.* Four years just flew by . . . I certainly did not want him to see me in my present condition. So I told him the truth, "*Don't come! I don't want you to see me bald. You can come when my hair grows.*"

He tried convincing me but I was adamant. Finally mom asked him to let go and visit later.

My father wanted to join office so he left with my mother for *Nasik. Anu-Di* and *Gargi* were with me. In absence of my mother, *Anu-Di* mothered me and spoilt me rotten. *Gargi* left after three days, reassured that I was fine. *Anu-Di* however, stayed back till my mother returned.

Anu-Di always admired my efficiency and was proud of my achievements. When she observed how adept I was in dealing with the side effects, her happiness knew no bounds. She would tell anyone, who called or came for a visit, about my strong will power and cheery disposition.

On *2nd October*, blood test was done and the report showed the *W.B.C. count* and *platelets* were low.

This time *Mr. Alex*, a roly-poly smiling male nurse (*also called brother*) came home and confidently administered the *Grafeel* injection in the sub-cutaneous region of the belly. The next day, he was home right on time; though the injection was painful . . . his cheerful disposition negated the pain. On *6th October*, blood test was done again and unexpectedly this time the *W.B.C. count* was again low. *Dr. Smruti* was informed and she advised me to take two more *Grafeel* injections.

My belly was sore from the two previous injections so I asked *Mr. Mark* to administer the injections in my thighs. On *11th October*, blood test was repeated and the *W.B.C. count* was normal this time.

Our life had become a blur of days running around in hospitals and clinics, taking doctor's appointments and visiting clinics for blood tests. We stopped counting how many times the blood tests were done! We also stopped counting the number of times Grafeel injections were administered! Previously the sight of blood troubled me, visits to hospitals and clinics distressed me but my cancer journey taught me to take everything in stride.

Acknowledge that there will be tough times and be mentally prepared so that they won't come as a big shock. My cancer journey taught me to get use to injections, the sight of blood and the typical smell of hospitals.

All doctors stressed on the fact that good nutrition is very important for cancer patient as this can help fight infection, maintain weight and increase strength. It can also help fight the side-effects of chemotherapy.

"Let food be thy medicine and medicine be thy food."

Hippocrates
(CIRCA 460-CIRCA 370 BC) Ancient Greek Physician and Father of Western Medicine

---

A strict diet plan was charted out—

- *Early morning—a cup of milk (I stopped taking tea and coffee).*

- *Breakfast—corn flakes with milk/ one bhākṛī with egg or vegetables/ dalia.*

- *Mid-morning—a cup of paya soup every alternate day/moong dal soup.*

- *Lunch—one chapatti/bhākṛī and some rice with vegetables, dal and fish.*

- *Mid-afternoon—one pomegranate.*

- *Evening—a cup of vegetable soup.*

- *Dinner-two chapatti with vegetables, dal and fish.*

Doctors told me that *bhākrī* made from multigrain flour (*nachani, soyabean, jowari flour etc. mixed with wheat flour*) was actually better than the refined wheat flour. *Dr. Nupur* knew about my fondness for burgers so she advised me to refrain eating them till my chemo got over. *Dr. Smruti* advised me to avoid eating raw vegetables so my mother boiled vegetables for me and surprisingly though not very fond of bitter-gourd (*karela*) earlier, now it enhanced my appetite.

We knew that pomegranate was one of the most powerful, nutrient dense foods for overall good health. *Punicalagins* from *pomegranates* were responsible for their antioxidant and health benefits. It showed remarkable anti-cancer effect (*Gargi found this information from the web*). Eating one *pomegranate* daily became compulsory for me. My father took upon himself to see to it that the fruit basket was always filled with *pomegranates*. *Gargi* told us that Vitamin C was good for cancer patients. Thus, I made a habit of eating *oranges* and *sweet lemon*.

The soups were always prepared fresh and were refreshing. The ingredients in the vegetable soups were mostly the same but variations were done if some fresh vegetables like *peas, drumstick, cabbage* etc. were available. I would drink vegetable soup daily and *paya* soup every alternate day. I would also have *moong-dal* soup or *yogurt, lassi, chaas* (*curd preparations*) etc.

Paya is the feet or trotters of goat or lamb, cleaned properly with no meat attached to it. *Paya* soup is extremely beneficial and is traditionally given to patients who are weak and needs to regain strength. If I maintained a good appetite then the credit for this would go to my mother. She always had some alternatives ready if I did not feel like eating something.

> *This is my story; others may have their own story to tell. I am not a medical doctor and it's my belief that what is good for me may not suit your purpose. It is my sincere advice . . . always consult your doctor . . . before making any change in your diet . . . as I did every time . . . I made a change in my diet chart.*

My favourite was the Vegetable Soup prepared by my mother. The ingredients used were—

- *1 Carrots chopped or grated*

- *1 Beet root chopped or grated*

- *4 Tomato chopped*

- *1-2 pieces (5-6 inch) Raw papaya chopped or grated*

- *1-2 pieces (5-6 inch) Bottle gourd chopped or grated*

- *1 tsp Ginger paste*

- *A small bunch of coriander leaves chopped*

- *A small bunch of spinach leaves chopped*

All the ingredients were put in a pressure cooker. Three cups of water was added followed by salt added for taste. It was cooked for 20 minutes (5-6 whistles). The liquid was then strained. It was the clear vegetable soup which I preferred.

I also liked Paya Soup. The ingredients used were—

- *4 pieces of Mutton Legs (cleaned paya)*

- *2 Tomato (chopped)*

- *1 Onions (chopped)*

- *5-6 cloves Garlic (chopped)*

- *1 tsp Ginger paste*

- *A small bunch of Coriander leaves chopped*

- *1 tsp Cumin Seeds powder*

All the ingredients were put in a pressure cooker Three cups of water was added followed by salt added for taste. It was cooked for 25 minutes (6-7 whistles). The liquid was then strained and the bone marrow was removed. Fresh pepper powder was added to enhance its taste.

The Moong dal soup preparation was simple—

- Moong dal—50 gms
- ½ tsp Ginger paste
- ½ tsp Turmeric powder
- Salt to taste

Washed and cleaned moong dal was put in a pressure cooker. Water, little ginger paste and turmeric powder was added. Salt was added according to taste. Boiled for 15 minutes. The liquid serves as a nourishing health drink.

Lassi (lussey), a customized preparation—

- 1 cup Yogurt
- ½ tsp Roasted and crushed cumin seeds
- Salt to taste

Yogurt was blended with little water manually in a pot. Salt was added for taste. Roasted and crushed cumin seeds were added to enhance its taste.

Chaas with variation to suit my diet—

- 1 cup Buttermilk
- ½ tsp Roasted and crushed cumin seeds
- Salt to taste

Buttermilk, which is the liquid left after extracting butter was blended in a pot with some salt and roasted and crushed cumin seeds. Coriander, grated ginger and diced green chilies which are added to accentuate the flavor of chaas were not added; as I was not allowed to take any raw vegetables.

Sheetal (*my nurse*), was meticulous and a talkative lady with a cheerful disposition. She asked for two printouts of my diet chart and medicine schedule. She pasted one set in kitchen and another in my bedroom. She made it a practice to offer me a glass of water every half an hour. She kept me engaged with her jokes and often exaggerated tit-bits about the people she met. Though confined within the four walls of my house, we remained updated about the happenings in our immediate neighbourhood, through her. I always knew who asked for me . . . who prayed for my recovery and I opened up to the positivity she brought around me.

One day I was searching for my crochet bag when my mother asked, "*What are you doing, Rina?*"

I said, "*Mā, I want to make some handkerchief edgings, I am not finding my crochet hook.*"

She was surprised, "*You want to make crochet designs, now?*"

I said, "*Yes, why not? Anyway Mā, I can't sleep in the afternoon so I will sit and try out some new designs.*"

Being a working mother, afternoon nap was never in my agenda before and now I found that it still did not figure in my routine. My mother presented me with colorful crochet threads, hooks and handkerchiefs.

I started making beautiful crochet designs for handkerchief edgings and presented the first six to my mother. Then I kept crocheting and presenting the beautiful handkerchiefs to *Anu-Di*, *Natasha* and *Bipasha*.

An important side effect of chemotherapy was that loud noise distressed me. I faced a major setback during the nine days of *Navratri*. The *Ramleela* ground was near my house where the mikes kept blaring as the *Ramayana* (*The story of Lord Rama*) was being enacted. Loud music from a nearby hotel where *Dandiya* was played upset me (*In dandiya as a part of merriment, men and women dance in a four beat rhythm, with sticks in their hands*). Life became unbearable between 7:00 p.m. to 10:00 p.m. The only way I could stay unruffled, was to keep the doors and windows shut and make my room sound proof.

> *More than physical, the emotional upheaval of cancer treatment is a torture. Yes I can vouch for that. The drastic change in my normal routine was demoralizing. I had to rationalize and sort out my life. I was vulnerable, edgy and the noise from my neighbourhood made me paranoid. There was disquiet, resentment and frustration welling up in me. So was it any wonder that I was suffering from insomnia?*

I had trouble falling asleep as a constant stream of chaotic thoughts crisscrossed my mind. If I slept, I woke up frequently during the night and had trouble going back to sleep. I remained restless throughout the night as I lay in bed trying to sleep. Disturbed sleep took its toll so I had to take the sleeping pills prescribed by *Dr. Smruti (first time in 47 years)*. I also had to take different medicines to overcome numerous side effects like nausea, vomiting, loose motion, constipation, headaches and body-ache etc.

It was common for everyone to say, *"Rina, think positive, stay positive."*

But where does the positive energy come from? How do I stay positive?

> *Well! From where did I get the positive energy, was almost like a story unfolding in front of me.*

If you really look, look hard enough, you will be able to imbibe the positivity that surrounds you. If each and every member of my family were caring, committed and optimistic then my friends were just that, my friends. They were attentive, supportive and good company. After my marriage we stayed at *Century Rayon Colony, Shahad*. We formed a group which consisted of four families and eight members i.e. *Benu* and self, *Alka* and *Babji*, *Sarita* and *Manjul* and *Anil* and *Sudha*. Each couple had two kids and we spent years and years of togetherness as our children grew up. There were outings, get-togethers, movies, picnics etc. where all the sixteen of us would be together.

> *Friends are always friends we knew that but when these friends became an important part of our family, is something we realized only after we went through a rough phase in our life.*

Our friends shared our sorrow and were with us every single moment when we felt lost or were troubled. Whenever required, they would help *Benu* or would take care of *Nini* and my parents. They would come home sometimes to spend some time with us. At times of emergencies when *Benu* had to go out urgently to purchase some medicine, *Alka* would babysit me. *Babji* and *Alka* made it a practice to be with *Benu* and my mom every Saturday. We found their positive energy refreshing. I realized that my friends stopped celebrating birthdays and get-togethers. When asked not to do so, they insisted that the moment I re-joined them, the birthday celebrations, get-togethers and outings would start again.

Being a Bengali it is a ritual to celebrate *Durgā puja* during the last five days of *Navratri*. During this period large idols of *Goddess Durgā*, her sons and daughters, *Ganesha, Karttikeya, Laxmi and Saraswati* are worshipped. We fast, offer prayers (*Anjali*), wear new dress, visit different *pandaals* decorated beautifully and help in the *langars*, distributing *bhog (prasad)* with friends and relatives. Our family friend, *Daisy* and *Susanto Dey*, knew that I was undergoing chemotherapy. Since, we could not visit and pay our respect to *Goddess Durgā*, from *13ᵗʰ-17ᵗʰ October 2010*, five days of *Durgā puja*, they made it a point to bring *prasad* for us and spend some time with us. *Such positivity! I was proud of my friends.*

My guide, *Dr. Naresh Chandra,* was extremely disturbed when he came to know about my cancer diagnosis. When he was told that I could not meet anyone he requested *Benu* that he would come home only for five minutes and meet me from a distance. I felt blessed when he encouraged me to get well. He was accompanied with his wife, *Mrs. Usha Naresh Chandra* and my friend *Dr. Geetha Menon (R.K.T. College).* Later he spoke to *Benu* frequently to remain updated regarding my treatment.

> *When I pondered on the reason . . . the source . . .*
> *of my positive energy . . . it was very clear that*
> *my friends, colleagues and family members were*
> *the source of my inspiration, strength and my*
> *awesome will power.*

We were constantly in touch with *Dr. Smruti.* She was extremely happy to note that my appetite was good and we were strictly following her advice. Regarding insomnia she said that since I never suffered from it before, it was only a matter of time that I would go back being my old self again. Her mantra was very simple, *"The day you stop brooding; stop being paranoid and anxious about chemo, is the day you drive insomnia away."*

The blood test was done on *16th October* as advised. The *W.B.C. count, platelets* and *S. creatinine* were normal. *CA125* was 59.2 U/ml. We rejoiced to see the *CA125* reading was fast approaching normal.

So much to learn—

- *Proper time management was vital; juggling between my medicines (both allopathy and homeopathy), drinking water, having breakfast, lunch, dinner, soups and fruits taught me that. Homeopathy medicines (eleven of them) continued throughout the day.*

- *It was also mandatory that food and water must not be taken, 20 minutes before and after taking homeopathy medicines.*

- *Doctor had however, advised to drink at least 3 to 4 liters of water daily. This was required to detoxify.*

- *Insomnia was due to stress, it would disappear as and when I relaxed.*

- *While every day brought in new challenges, the love and support of family and friends were the key factor that helped me to get through difficult time.*

Chapter 9

Third chemotherapy and the uncertainty...

My parents returned to *Shahad* on *18*th *October* as my third cycle of chemotherapy was scheduled for the next day. This time *Benu* wanted to drive our car but my parents advised him against it. *Mr. Bhasker Pansare* was an excellent driver and he would take care while driving so they wanted him to drive.

In these few days *Mr. Pansare* had become attached to me and started addressing me as *didi (elder sister)*. He knew that the doctors had advised me to have soup and coconut water. So he brought fresh raw papaya and coconut grown in his farm, for me. He also brought pomegranates from *Nasik*, as good quality pomegranates were not available in *Shahad*.

My dad was shocked to see that his daughter was so frail that she could not stand or walk without support. My mother noticed that sitting, I was confidence personified whereas the steel in my voice would disappear and I would look for support the moment I had to stand. She patted my cheeks, blew a kiss and said softly in Bengali, *"This is just a passing phase."*

Yes, I was convinced that it was transitory phase. Few days back, it would embarrass me to take help . . . but then I figured out, "*What's the big deal?*"

My cancer journey made me sensitive to the love that surrounded me. I started treasuring the unconditional love and attention showered on me. There was no humiliation in accepting help and this took me back to my childhood days, when I trusted that someone will pick me up if I fall, hold me and cuddle me.

It was strange but true, "*I began to enjoy my dependency.*"

My father however, looked deeply troubled so I told him, "*With you on one side and Benu on the other, I can walk with confidence, don't worry Bābā, I will not fall.*"

But my condition bothered him. It was written on his face.

Benu proposed that next day we leave home early in the morning so that we could be ahead in the queue, waiting for *Dr. Smruti's* appointment (*Where it was strictly first come first basis*).

We reached *Bombay Hospital* by 8:00 a.m. In the lobby we bowed with clasped hands before Ganapati. Cancer had messed up my life but I was determined to pick myself up. Asking for his protection, I repeated my prayer, "*Take care, Lord Ganesha . . . I trust you with my future.*"

Dr. Smruti's chamber was in the first floor. The lift was taking time so I climbed the stairs slowly. This surprised my dad he admonished, *"Why Mamoni, Why?"* But he accompanied me. Poor thing, he could not leave me alone to climb the stairs.

We patiently waited for our turn in the waiting room. We were not late for our appointment but there were many who came earlier than us. We learnt that patience is a virtue but the lesson was pretty painful. After a long wait, we could finally meet *Dr. Smruti*.

We knew that my father was worried so after the check-up, we were not surprised when he asked *Dr. Smruti*, *"Have you seen her, she is not able to stand without support."*

Doctor reassured him, *"Don't worry, weakness will go eventually."*

Acknowledging his skepticism, *Dr. Smruti* asked him to have faith in the advances made in modern medicines and to be patient since his daughter was responding quite well to chemotherapy.

She told him, *"Your daughter is smiling, talking, taking interest in her surroundings and eating proper meals, this means, she is fine."*

She asked him to get me admitted for the third cycle of chemotherapy after she noted that the blood test report showed that *W.B.C. count, platelets, S. creatinine* were normal and *CA125* was almost normal.

After admission, we went to the 9th floor. There we saw our family friend, *Arun Dana* and his wife *Sudeshna Dana* from *Nasik*, waiting for us. *Arun-Da* was *Ashish-Da*'s childhood friend and our family friend and he was like a brother to me. We sat talking for a long time, sharing our experiences with them. The sisters from chemotherapy section made arrangements and after sometime requested the visitors to step out. The drip was started for *Taxol (300 mg)*, they kept watch on the number of drops falling per minute in the tube.

They told us, *"It should neither be fast nor very slow."*

After an hour the sisters left. I started feeling disoriented and my father sat near me soothing my nerves, *Sonali, Benu, Arun-Da* and *Sudeshna* were talking softly. As *Taxol* slowly entered my system, I was benumbed with sleep. I must have slept because suddenly to a flurry of activity woke me up. *Sonali* was greeting a lady. *Who was she?* She walked in and wished my father. She bowed and touched his feet for his blessings. *Who was this lady?*

Sonali brought the lady in front of me and asked, *"Rina, do you remember Nupur (Jhoomma)?"*

Of course, I could not recognize her, but her name was familiar. *Yes! She was my childhood friend Jhoomma! When did we last meet? Jhoomma* told me that we had last met when our parents were posted to Chandigarh. We were in seventh standard; probably twelve years old. She told us that she had once met *Ujjal-Da* in *Lucknow* when he was in the Army. *Jhoomma* had changed drastically; the thin and lanky girl was now a beautiful and smart lady, she was now *Lt. Col. Nupur Chanda* working with *Indian Army*. It was a nostalgic moment for us because we were meeting after a gap of about thirty years. Later in the day, I met *Sonali's* brother *Shuprobhat* for the first time. He had come all the way from *Kolkata* to meet me.

Dr. Priyanka paid us a visit even though it was her day off. She was aware that I would be admitted for my third chemo so she had taken pains to meet us. She spent about an hour with us, talking about the work she was doing, her tenure in *Bombay Hospital* and her family. My father had this special quality to attract people. They felt so comfortable and at ease around him that they discussed their life story with him.

Dr. Indu Nair, this time asked me to tell her about my family, my job as a professor and my hobbies. She realized that my unfulfilled dream was to write a book.

She asked me, "*Why did you not write till now?*

I asked her, "*Where was the time?*"

She smiled and told me, "*Now you have time, so start writing. Write your book; fulfill your dream to become an author.*"

Slowly she warmed up to the idea and tried convincing me, "*You are a Professor, writing a book is easy for you. Yes, this is the right time to write a book, so why don't you write it."*

After she left, I was thinking about the events of the day. We had visitors from *Nasik* and *Kolkata*, I met my childhood friend after thirty years, the conversation with *Dr. Priyanka* and finally and most importantly *Dr. Indu Nair*'s words of encouragement. *Write a book! How could I write a book now, I wondered? Was this the right time to write a book? Dr. Indu Nair* was so positive; her attitude was so right. It filled my heart with joy and inspired me to write my book.

Yes, in spite of hours spent in the waiting rooms for doctors, in hospital for chemo, blood tests, scans, for the reports etc. I would make time and fulfill my dream.

I told my father, "*Bābā, I want to write a book.*"

"*Yes, yes why not.*" He cheered me with a huge smile on his face, "*Good! Good!*"

I said, "*But Bābā, now I don't want to write a book on Genetics or Biotechnology, I want to write a book on cancer.*"

This surprised him, "*You decide what you want to write; I will provide the diaries for you to write.*"

Sonali was enthusiastic, "*Cancer? Tell us what you will write about cancer?*"

"*Well! It will be a memoir on the struggle and triumph of a cancer patient,*" I said.

Sonali told us about her experience with cancer patients in Army hospital and *Dr. Nupur* and *Dr. Priyanka* joined us sharing their experience in this hospital.

I slept peacefully that night though the intravenous continued through the night. I dreamt of becoming an author, busy writing books. My imagination knew no boundaries and the next day, I woke up with a pleasant feeling because somehow I knew that the dream of writing a book would not be a dream anymore.

Carboplatin (700 mg) was given the following day. *Benu* had gone to the airport to receive *Gargi*. It was very quiet and we were feeling lethargic. My father was talking to me in his special baby language. *Sonali* was laughing at something he said when *Gargi* walked in with *Benu*. Her presence radiated warmth, love and joy. The room brightened manifold with her mere presence. *Gargi* did some cat walk in a new dress she had purchased from *Fashion Street* and presented a beautiful scarf to me.

I missed *Nini* during these special moments. She was busy with her college and coaching class. We did not want to expose her to the harsh reality of cancer treatment as we thought it might have an adverse effect on her. So my mother stayed with her at home and neither of them visited the hospital during the chemo cycle.

Dr. Priyanka liked the strong ties in our family and appreciated the positive attitude and strong will power she observed in our family members. She mentioned that our bonding with each other helped us to enhance our feeling of well-being and also helped us to find the strength to deal with cancer.

Dr. Nupur visited at least three to four times a day. She told us that patients who were dealing with cancer were devastated both physically and emotionally but patients who were positive in the face of terrible adversity were inspirational for a doctor. Our family had the right attitude towards cancer and she often quoted our example to other cancer patients.

At the time of discharge, Dr. Smruti advised—

- *Schedules must be adhered to without fail.*

- *Eat regular meals.*

- *Drink lots of water to drain out the toxins and stay hydrated.*

- *Get the CT scan done for abdomen pelvis.*

- *Get CA125 and other blood tests done.*

- *After twenty one days return, for a follow up.*

- *If hepatomegaly does not disappear, an extra chemotherapy cycle would be considered.*

- *If CA125 was below 35U/ml and other blood reports were normal, only then the doctors would consider surgery.*

Due to the trauma of having a cannula struck (*IV catheters*) in my hand for two days, the back of my hand was swollen and very painful. The nurse rubbed an ointment of *Heparin and Benzyl Nicotinate* (*Thrombophob*) for relief. By now my painful bruised arms bore the testimony of the three cycles of chemotherapy and repeated blood tests.

Dr. Smruti's student had come to meet us when she saw how painful my hand was. She told us about the use of port, groshong line etc. which remain in place for months even years. She told us that through the port, chemo drugs and other medicines could be given and thus no more needles sticks in the vein, throughout the treatment. Well this was news to us and we wanted to know more about it. The discussion went on till *Dr. Nupur* came to meet us.

After the briefing, we started for home. As before, we carried two *Grafeel* injections with us. The journey back was uncomfortable but *Gargi's* presence was helpful.

The same day I realized that Bombay hospital also called Bombay Hospital Institute of Medical Sciences (BHIMS) had two buildings. There were an old and a new building, which was surprisingly on either side of a service road. I always went straight to the new building to first meet Ganapati in the lobby then Dr. Smruti and finally for chemo, to the hospital room which was housed in the same building.

The old building had the administrative building, consulting rooms and the Operation Theaters. Both the buildings were connected from inside, so there was no need to cross the road every time the need arose. There was however, a maze of confusing corridors one had to traverse to reach your destination. No wonder Benu always took lot of time to complete the administrative procedure for my admission.

At home, as per schedule the blood work was completed. The blood reports showed the *W.B.C. count* was low. Two *Grafeel* injections were administered and again, after two days blood test was done. This time the report was normal.

My third chemo was over and the physical changes in me were quite severe. So how did I camouflage them? Well! Beautiful scarves concealed my baldness. I refused to wear a wig. Below dignity! Why? I always felt that you could easily spot a person wearing wig. So, definitely no wig for me! Other changes were such that I could not do much to mask any of them except wearing a cloak of positive attitude.

The changes in me after chemo—

- I was bald.
- I lost my eyebrows and eyelashes.
- My teeth and nails turned black.
- There were dark circles round my eyes.
- My skin was pigmented with dark patches.
- There were blood spots and rashes on the skin.

After two days, bone and joint pain started with a vengeance. There was debilitating pain and discomfort in my hips, lower back, knees and shins. At times it felt as if someone put a heavy weight on my body and it was difficult to move even an inch. My mother always found innovative ways to combat these aches. Sometimes she would give me hot water fermentation, hot water bottle, hot towel or electric belt for heating. By now we knew that within a week, the pain would subside.

An important side effect of chemotherapy was my aversion to any kind of strong smell. *Geeta Bhakare* (*cook*) while cooking kept the doors closed because tempering and strong aroma caused nausea. Surprisingly though, I could eat almost everything that was served. *Benu* was told about the health benefits of walking cat fish (*magur fish*) so it was cooked almost daily. We were bewildered that the strong fish smell did not trouble me while eating.

My daughters used powder, perfume or cologne cautiously as the fragrance disturbed me. I was so sensitive to smell that *Bharati Mane* (*maid*) could not use phenyl while swabbing the floor or use scented gels to wash utensils because even a whiff of smell could cause nausea.

Loud noise troubled me from the day my chemo started. I developed severe head ache when an inter-school sports events was conducted in a school near my house. The noise due to the microphones used to make announcements or for commentary was unbearable and the continuous cheering by the supporters was nerve wracking. The sports event started in the wee hours of morning and continued till late evening. This event went on for many days and upset my equilibrium. *Sheetal* tried to reduce the noise level by making the room sound proof.

I became so sensitive that small thing like speaking on phone, watching television became troublesome because the sound from the speakers and moving images of television made me dizzy.

Notwithstanding these irritants I tried to remain calm, energetic and in total control of myself. Meditation and Praṇāyama helped me considerably. I also recited Hanumān Chalisa, Gâyatrî mantra and Sāi astha-shatnamani regularly.

I was paranoid when my chemo had started. Circumstances were such that even strong person like me . . . when diagnosed with cancer . . . wobbled. Don't blame me!

But the same circumstance also taught me that there was no use worrying. Doctors were doing their job well so all I had to do was to stop worrying and think of self-healing. First thing in my agenda was to sleep well . . . so the day I convinced myself that "all is well" is the day I stopped taking sleeping pills.

Insomnia! What insomnia?

I could sleep every night without interruption after that.

A few strengthening facts—

- *I knew these changes would not last forever, as all things must pass.*

- *I knew that this was just a temporary phase.*

- *Though I was physically weak, I was mentally very strong.*

I somehow liked it whenever *Gargi* would softly run her hands on my arms and legs. Her touch was magical and had the most calming effect on me.

Gargi loved singing. Her soft and sweet voice was captivating. Whenever she sang in her vibrant and melodious tone, it elevated all of us to an altogether different zone. *Nini* loved to prance around, dance and break into a jig occasionally. Both of them choreographed dances, recited poem, walked the ramp, read SMS jokes and they called this as my entertainment time.

Happiness is to be surrounded by people who
spread lots of love and laughter

In all this fun and frolic, *Benu* and my mother often forgot about their worries and would join them. Laughter is the best medicine and my daughter's antics always made us laugh and it turned out to be a great stress buster for all of us.

As I was struggling to keep physically fit,
spirituality in its essence was awakening my
inner self and my efforts to keep cancer at bay,
was helping me grow spiritually.

One day, around 6:00 a.m., I was sitting on a chair enjoying the morning breeze, at home. I was half asleep or half-awake . . . in a trance, maybe . . . when I distinctly heard a voice coming from the photograph of *Śrī Sāi*, *"You will be fine, but take care of your mother."*

Mystified, I looked at the photograph. *Was it a dream . . . or was it a hallucination!* The atmosphere was filled with some kind of energy, a sort of movement . . . I don't know, what it was but I was wide awake and shivering with excitement. I shouted, "*Mā . . . Mā . . . come here . . . come soon.*"

My mother came running, "*What happened, dear?*"

I told her, "*Sāi Bābā just spoke to me . . . he told me I will be fine but he also told me, you have to take care of your mother. Mā . . . what will happen?*"

My father had also come into the room thinking that there was some emergency. He told me calmly, "*Good, you will be fine and don't worry about your mother; we will see that she remains fit and fine.*"

My hunch was that he did not believe me. I looked at him reproachfully and then turned to look for support from my mother. I was relieved that she believed me.

Benu sat beside me astound, he murmured, "*I am a devoted Sāi bhakt, but Sāinātha has neither given me darshan nor spoken to me. You are so lucky, you got his darshan. He has spoken to you, you are blessed Rina, really blessed.*"

Did I qualify as Sāi bhakt? No, I considered *Benu* and my mother as devoted *Sāi bhakt . . . I just tagged along.*

But Yes! I was a determined lady. Yes, determined to walk the path with the belief that with *Sāi's* blessings the hurdles in my cancer journey would disappear.

Dr. Mulgaonkar called me regularly. One day we were discussing about the vast literature available on internet regarding cancer and its side effects. She knew about my inquisitive nature, how I surf the web for hours together to get information.

She must have felt something because suddenly she said, *"There is lot of detailed information on internet about cancer, I advise you, not to access them."*

Surprised, I asked her, *"Why madam?"*

She told me, *"I know, you will try to dig out information about every little thing. You will take unnecessary stress. But I feel that you are in right hands, in a renowned hospital, under the care of well-known doctors and you have a great family so you should not think about anything else but to get well soon."*

Her concern touched my heart. Don't ask me why? But something clicked. I told my mother what *Dr. Mulgaonkar* had told me. She felt whatever madam said, made sense.

So my resolution was, *"Will not access the web for cancer related queries, from now on."*

When my daughters heard of my resolution, they introduced me to some games on Facebook. Surfing the net to read about cancer, had become an addiction. It was initially difficult to stop accessing the web for cancer information but gradually my attention was diverted towards these games. I found them rather interesting. I started spending more time on them. So, farming in *Farmville* and building a city in *Cityville* became my passion.

Chemotherapy meant, I stayed home mostly and if I ventured out, it was only to visit hospitals or clinics.

But I did not miss going out. Why?

The entire world . . . entered my little room.

How was it possible? Well! My best friend . . . World Wide Web!

I started making friends, worldwide . . . chatting with them, taking interest in their life. I found a number of my Facebook friends were suffering from cancer. As I spent a chunk of my time on Facebook, *Ashish-Da* started teasing me, *"Facebook addict . . . you are turning into a Facebook addict."*

While I started recuperating, it was disclosed to me that *Gargi* was almost homeless as the *PG* in *Hyderabad* (*which I had arranged for her*) was closing. The boarders were asked to search for an alternative accommodation. This happened a week after *Gargi* got the cancer news. She decided not trouble us with her predicament till she found an alternative accommodation. *We were stunned but happy that our little girl was all grown up!*

I congratulated her, *"Gargi, I now know for sure that you are mature enough to face any adverse conditions without panicking."*

She chuckled and told me reproachfully, "*Mā, I am still your baby.*"

I laughed and cuddled her, "*Yes, baby.*"

Benu advised *Gargi*, "*You need not worry about your mother, so much. Now that we are able to cope with chemo, you need not come here so often. You should come only after you finished your project in December.*" *Gargi* was not very happy about it, but she agreed.

> *My reading of the situation—*
>
> - *The involvement of your children with you is much more than what they may express.*
>
> - *They rationalize their decisions, based on circumstances and act accordingly.*
>
> - *Adolescent children are vulnerable, but your child might surprise you with their maturity.*

Gargi left for *Hyderabad* and my father for *Nasik*. I was with my mother, *Benu* and *Nini*. *Benu* resumed office. In the morning my mother and *Sheetal* stayed with me.

We were busy rescheduling our life when it was brought to our knowledge that Mrs. Swamy who resided on the top floor in the same building, was also suffering from cancer. She was operated and her sixth chemotherapy cycle was underway.

We were stunned to hear this and wondered how was it that two people from the same building were suffering from the dreaded disease. Incidence of cancer seems to have increased manifold. We knew some of our friends were cancer survivors and some who had fought valiantly. There were also few who had concealed cancer diagnosis for the fear of stigmatization.

Misperceptions of Cancer diagnosis—

- *Instills the fear of stigmatization . . .*

- *Some think of cancer diagnosis as something to be ashamed of.*

- *There is a feeling of guilt.*

- *They feel that they are being punished, for having done something wrong.*

- *They are anxious that they will be a financial burden to their families.*

- *Worried that people would avoid them because of their history with cancer.*

- *Worried that getting their son and daughters married would be a problem.*

- *Believing that cancer can only mean death.*

Nini's birthday was on *29*th *October*. *Nini's* friends turned up at 12:00 a.m. (*night*) with a huge cake and cards to celebrate her birthday. There was a festive atmosphere as *Benu* arranged for a chocolate cake (*Nini's favourite*) and other snacks. We celebrated *Nini's* birthday at home as she wanted to celebrate it with me.

One day, in a conversation with *Dr. Pejaver*, she wanted to know, "*Are you wearing a scarf or a wig to cover your head.*"

I told her, "*I wear a scarf.*"

"*You sound depressed,*" she asked and then told me, "*Don't be. Your hair will grow back again.*"

She then told me about her sister-in-law *(bhabhi),* who was a cancer survivor. She said, "*Moitreyee, my bhabhi had very long hair, which grew almost to her waist. She became completely bald as she underwent chemotherapy. She also wore scarfs to protect her bald head. Now her beautiful hair has grown back, better than before. She is a cancer survivor and now she is totally cured.*"

I then shared with her the pet names I acquired from my daughters. She began to laugh when she heard the name . . . "*Gulli*".

Laughter is undoubtedly the best tonic; good for your emotional wellbeing.

Dr. Pejaver then shared her experience about her sister-in-law with me. How they kept her happy during that period but she rather liked my daughter's innovative style of keeping pet names.

Advice to friends—

- *Cancer is a non-communicable disease but the patient undergoing cancer treatment is going through a major upheaval in life.*

- *Cancer patient undergoing chemotherapy may suffer from hair loss. If they do, it affects the patients to a great extent, drains them emotionally.*

- *Some patients are emotionally stable, knowledgeable and know that their hair will re-grow when chemotherapy stops.*

- *But when friends and colleagues discuss, assure and underline the truth, it helps the patient immensely.*

5th *November, 2010* was Diwali, *"The festival of lights,"* we enjoyed lighting lamps and performing the rituals. *Nini* made beautiful colourful rangoli in front of my house, but the noise and the smell of the bursting crackers spoilt the fun. Our friends *Himanshu* and *Monica* were with us to celebrate the occasion.

> *All my doctors were very vocal about the fact that health should always be the first priority. The schedule (chemo, blood tests and various scans and follow-ups) chalked out by the doctor should be followed meticulously. There was no scope of deviation. Festivals, birthdays etc. did not count. They insisted that excuses would not be tolerated. Dr. Nupur often cited examples of patients who delayed chemo or surgery due to some festival or other event in their family and later suffered, sometimes at the cost of their life.*

So as per schedule blood test was done on 4th *November*, a day before Diwali. The report showed the *W.B.C. count*, *platelets*, *S. creatinine* was normal. *CA125* was 14.9 U/ml.

On *8th November 2010*, we were at *Bombay Hospital* for *CT* scan of abdomen and pelvis. I was advised not to eat or drink anything several hours before the scan. We were called at 9:00 a.m. We filled a form giving complete medical history and submitted my earlier scan reports. After half an hour the nurse supplied a bottle filled with a coloured liquid and a glass. She asked me to finish the liquid, one glass full according to the timings indicated on the glass. The liquid was tasteless. The nurse also asked me to remove any metal I wore like my jewelry, clips etc. as it would interfere with the scan. But then since the start of my cancer journey I stopped wearing them altogether, also I took care not to wear any clothing which had metal buttons so it was not a problem. *Benu* was with me in the waiting area, we read newspapers, listened to music and finally I was called in for the scan by 1:00 p.m. It was freezing in the scan room. I was made to lie on the bed of the *CT* scan machine. My experience was not pleasant because the nurse had to insert the needle at least thrice before finding a proper vein. The machine started whirring and the nurse asked me to raise my hands above my head. The computerized voice of the technician guided me when to breath in, hold my breath and then breathe out. This went on for several cycles and finally it was over. The nurse came in removed the IV and that's it.

At home, firm in my mind about writing a memoir, my decision was *now or never.* My father kept his promise and presented me few new diaries for writing my memoir. Inspired by *Dr. Indu Nair* and with my family's encouragement, I started jotting down my thoughts and my experience regarding cancer.

However, the first barrier encountered was that I found it difficult to hold a pen since my fingers kept shaking. Second barrier was that every time I held a pen and started to write, it would slip from my fingers.

So to my chagrin neither could I hold a pen nor could I write. My exasperation prompted *Benu* to call *Dr. Smruti* and tell her about my predicament. Doctor however, assured that it was just a passing phase. My fingers would stop shivering the moment chemotherapy cycles stopped.

Did that stop me? No! It did not! Distressed about my difficulty in writing, I started finding out alternatives.

If you have the inclination, no one can stop you.

I could not write, Fine! But I could type! Fantastic! So typing on my laptop was the best option. And this was the first step in the realization of my dream, to write a book.

Initially I wrote the events and dialogues as small notes describing something that urged me to fight, something which made me laugh or cry. I started from the beginning . . . the first day of my cancer journey. Totally wrapped up in my thoughts, I started experiencing a myriad of emotions and had plenty to write.

Yes! it was a life's lesson . . . though I was not a medical doctor . . . it was my cancer journey . . . a true story which I could share with all the multitasking working mothers, who are very dear to me and like me, needed information, counseling and the courage to face such adversity.

Writing about positive attitude, strong will power and the invincible faith in God to accomplish one's goal, was cathartic. Spreading to one and all, the importance of holistic healing was mandatory.

I was entertaining a thought; whatever I may be able to write, the purpose of my writing the book will remain incomplete if I do not focus my sincere attention to the contribution every person made in his or her own way.

How not just the cancer patients but family members, friends and colleagues contributed in the healing process was the message I wanted to spread.

Every event of my cancer journey was important.

However, Reality struck while jotting down about some recent events on my laptop, I wondered why to write a book on cancer?

All this stuff was very different from the usual scientific papers I wrote.

Who will publish my book?

Will anyone read my book?

I am not a medical doctor so I could not give advice.

All I could do was to write about the events during my cancer journey and about what helped me to face the hurdles.

But something in me prompted me to keep writing.

If my book could make a difference in the life of even a single cancer patient, then my life would be worth the struggle.

Well! I am writing this book to tell everyone that—

- *Cancer does not happen in a day. Be alert to any symptoms, any change in your body.*

- *Cancer is an inconvenient truth; but there is absolutely no reason to hide the truth.*

- *Do not delay investigations; hiding cancer diagnosis can lead to an increased risk of death.*

- *There is no stigma attached. It should not instill the fear of stigmatization.*

- *Stigmatization deters patients to seek the help, they need . . . delay leads to complications . . . death.*

- *Evaluate the screening options available, finance available and decide your course of action.*

- *Cancer is not a death sentence.*

- *Cancer diagnosis is not a shame.*

- *It is a non-communicable disease.*

- *Always let your family members, friend and colleagues know; their prayers and good wishes surrounds you with positive energy.*

- *Be open to the love and the affection that surrounds you.*

- *Holistic healing helps where everyone contributes in healing of the mind, body and soul.*

- *Educate the society and eradicate the myths surrounding cancer.*

Chapter 10

Surgery and there after . . .

On *9*th *November 2010*, we were at *Bombay Hospital*. This visit was momentous for us because my doctors would either ask me to undergo few more cycles of chemotherapy or would decide on surgery. A crucial decision, for which they would first study my recent blood test and *CT* scan reports, analyze them and only then give their verdict.

In my private conversation with Ganapati, I requested him with an intense yearning in my heart, *"Please Gannu, please see to it that I don't require an extra chemo."* I was not alone there because *Benu* stood beside me praying.

Benu went to collect the *CT* scan report. We then waited for few hours before we could meet *Dr. Smruti*. Doctor went through the reports. *CT* scan report for chest, abdomen and pelvis showed, *"Complete resolution of ascites, focal peritoneal deposits, left side pleural effusion and marked resolution of omental thickening. The bilateral ovarian masses showed moderate resolution and no new lesions were detected. The liver was normal and no localized solid or cystic mass was identified."*

Blood tests showed, *"White blood count, S. creatinine and blood platelets as normal and CA125 at 14.9 U/ml."*

Dr. Smruti was satisfied with the reports. She sent the reports to *Dr. Prakash Patil*. He was surprised to see the *CT* scan reports. The hypo-dense area in IV lobe of the liver, which was a cause of major concern, had completely disappeared.

Dr. Patil murmured thoughtfully, ***"It is a miracle."***

We rejoiced when he confirmed, *"Yes, the cystic mass on the liver has indeed disappeared."*

We remembered *Dr. Bhattacherjee's* claim, *"The cystic mass on the liver will disappear only with homeopathy."*

I don't know how this miracle happened. *Was it due to chemotherapy or homeopathy? But the moment, Dr. Patil proclaimed the disappearance of the cystic mass from the liver, a miracle, my faith of being completely healed was reinforced.*

> *You will always encounter problems in your life but have faith that something good is waiting ahead for you.*

Dr. Patil explained to us that since the cystic mass from liver had disappeared, extra cycle of chemotherapy was not required.

So! Every cloud has a silver lining. We were thrilled that after three cycle of chemotherapy, the cystic mass on the liver had disappeared.

Dr. Patil saw the huge smile on my face and added, *"Not only that, there is complete resolution of ascites."*

We nodded *Dr. Smruti* had told us after the first cycle of chemotherapy, the peritoneal fluid had disappeared (*resolution of ascites*), but today, the *CT* scan report confirmed her prediction.

Dr. Patil elucidated further that since *CA125* was at 14.9 U/ml, he would decide on the date for surgery. After consulting his itinerary and few more doctors (*his team of doctors*) on phone, he informed us that he would perform the surgery on *15ᵗʰ November, 2010.*

We immediately called my father and informed him about the doctor's verdict and the date of surgery. We also asked him to inform *Dr. Bhattacherjee* about the reports. As we were leaving the hospital, we gathered in the lobby, stood praying in front of Ganapati, we thanked him for his blessings. I bowed with folded hands, assured that *God* listens to the prayer from a sincere heart, *"Thanks Gannu . . . the extra chemo was not required. I will be back after five days for the surgery . . . Thanks for taking care."*

Proper arrangements were made at home as this time my stay in the hospital would be for a longer period. My parents arrived on *13ᵗʰ November* night. As per the advice of *Dr. Patil*, I was admitted in *Bombay*

Hospital on *14*[th] *November*, a day before the surgery. We entered the hospital and I stood in front of Ganapati with folded hands praying, "*Please bless me and give me the strength to overcome the ordeals, struggles and difficulties.*"

On admission the pre-operative preparations started and went on throughout the day. The doctors prepared me mentally and physically for the surgery.

First, *Dr. Pratima* came down to meet me. Surprised to see her after a long time, I probed, "*We have not seen you after my first chemo, where were you, doctor?*"

She smiled and said, "*Yes, I underwent hysterectomy and had complications during the surgery.*"

Once she had told me about working ladies and how they neglect their health. I understood that . . . *God spares no one.*

I asked her softly, "*How are you now, doctor?*"

She laughingly told me, "*Fine, but you know, doctors are usually atrocious patients.*" She then spoke about her surgery, complications that occurred and also about the doctors who had operated upon her.

Dr. Pratima told me, "*I will not be present for the surgery as the expenses are already high and if I do come, it will further add to the expenses unnecessarily.*"

We felt that doctors were needlessly blamed and made scapegoat for the rising cost of healthcare expenditure. Here was my doctor trying to help us by reducing our medical expenditure. This gesture of her was appreciated by our family members.

But I wanted her to be there! She saw my expression, laughed and assured me, *"You will be operated by the best cancer surgeon of this renowned hospital. Be assured that you will be looked after well."*

She explained, *"Anyways, there is a close connection between mind and body. Patients with 'fighting spirit' do much better than those who give in to their illness and you are definitely a very strong lady."*

Dr. Nupur and *Dr. Priyanka* had accompanied *Dr. Pratima.* In an effort to reassure us, they informed that as students they would observe the surgery. My father asked them how long the surgery would take. However, they were not very sure since the time taken varied from patient to patient.

We were busy talking to the doctors when a gentleman entered the room and introduced himself as *Dr. Jadliwala.* This was the first time we met *Dr. Jadliwala.* He was accompanied by his student. We found the doctor to be a very friendly and genuine person. He explained to us about his role in the surgery. *Dr. Pratima, Dr. Nupur* and *Dr. Priyanka* left after wishing me well for the surgery.

We were busy clearing our doubts with *Dr. Jadliwala.* My father asked him, *"Doctor, how long will the operation take?"*

Dr. Jadliwala smiled, "*It can take few hours . . . depending upon the complications. Don't worry unnecessarily, she will be fine.*"

My father was trying to find out how much time the surgery would take, but the doctors were evading his question and not committing themselves.

Thereafter, we had the opportunity to hear from *Dr. Prakash Patil* about details regarding the surgery. He patiently answered all our queries and we were amazed to see his confidence, his gentle manners and his vast knowledge on the subject. He gave very simple explanation, choosing his words carefully and honestly.

He emphasized that it was a major surgery which could take two hours or more. He explained that he could not confirm how much time it would exactly take, as only after opening up he could clearly see how much the cancer had spread.

The doctor had prescribed a medicine which would clear my stomach and he advised me not eat or drink 12 hours prior to the surgery. Clearing my stomach was a messy affair as I had to run to the toilet after every five minutes. Oh God, it was tiresome!

After few hours things normalized, *Benu* was sitting with me and talking about the surgery when out of the blue realization hit me, "*What if I died on the operation table? What if my sojourn on earth was coming to an end?*"

My restlessness, my tumultuous emotions prevented me from thinking anything positive. My overactive mind seems cluttered. *What could I do to ease my wandering mind?*

I accused *Benu*, "*You are not worried?*"

He was surprised, "*Why, why should I be worried?*"

Here I was unable to control my mind from thinking the worst. The chaos in my head was eating me up and he was asking me, why he should be worried. I felt like boxing his nose.

Then he calmly told me, "*You are in the best hospital under the care of best surgeon and you are a strong lady! So why should I be worried?*"

"*God knows why, but I am feeling very restless?*" I told him "*My mind is wandering over my unfinished duties and commitments.*"

"*What are you talking about? What duties and what commitments?*" he asked surprised.

I emotionally told him, "*In my little world . . . my dreams will remain unfulfilled. Dreams of seeing Gargi receiving her degree . . . Gargi working as a professional and Nini studying in a good professional college . . . there are other dreams . . . where we are enjoying together . . . my daughters getting married . . . grandchildren . . . these dreams will remain unfulfilled if . . . I am no more.*"

I told him, "*I know, No one in this world is indispensable, that is the harsh reality . . . but I want to be indispensable, for my family.*"

Almost hysterical, I started imagining how helpless my daughters would be if the worse happens. Both were of age when they needed their mother the most.

They do not deserve this . . . neither do I!

These thoughts were traumatic. Though distraught and panic-stricken, I tried to stand back and be objective, give direction to my thoughts as I did not want to aim in the dark. Nevertheless I failed miserably.

Anxiety was building up, distressed I cried, "*If I don't return from the operation table . . . Will you take care of my kids? How will you manage? What will happen?*"

Benu's eyes welled up with tears. With unfathomable tenderness, he held my hands and said affectionately, "*Don't worry, you are not going anywhere. Sai Bābā is with us, he will take care.*"

His softly spoken words were poignant and healing. I wiped the unshed tears from my eyes. My breath came out shallow and ragged but I could feel deep in my heart that everything was going to sort out.

Next day, as instructed by the nurse, I was ready by 6:00 a.m. and was reciting *Hanumān Chalisa* when the ward boy came with a stretcher to take me to the operation theatre.

I looked at the stretcher and told him, "*I will walk down or take the wheel chair.*"

He said, *"Rules are rule, you will use the stretcher."*

I felt like a fraud when the nurse asked me to lie down on the stretcher and then she carefully covered me with a sheet. However, recollecting how I had fainted on my first day in the hospital, I decided to keep quiet.

My parents were late so *Benu* called to inform them that we were proceeding toward the operation theater. We got the news that they were held in a traffic jam near the hospital. But *Benu* was with me, holding my hand as I was wheeled towards the operation theatre. It was a very somber moment for us, I don't know what he was thinking but I wondered, *"Is this the last time I will be seeing him?"*

"Think positive Rina! Think positive!" I admonished myself.

There is a beautiful white statue of *"Lord Satyanarayan"* in the passage beside the operation theatre. The ward-boy told us, *"Offer you're your prayers here, he listens to us."*

Benu and I prayed for his blessings. *Benu* received a call from my mother. She informed him that they were held up in a traffic jam. We felt bad but could not blame them as we were well aware of the atrocious *Mumbai* traffic.

The ward-boy told us that it was time to go inside the operation theater. *Benu* wished me *Om Sāi Ram.*

Then a door was opened and I was slowly wheeled towards the operation theatre.

The door closed behind me and the atmosphere inside was very different. It appeared to be a waiting room where the air conditioner was working in full blast. I looked around, the room was well sanitized and squeaky clean. Walls were soothing teal colour, sisters were wearing light blue apron busy with some preparatory work and there was a kind of hush in the room. Let me not deceive myself, I actually felt neglected, a sense of dread was slowly creeping in and I started shivering.

Was I shivering due to cold or out of fear?

I am a firm believer of *Nām Smàraṇ* or chanting of one's Lord's name so I started reciting *Sāi-astha-shatnamani (Asthothram)* and later *Hanumān Chalisha*. This ceaseless chanting were an eternal spiritual guides and sources of inspiration for me.

I strongly believe that if we take shelter with
God, the journey becomes much easier.

Dr. Jadliwala came to meet me. He introduced himself again. His cherry demeanor and warm smile was reassuring. His mere presence was calming. He took my hands in his when I told him that the waiting was making me nervous. He smiled and comforted me, *"Don't worry at all, Dr. Patil and I will be present for the surgery."*

He then explained, *"The cysts in the ovary might be closely aligned to the ureter"*

I asked him, *"What will happen then?"*

He answered, *"During surgery, the ureter should not be scarred or damaged so I will be there to keep watch, if required, will put a stent."*

This made me curious. As a researcher, my inquisitiveness pays and this was an entirely new world for me, quite different from my work so I started asking questions. There were plenty of questions. But it was to his credit that *Dr. Jadliwala* patiently answered all my queries. His positive attitude was contagious soon my nervousness vanished.

I was taken to the operation theatre where surprisingly some soft music was being played in the background. It had a soothing effect on me. I was transferred to the operation table and introduced to a group of doctors by *Dr. Patil.*

As I looked around, there were huge lights, sterilized instruments and equipment in the operation theatre. Doctors and nurses were working silently, the highly sterile conditions, sophisticated machine, the hush in the operation theater caused trepidation, a sense of fear and I panicked. I closed my eyes immediately and surrendered to the Divine Lord entirely (*without reservation*).

Silently, I started calling Sāi Bābā to take care as I believed in his unconditional love.

Then I heard a soft voice calling my name, *Mrs. Saha, Mrs. Saha* can you hear me, I am your anesthetist, *Dr. Arora*, I will inject . . .

After gaining consciousness, I found myself in a different room. Nurses and *ward-boys* were busy looking after patients; my eyes were searching for some familiar faces. There weren't any. I did not know the time as there was no clock around. This looked like a recovery room. There were other patients, who like me had undergone surgery. Some were conscious and some still unconscious. I wondered how many operation theatres were there in *Bombay Hospital* . . . there were so many patients in the recovery room.

My mouth and throat was parched so I called the nurse standing near me and asked for water. The nurse was happy to see me conscious but ignored my request for water. I was not very happy when she ignored my request twice, but could not do anything about it.

I tried to recollect the scene in the operation theatre, *Dr. Arora* calling my name and how I felt something rush to my throat, mouth and nose and after that . . . *nothing . . . and here I was. No! There was this vague recollection . . . someone calling out my name repeatedly; tapping my cheeks . . . well it was hazy. When did it happen before or after the operation?*

Well I was happy to be awake. Thanked God profusely that I did not die on the operation table. Concentrating on myself, I moved my finger slightly and then tried shifting my legs. I was engaged in discovering these small details when I felt someone was standing near my head and watching me.

I turned my head but could not see anyone. However, when I focused my attention at a point in the middle of my forehead and meditated, there was this lovely feeling of his benign presence, *"Yes! He was definitely present! Sāi Bābā was with me!"*

This filled me with gratitude. I remembered having read in *"Śrī Sāi Satcharita"* his famous quote, **"My eyes are ever on those who love me."**

I wanted to stay awake and soak in his presence but the anesthesia was working. I must have dozed off because suddenly I was wide awake again as realization struck; *His Holiness Śrī Sāi Bābā was talking to me! Yes! He was talking to me.* I tried to look back again but could not see anyone there. *Was it hallucination?* Because unquestionably I heard a whisper, *"I was with you, don't worry, you will be fine."* I felt his presence but could not see him.

"Why fear when I am here."

Śrī Sāi Bābā of Shirdi (Unknown-1918)
Spiritual Master, Saint, Sadguru, Fakir and Avatar

Yes! No worries because Sāi was with me. Also deep in my heart, there was this conviction that *Benu's* faith in *Śrī Sāi* brought him to me. What did he tell me yesterday, *"Sai Bābā is with us, he will take care?"* His words came true. *I was convinced that the doctors will tell me that the surgery was successful. Yes! Everything will be positive from here on.* I felt within me the touch of something positive, beautiful and truthful. I felt blessed and started chanting *Om Sāi Ram . . . Om Sāi Ram . . .* my voice, tremulous with joy.

After some time, I was wheeled out of the recovery room. *Benu, Ashish-Da, Arun-Da* and my parents were waiting for me. My father's expression was that of relief, my mother, *Ashish-Da, Arun-Da* and *Benu* were smiling, but all of them were surprised to see me conscious. At once everyone started waving and calling out my name, *Rina . . . Rina.* I smiled and acknowledged their presence but kept chanting, *Om Sāi Ram . . . Om Sāi Ram . . .*

Benu saw my lips moving, his voice was tremulous with joy. He exclaimed, "*Mā, look . . . look, she is awake . . . she is trying to tell us something?*"

My mother came near me, heard my ceaseless chanting of the holy name and started chanting . . . *Om Sāi Ram . . .* with me and within no time all my relatives joined us chanting . . . *Om Sāi Ram . . . Om Sāi Ram.* After that I remembered, being wheeled into a lift and my mother accompanying me but nothing after that. I woke up and found myself in the *ICU* with tubes inserted in my body.

I counted them . . . there was a catheter for urine,
a drainage tube from my side—there was blood
in it, tube in my nose plus a central catheter
vein in the neck. I could hear the beeps from an

*instrument nearby . . . a clip like attachment on
my finger and finally I could also see a beautiful
nurse by my bedside.*

*Yes! There was some hazy recollection of adjustments
being made and a female voice prompting me to inhale,
exhale, turn . . . my memory was obscure . . . but yes,
she must be the one . . . shifting me, adjusting the tubes
etc. and her name was Jennifer, I knew because she was
wearing a name plate on her uniform.*

I told her, "*Jennifer, I am very thirsty, give me a
glass of water, please?*"

She smiled but promptly refused, "*No . . . No . . . no
water.*"

My lips and throat were dry so I requested my
father standing beside me, "*Please . . . please . . .
please . . . Bābā, I want water.*"

My dad asked *Jennifer*, "*Can she be given little
water, her throat is parched?*"

She was sympathetic but she told him gently, "*Your
daughter will start vomiting if she drinks water.*

*I felt like throwing a tantrum but thought better
of it. My mission was to procure some water so
something had to be done. I thought for some
time and then asked Jennifer to give me some
ice-cubes.*

Ice-cubes! Ice cubes?

Jennifer looked surprised by my request for ice-cubes. *Stunned her, did I? Good, my ploy was working!*

My intention was to procure some water *by hook or by crook,* so I told her soberly, *"I understand what you are telling, Jennifer. Give me some ice-cubes; I will only rub them on my dry lips. I promise not to gulp them."*

She looked at someone for permission. Followed her glance and found *Dr. Patil* sitting and writing something. He nodded, so *Jennifer* brought some ice-cubes and with the help of cotton started dabbing my face and lips. *At last, it was a great respite for me and very soothing to my dry, cracked lips.* Mission successful!

After sometime, doctor finished whatever he was writing. He came and stood beside me. He had good bedside manners. He asked me gently how I was feeling now. Well! After the ice cube rub I was really feeling good. I asked the doctor to tell me about the surgery in detail and prized a look of surprise, out of him. He started by telling me that *pan-hysterectomy* was done and when asked what was that, he started explaining. While he explained, his voice was very soothing, there was a strange kind of hush in the *ICU,* it kind of made me feel sleepy and slowly I drifted off to sleep.

Next when I woke up, it felt as though I was burning up, there was this unbearable pain in my abdomen and pelvis. *Dr. Patil* was still there talking to my father and *Benu*. I requested the doctor to give me some anesthesia so that the pain would go. *Dr. Patil* explained that four different painkillers were already administered, so he could not give anymore.

His reasoning though sensible, did not interest me the least. I shouted, "*First, you don't give me water and now when this excruciating pain is killing me, you say you cannot give me anymore painkillers.*"

But the doctor coolly smiled and said, "*Bear it just for some time; you will be fine, soon.*"

I looked at my father with tear in my eyes and grumbled, "*It is better to die than bear this pain.*"

I saw the look on his face and immediately felt guilty of my tantrums. I chided myself, "*You ought to be ashamed of yourself, Rina. A person like you, to go on crying in this way! It was disgraceful, really shameful!*" I caught hold of his hand and with a tearful smile promised, "*I am your strong daughter Bābā, I will face it.*"

He stood beside me silently, soothing my forehead with his fingers. I liked the touch and slowly felt at peace. I must have dozed off because waking up I found *Arun-Da* standing beside me.

Arun-Da exclaimed, "*Hats off to you bhabhi, even after a major surgery you are awake and possess the energy to talk and make yourself heard loud and clear.*" I told him about the pain. He was sympathetic because he was operated recently. He advised me to bear the pain as it would soon pass. He then told me that *Dr. Patil* had told them that the surgery was successful.

After he left my mother entered and stood beside me and tried to give me courage to bear the pain. She said, *"Stay calm dear, why don't you try to sleep?"*

I complained, *"Can't sleep, Mā . . . this pain is killing me."*

She started patting on my head and caressing my face which was somewhat soothing. I was surprised when she hugged me and said, *"We will leave now, we will come back tomorrow early morning."*

Astonished, I asked, *"Going . . . so soon? Why? What is the time?"*

My mother then told me that the surgery took five and half hours and that it was six in the evening. Almost twelve hours passed and I completely lost track of time.

I became emotional when my mother hugged me again. I could not hold back my tears as she comforted me. Though the incident seems to be inexplicable, I told her about my experience, when I felt that *Śrī Sāi* was with me.

She exclaimed, *"So, that's why you were chanting Om Sāi Ram."*

*Yes Mā! He was present . . . Mā, Sāi Bābā was
with me.*

My mother had tears in her eyes, "*You are blessed, Rina . . . Really blessed.*"

> *My mother a true Sāi Bābā devotee prayed that he should give us solace and comfort throughout our life. My mother felt that he was aware of us, watching us and knew what was going on, for without his blessings we would find it difficult to get over the hurdles in our life.*

She made a promise, a *sañkalp*, "*We will come to Shirdi and offer prayers as soon as Rina's treatment gets over and she gains a little strength.*"

I must have slept after my mother left because I found myself waking up to a very lovable voice of *Dr. Nupur*.

She asked me, "*How are you feeling, dear?*"

I told her about the unbearable pain but she only nodded and coaxed me to think of something that would take my mind away from the agonizing pain.

I asked, "*Like what?*"

She said, "*Think of funny moments or focus on people you love like your husband or events relating to your daughters. Somehow try to block the pain out.*"

She started examining me with a stethoscope, pressing it at different places on my abdomen. She was listening carefully.

I found this very interesting. *"What are you doing,"* I asked.

She told me, *"I am listening for sounds of movement, from your abdomen."*

She smiled and asked, *"Did you pass gas?"*

I shook my head and thought, *"Awkward question. I did or did not, pass gas? Big question, well! I could not remember."*

She explained why it was important to pass gas and why movement in the stomach, small intestine, large intestine and colon was important, after surgery.

She expressed her respect and admiration for *Dr. Patil's* patience during the surgery. She related how he painstakingly removed the cancerous organ, tissues and cells during the surgery, which took five and half hours. She reiterated that I was operated upon by an incredible, knowledgeable and master onco-surgeon. It was a moment of joy and happiness when she told me that she witnessed the entire surgery from start to finish. I started asking for details and she happily answered all my queries.

After she left I followed her advice and tried to recollect some interesting tidbits of our family, some beautiful memories, sadly I could not remember any, I tried to dwell on some important incidents relating to my daughters, funny moments, future events, but the excruciating pain did not allow me to do any such thing.

I tried meditation but could not concentrate properly. Nothing worked even after trying every trick to stay calm. This pain was crippling me. It was slowly and steadily making me lose control over my mind and like a fool I started moaning.

Moaning was due to pain but it embarrassed me. *Come-on! A respected Professor could not moan like this! But what to do I could not help it! Moaning relentlessly, I thought why does a person moan when in pain? Does modulation while moaning help in decreasing the pain?*

Moaning was a new experience, making so much unusual noise, unpleasant sounds to overcome the pain, was something different. I tried experimenting, if I stayed quiet—did it increase the pain?

I also tried to find out whether moaning really helps in reducing pain?

While I continued moaning, my scientific approach was working overtime, trying to judge which pitch of moaning . . . loud . . . medium or low would help me.

Could anyone guess what I was doing?

It was little dark when I suddenly heard another patient screaming on top of her voice. It looked as though she was in considerable pain.

I asked *Jennifer*, "*Who is she?*"

Jennifer told me, "*She is an aged lady (moushi) who was also operated this afternoon.*"

The old lady was crying in pain, bawling on top her voice and then she did the unexpected. She forcefully pulled out the drainage tube, yelling on top of her voice. There was lot of commotion as the nurses and *ward-boys* ran to stop her from doing further damage. They asked her to stay quite as she was disturbing other patients. There was lot of activities as some of the nurses scolded her and some were kind as they cleaned her. Thing started settling down after a while but the nurses decided to keep watch on her.

The respite however was short lived; the commotion commenced again when the lady became violent. She pulled out the intravenous infusion from her arm and started vomiting. The *ICU* was now filled with the unpleasant vomit smell and the commotion restarted. I could see the nurses running towards her and hear them warning her again and again, "*If you don't behave yourself, we will strap you to the bed.*"

They asked her, "*Why are you doing this, Moushi? Don't do it again.*"

The lady kept complaining but slowly things were getting back to normal.

I suddenly realized that in all this drama and commotion, almost like a miracle . . . my pain had completely disappeared. I was astonished . . . no

pain . . . no pain at all . . . due to distraction . . .
pain had completely disappeared.

Benu walked in complaining that entry in *ICU* was being restricted. They had relaxed the rule in my case, but the nurse was allowing only one visitor per patient now. When I asked him what kept him away for so long. He said all our relatives were leaving one by one so he was seeing them off.

He then smiled, "*Pain gone?*"

I nodded and told him about what *Dr. Nupur* had said and how the dramatic situation that transpired in the *ICU* helped me forget my pain.

Benu told me that *Dr. Patil* had made detailed notes on my surgery with explicit diagrams and asked him to laminate the pages, file them and keep them properly.

He then told me, "*Dr. Patil showed the cancerous cysts, ovaries, uterus, appendix and some other cancerous parts which were removed during the surgery to the entire family.*"

I asked him, "*What did you see, how big was the cyst?*"

He told me, "*There were two; one small, almost like a table tennis ball and second was big, the size of a small coconut.*"

I enthusiastically asked him, "*Did you click photographs?*"

He clapped his hand on his forehead as he realized his folly. He told me sheepishly, "*It did not strike me at all; none of us had the presence of mind to click it.*"

I felt bad about it and angry that all of them had seen the cancerous organs, except me. They knew about my inquisitive nature, always curious, wanting to know about things in detail, how could they forget? *Benu* knew his folly so he quickly changed the topic.

He said, "*Do you know, your father was upset because he could not meet you before the surgery. Later, he kept watch, which patient was taken in the operation theatre and at what time did the patient come out. He realized that your surgery was taking time and was nervous. When after four hours, we got the news that you were still in the operation theatre, he felt something is wrong and started weeping. He was terribly upset and kept repeating, something has happened to my daughter . . . something has gone wrong.*"

I wondered why my mother hid this piece of information from me. *Benu* laughed, "*Your mother was no better. She was standing in front of Lord Satyanarayan, praying for hours together. We had to force her to sit with us in the waiting room.*"

I asked him, "*What did you do in the waiting room?*"

He said, "*We watched cricket match live telecast on TV. The operation was taking so much time; your parents were restless so we could not enjoy the match.*"

I enquired, "*Why did you not take them out somewhere for tea or lunch?*"

"*How could I?*" he asked "*There was heavy shower since morning and it is still raining.*"

What! Raining! This surprised me. When I was wheeled to the operation theatre, it was a bright sunny morning. *Rains in November!*

On the third day, early morning, I was shifted to my room from the *ICU. How weak I was!* Just moving from the bed in the *ICU*, to the stretcher (*whose height was more*) was strenuous. But the nurse and the ward-boy's efficient maneuvering made the switch easy. As the ward-boy wheeled me through a maze of corridors, lifts etc. to my room in the 10th floor in the new building, I felt exposed, sensing the inquisitive eyes of people we met on the way. I cocooned myself by closing my eyes but kept my mind's eye open and listened to the conversations of other patients, the ward-boys greeting others, the bickering between the ward-boy and the nurse accompanying me. In my room, the switch from the stretcher to the bed was again time consuming and troublesome. The entire procedure exhausted me and I went to sleep. I woke up only when *Dr. Patil* came for visit. *Dr. Patil* told me about the cysts in the right and left ovary and explained due to metastasis how cancer had spread.

He said, "*Pan-hysterectomy, appendectomy* and *4 layer of complete Omentectomy were done.*"

Tongue twisters! What did they mean exactly?

Well! We sort of understood something about human anatomy ten minutes after doctor's explanation. Well! My anatomy would be minus few organs but Survive! Surely I will!

My father asked the doctor about the recurrence of cancer. *Dr. Patil* said that he searched minutely and painstakingly removed every speck and every spot. He removed *4—layers of omentum* and also the *appendix.* He said that not *hysterectomy* but *pan-hysterectomy* was done. *Dr. Patil* assured that the cancer cells were removed completely and that was the reason why the operation took so long.

Though what the doctors said, reassured me . . . but . . . somewhere in one corner of my mind there was this little question, "*What if a tiny speck . . . one cancer cell remains, then what*?

"*What if cancer returns?*"

Questions and more question crowded my head . . . I saw *Dr. Patil* talking to my father. Doctor was telling him that he was happy to see my progress. When I asked him again about the surgray, he patiently answered all my questions.

"Every time you are tempted to react in the same old way, ask if you want to be a prisoner of past or a pioneer of the future."

Deepak Chopra
Indian American Author, Holistic health/New Age Guru and, Alternative Medicine Practitioner

Doctor then advised *Benu* to give me coconut water (*100 ml*) three times a day. *Arun-Da* was beside me, I asked him, *"Will coconut water be sufficient because I can already feel the hunger pangs?*

Arun-Da told the doctor about it. Doctor laughed and said that it was a very good sign. He instructed the nurse to let me have some semisolid milk-rice porridge for dinner.

The whole day I slept and surfaced only when *Dr. Jadliwala*, *Dr. Smruti*, *Dr. Pratima*, *Dr. Nupur* or *Dr. Priyanka* visited. It was late evening when I suddenly woke up on hearing *Benu* talking to *Gargi* on phone. I asked for the phone and started speaking to her. *Benu* asked me to wish *Gargi* as it was her birthday.

"It was 18th November! How could I forget my darling daughter's birthday?" After wishing *Gargi*, I asked for her forgiveness, *"I should have remembered your birthday, I am sorry, dear."*

With a break in her voice *Gargi* replied, *"No, Mā, God is great! You are speaking to me; I can hear you . . . Mā that is enough for me."*

Since cell phones were not allowed in the *ICU*, I could not speak to either of my daughters after my surgery.

We discussed about my divine experience of *Sāi Bābā's* presence during my surgery. She had heard about it from our family and she felt that we were certainly blessed. She was happy to hear my voice but asked me to hand over the phone to *Benu*. She did not want me to exert after the surgery.

Later *Benu* told me that even he had forgotten that it was *Gargi's* birthday. She had called after her office and temple ritual and told him, "*You and Mā have forgotten my birthday for the obvious reason. All I want for my birthday is that Mā should get well.*"

She then told *Benu* that she did not want to eat the dry tasteless food provided in the PG so she would order a *Chinese* take-out.

I found that post-surgery, the role of physiotherapist was extremely important. Two young lady physiotherapists of my elder daughter's age visited three times a day. They demonstrated and encouraged me to move my limbs and do some simple exercise to avoid *deep vein thrombosis*. They told me it was formation of blood clot in a deep vein and it was potentially a life threatening complication.

I did not want that so I decided to exercise. Though these exercises looked simple in my present condition, it took lots of effort from me.

> *These exercise were simple—*
>
> - *The ankle-pump exercise that is bending ankles up and down.*
> - *Rotating feet for a few minutes, moving them up and down.*
> - *Lift leg one by one.*
> - *Bend knees one by one.*
> - *Change position frequently by shifting from back to side.*
> - *Practice lung exercise by coughing and deep breathing.*

Dr. Patil's student came to examine me on the fourth day, he asked me jovially, *"Mataji, kaise ho? (Mataji, how are you?) Bhook lagti hai, kya? (Do you have an appetite?)*

I was stunned because I was never addressed as, "*Mataji*" earlier. *Teacher, Madam, Auntie was fine, but Mataji?*

Mataji usually refers to an old lady. Did I look that old?

Well! The young doctor must have seen the few grey hairs on my bald head. No wonder, he called me *Mataji.* I did not know whether to laugh or cry . . . *Mataji indeed!* But then, humour is the best antidote to life's absurdities so I grabbed the opportunity. I answered in an old women's voice, "*Betā, theek hu, par abhi bhi kuch takleef hai*? (*Son, I am fine but I still have some problems*).

I started telling him about my aches and pains one by one and flooded him with questions about the tubes which were inserted in my body. I pointed my finger at one and asked him, what its function was. Then I pointed at another and so on. He went on addressing me as *Mataji* and patiently answered all my queries. I really appreciated his patience and realized that one day this young man will turn out to be a very good doctor. However, *Dr. Patil* spoilt the fun when he entered my room after a while and I had to revert back to my normal self. The trainee doctor looked in askance at my transformation.

I explained *Dr. Patil* gleefully how, for the first time I was addressed as "*Mataji*" and had a great time pulling his students leg. *Dr. Patil* told his student that this *Mataji* is a professor teaching in a college. We started laughing when he started telling about how I had scolded him after surgery for water and pain killer.

Doctor told me, "*Well, laughter is the best medicine.*" He also told me it was a good sign that I was ready to laugh.

> *Through humor, you can soften some of the worst blows that life delivers. And once you find laughter, no matter how painful your situation might be, you can survive it.*
>
> *Bill Cosby*
> *American comedian, Television producer, Veteran stand-up performer, Author and Activist*

After they left I asked for my scarf but due to the tubes from my neck and nose, covering my head was problematic. By now the effect of anesthesia was slowly wearing off so I was sleeping less and was awake for a longer period of time.

There was accumulation of cough in my chest so steaming was done thrice a day. It was fun to gobble and inhale hot steam coming out of a nozzle.

There were some breathing exercises to be performed regularly. The nurse presented a small instrument which was a plastic box with three partitions. Each partition had a coloured ball (*green, yellow and red*). She asked me to blow into the pipe attached to the side of the instrument. When I blew nothing happened. She asked me to blow hard, this time the ball jumped up in the first partition. She said if I blew very hard, all the three balls would jump together. But I had just enough strength to blow the first ball half way. This exercise was done after every two hour.

The physiotherapist brought a plastic pouch filled with a fluid. One end of a tube dipped in the fluid and through the other end she asked me to blow bubbles. The child in me loved these exercises. We called them fun exercise.

That evening our friends *Sarita, Manjul, Anil* and *Sudha* came to meet us. We spent the entire evening gossiping about the hospital, doctors, the surgery etc. Their company refreshed us.

The next day, *Dr. Patil* told me, he would take me for a short walk. His statement stunned me, I asked,

"You have put tubes into me at so many places and how do you expect me to walk?"

He told me, *"Simple, we will put all the pouches in plastic bags. One bag, Sonali will hold and support you from one side. The other bag, I will hold and support you from the other side, don't complain, start walking."*

He instructed me to roll over onto my side, bend my knees and hang my legs over the side of the bed. Then use my arms to lift my upper body and sit on the edge of the bed. He directed me to leave my legs hanging for few minutes.

He advised, *"Stay still for a moment to make sure you're steady"* and then he asked me to push with my arms and stand up.

It sounded simple but when I tried to follow his instructions I could not get up. *Sonali* helped me, *"I can't . . . I am feeling giddy,"* I protested. Doctor instructed me to wait and then try again.

I panicked, *"I will fall . . . my legs won't hold . . . I feel shaky."*

But everyone encouraged me, *"Put your foot down and slowly stand up."*

As my feet touched the ground, it buckled. My orientation was totally disturbed as there was a woozy sensation in my head. *I looked at my foot . . . they looked normal . . . why were they not supporting me?*

Determined to walk I pressed my foot on the ground for some time and then told *Dr. Patil* that I was ready to walk. It was not easy but I found that my doctor and *Sonali* were efficiently maneuvering me. They took me out of the room, into the passage and towards the glass doors from where I could see the outside view. The bright sunshine almost blinded me.

Doctor asked for a wheelchair and advised me, *"Relax, enjoy the scenery and sit for at least half an hour."*

Rubbing my eyes I grumbled, *"Half an hour is too much, light is too bright; it hurts my eyes, my head is heavy and I am not comfortable."*

I wanted to go back to my room. Squinting from the bright sunlight reflecting off the glass panes, I told *Sonali,* *"Sunlight is too bright; I am not able to tolerate it."*

Dr. Patil warned me, *"No excuse, I will be watching out for you."*

Sonali was sympathetic. She assured me that the moment *Dr. Patil* left she would take me to my room. *Sonali* however said, *"Thank God it not raining today and don't worry, you will get accustomed to the sunlight."*

Later, the physiotherapist taught me not only to get out of bed but also to get back into to bed safely. Now it became a task to be performed almost every two hours. *Benu, Sonali* or my father would take me out for a short walk in the passage.

My mother, the pillar of strength for us, visited only after *Nini* left for college. Her cheerful greeting always brightened the atmosphere in the hospital room. She described all the tit-bits happening at my place. It was hilarious to hear that *Nini* and she would watch horror movies or series on paranormal activities (*their passion*) and then get scared later. She threw up her hands in mock horror as she told us about the tough time she had, making *Nini* eat green vegetables. She said that they would stand by the window to watch the storm beating up furiously, the dark clouds, lightening and the thunder.

There were heavy rains in *Mumbai* in the last few days and my mother complained how *Mumbai* rains and roads were conspiring against her. She asked me, "*Rina, where are the roads here, there are only potholes and more potholes.*"

Regarding the roads in *Kalyan,* she chuckled, "*Who needs to go to Esselworld! Your roads are the best . . . for a rollercoaster ride.*"

She said on the day of surgery in spite of travelling by car and using an umbrella she was wet, while entering the hospital. It rained the whole day. She giggled, "*It does not rain here, God opens the tap and water comes pouring down.*"

She was like breath of fresh air with her witty comments and cheerful disposition. Her positive thinking always moved us to face life with optimism. But the best part of her visit was that she brought lots of tasty home cooked food for us. She knew that the hospital provided vegetarian food so she always packed eggs or fish curry for us.

> *She was my mother but more than that she was my true friend who knew my weaknesses but showed me my strengths.*

Chapter 11

Post-surgery . . .

Next day in the hospital, we were enjoying the morning view from my hospital room when *Dr. Jadliwala* walked in and started examining me.

A cheerful soul, he radiated warmth and good cheer. There was a twinkle in his eyes, when he asked *Benu*, "*I heard she is a very good patient.*" I shook my head and hid a tiny smile, so *Sonali* was at it again.

Benu grinned, "*Yes doctor, we keep hearing that from everyone here.*"

I told *Dr. Jadliwala*, "*Sonali, my bhabhi is spreading this information. She is my greatest admirer.*"

Sonali was from the medical field. She was extremely vocal about her admiration for me. She was in awe of my tolerance, self-control and courage. *Sonali* would press my hands, pat my cheeks or just hug me and tell, "*Rina . . . I have yet to see a patient like you. What a positive mind-set! Great . . . keep it up.*"

After *Dr. Jadliwala* left, *Dr. Smruti* entered the room. After some advice regarding post-surgery care, she observed that the few remaining grey hair were getting entangled with the tubes.

She asked me, "*Why don't you cut these few remaining strands?*"

I told her, "*They are my faithful ones, See! They didn't fall like my black ones.*"

She said, "*Fine, but cut them now, your hair will grow much better than what they were before.*"

This was the second time she advised me to cut my hair. Her smile encouraged me to listen to her. It was decision time and I was ready to rise above '*moh-māyā*' and cut my hair.

All the doctors were happy with my progress but they were more impressed by my attitude. I was a model patient according to them, the sisters and my family members.

Why? Was it because I followed doctor's advice scrupulously? Or was it because I did not whine or complain? True! After the ICU episode there was nothing to complain about.

> "*Yes, the right attitude was that I was not ready to be bogged down. I was determined to get well—without wasting time in throwing tantrums.*"

Everyone praised me except *Dr. Patil*. He asked my father, "*How many times did she go for walk?*"

My father said, *"She walks with our help, without complaining, religiously every hour."*

We started laughing he murmured, *"Well, she was complaining a lot yesterday."*

> *It was very difficult to please the man. Stringent and meticulous, well! It was a good patient— doctor combination because I was the same— stringent and meticulous.*

After examining me, *Dr. Patil* started cleaning the wound. He showed me the stitches. *I was surprised to see that the wound was stapled. Instead of using threads he used metal clips! How ingenious was that!*

I exclaimed, *"Clips! Benu see they look like stapler's pin."*

Everyone in the room crowded to see the clips. *I proudly showed the trophy I carried now. There was a huge vertical cut, traversing my belly. God! It looked as though doctor had cut open my entire belly.*

We tried counting the number of clips but there were too many. Doctor advised the nurse to keep the area clean and dry. This would allow the incision to heal. He did the dressing again and told me that bleeding was less and there was marked improvement in me so he might consider giving me discharge from the hospital within few days.

Later, when *Dr. Nupur* came for a visit, we told her what *Dr. Patil* had said earlier. *Dr. Nupur* told us,

"During the surgery, Dr. Patil had taken care so as to have minimum blood loss. Even now you can see there is hardly any bleeding."

At the time of discharge, both *Dr. Patil* and *Dr. Pratima* were present and they decided that after fifteen days, *Dr. Pratima* would remove the clips. *Dr. Pratima* asked my dad how we were going back. When my dad told her that we had a car, she advised him to drive very slowly so as not to cause any harm to me. My stitches were still tender and the pothole ridden roads of *Mumbai* were dangerous.

Doctor also advised me, *"Don't get your dressing wet."*

I wanted to know, *"Can I take shower?"*

She smiled, *"Yes, you can. Protect the area with a water proof cover to stop it from getting wet."*

Dr. Patil advised—

- *Walk for few minutes, several times a day.*
- *Avoid strenuous exercise such as lifting or carrying heavy objects.*
- *Take all the medicines on time.*
- *Follow the diet schedule provided.*
- *Drink lot of fluids to help rid the body of the drugs used during surgery.*

This time, my stay in the hospital was for eight days and we paid the hospital charges of ₹ 3,50,000. *Dr. Pejaver* had informed me that, as a professor, I was entitled to medical reimbursement. However, medical reimbursement could be claimed either from my college or from *Benu's* office (*any one place*). *Benu* advised that we should not be bothered about what I could claim from my college but single mindedly think of getting better.

The huge amount paid, every time I was discharged from the hospital after my treatment, however disturbed me.

At home, we noticed that a special bond, an amazing attachment, never seen before had developed between my mother and *Nini*. Both of them were straight-forward with a dominating personality. They were very similar in their looks and behavior so we were worried that in our absence, they might argue over small issues. However, we were pleasantly surprised to find that their being together day after day, insecurity about my wellbeing and search for consolation and security from each other, brought them close. Fear, pain and loneliness had drawn them together. We found them sharing jokes, reading short stories, watching horror movies (*favorite pass-time*) and looking after each other's needs. They would dance around the house with uninhibited joy if they heard a catchy song they particularly liked. They found solace in each other's company.

Nini, a proud owner of a scooty was ever ready to go to the shop and buy whatever her granny asked for. My mother told us that when we were at hospital, one day *Nini* thumped the back seat and invited her granny to ride pillion. When my mom looked scandalized *Nini* exclaimed, *"Oh Thamma! Don't get scared, we won't tumble."* This was a new development in their relationship and we were delighted to see their togetherness.

Ujjal-Da who was working for a project in *South Africa*, did not visit as I had asked him not to, but he kept enquiring about my treatment. One day, he told mom that he called his *Guru* in the *US* and had arranged for *puja* and a *havan* (*worship through the use of sacred fire*) for my recovery.

He told my mother, "*Mā, a Fākir has told me that some negative forces were working against Rinki for years and she has been resisting it but ultimately she succumbed to it*."

He told her, "*Tell Rinki, she will be fine now*."

It appeared that everyone had joined force to pray for my recovery. After surgery my movement was slow as the wound was still painful. *Sheetal* helped me to walk around in the house. She assisted me while exercising and taking shower. I wore a protective abdominal belt while bathing. It was a big chore and an important agenda in our daily routine.

My mother had started growing green leafy vegetable in pots. This became a major attraction for us. My mother was a resourceful, talented lady with a green finger. These green leafy vegetable and wheat grass grown in pots was not only a healthy supplement when used in a soup but it provided an outlet for our emotions. We started spending time gardening and experienced a range of emotions like we would be delighted to see the seeds germinate or annoyed to see an ant or white fly causing damage.

At home, I asked my mother a favour, "*Mā, will you cut my few remaining hair?*"

My mother said, "*Let them remain, why you want to cut them now?*"

I told her, "*Dr. Smruti asked me twice to cut them. Anyway Mā, they are disturbing me. So will you please cut them for me?*"

She had tear in her eyes when she cut the last few remaining grey hair.

It was *4*th *December, Benu's* birthday. My mother prepared some milk-rice porridge (*called payesh in Bengali*) and *Nini* brought a cake. We celebrated his birthday with our friends, as they turned up to wish him. *Arun Dana* had heard from my brother regarding my surgery. He desperately wanted to meet me so one day he came all the way from *Nasik* to *Shahad* just to meet me.

After surgery, my weight was 62 kg, lost 13-14 kg. Well! That was something great. Everyone at home started joking about me fitting into my daughter's clothes. It pleased me to admire myself in the mirror. What did my daughters call me few months back? *Rolly-Polly, Kidney bean and what not! Now they kept quiet. Ha-ha really quiet.*

After fifteen days, we were at *Bombay Hospital* and to our surprise we found, *Ashish-Da*, *Sonali* and *Anjan* waiting for us. I wondered whether removal of the staples was painful because all my relatives had joined force to be with me. All of us went to *Dr. Pratima's* chamber. *Ashish-Da* hugged me and asked me to be strong. My father and *Sonali* informed me about the slight bearable pain that I would experience. They were speaking from experience as they were operated before.

In the doctor's chamber, *Dr. Pratima* along with *Dr. Priyanka* assured me that the pain would be no more than an ant bite. They were right because there was no pain and I watched with interest how they worked in tandem.

They were using a small instrument, a needle-nose-plier and pressing the staple in the center to bend it to form a *"capital M shape,"* due to which the ends of the staple would come out of the skin slowly without hurting me. Thanks to the modern techniques, removal of the staples was a quick and painless procedure though there were around fifty of them. I was then advised to protect my wound using abdominal belts while traveling and climbing stairs. *Dr. Pratima* explained a technique to climb stairs without exerting. She told me that climbing stairs was better than taking a lift but I should not strain myself. Doctor directed me to come for the next chemotherapy cycle after a month.

Out of the doctor's chamber, I saw the glum faces of my family hogging almost all the chairs in the waiting area and grinned to see their expressions, when

I told them there was no pain. They thought that I was faking it but when I explained about the procedure, they felt reassured.

At home, I was thrilled to notice my hair growth in the next few weeks. Whenever I looked in the mirror *Nini* would run and bring a scale to measure the length and shout, *"1mm . . . 2mm . . . and after few days, 1 cm long."* I was pleased to see my shiny bald pate covered with short silky black hair.

My family and friends presented me some books to read. There were books on yoga from *Mrs. Ubhan,* spiritual books from *Mrs. Bhatta,* research papers from *Snehal* and the latest issue of *Bionano frontiers journal* in which my review article was published, from *Dr. Jamdhade. Benu* presented a book *"Diet cure for common ailments"* by *Dr. H.K. Bakhru.* I liked a portion of the foreword written by *Dr. R.G. Krishnatray*—*"Man, the highest creation of God, is, by divine plan, born healthy and strong. It is when the nature's rhythm and cycle are upset the human system loses its natural capacity to renew and rejuvenate itself."* I loved to read the book which stressed on nature cure and belief that, *"Nature alone possesses the power of healing."* Once I flipped through the pages and discussed about nature's cure with my family. The discussion ended with my mother telling us that as a child, I refused to eat green vegetables and *Benu* response was, *"She still does that."*

It was hilarious when *Nini* questioned, *"Guess Thamma! From whom I have inherited this gene?"*

I immediately placed the blame on my father, *"Don't blame me please! I have inherited it from Bābā."*

But later, my mother started incorporating more vegetables . . . in different forms, in my diet.

On *15*[th] *December*, blood test was done and the report was normal for *W.B.C. count*, *platelets* and *S. creatinine*. *CA125* was 6.0 U/ml. After my surgery I noticed that there was pin pricks and some tingling sensation in my toes and fingers. It was not painful but it was irritating and frustrating because I kept scratching and the sensation still persisted.

I was always a busy multitasking lady with no time for leisure, managing both home and college. But now I learnt that life goes on at its own pace even if you are not multitasking.

The monsoon rains had started receding and there was a hint of chill in the atmosphere. In these few days, I started enjoying a great deal of leisure. I sat for hours in the balcony and felt the soft gentle breeze touching my face. *Benu* and my mother would grab a chair and sit with me in the balcony. We would watch the sunrise in awe as the golden brilliance, orange and gold hue, of the rising sun kept us spellbound.

For years, with my busy schedule, I failed to appreciate the beauty that surrounded me. But now my mind was filled with the beauty of my surroundings. They say, nature expresses herself most harmoniously and it speaks to us when we know how to listen to it . . . understand its language.

There are five *Cassia fistula* trees (*Indian laburmum or amaltas*) and two *Spathodea campanulata* trees (*fountain tree or pichkari*) in the little garden in front of my flat. But what I found interesting was that the *Spathodea tree* was the house for a "*pair of owls*." These small, brown and white coloured spotted owls were beautiful. Being nocturnal birds, they were usually very quiet in mornings but their hooting could be heard late night. However, during daytime, they would become alert if an intruder tried to venture near their nest. Their nest was nothing but a big hole in the branch of the tree. They vigorously defended their nest. Attacks on intruders were vicious and brutal. The pair would take turns to be with the young one or sit together on an adjoining branch. There was often mutual preening; with the pair perched close together and there would be lot of cheek rubbing, which was a pleasure to watch. They would talk to each other making a wide variety of calls. In these few days I grew attached to them, every time I heard their call, I would run to the balcony to see what happened. In the days that followed I saw their little one grow and fly away.

As a student and Professor of Botany I have been for many field trips, excursion, hiking or nature trails but this was a totally different experience for me. Standing in my balcony I could relate to nature. I found out that the *Cassia tree*s were visited by a herd of about fourteen parrots for the fruits (*pods*). It was a beautiful sight to see so many parrots flying up in a wild flutter, in harmony with nature. They sat on the spreading branches and chattered noisily. These noisy but beautiful birds visited the trees from mid-morning to late-afternoon. I loved to talk to them making sounds to attract them but they would listen and then ignore me. They were very striking and attractive so I tried to paint them. Since the paintings did not come out well (*as my fingers were not stable, would shiver after chemotherapy*), I clicked photographs of these talkative, noisy little birds.

Two watchdogs, *"Marshal" (German shepherd)* and *"Bruno"* (*Yellow Labrador Retriever*) were kept for the security of the colony. Their kennel was next to my building. Earlier I had seen them doing rounds as their duty. But now it was a pleasure to watch them get formal training to sniff dubious objects, play and bathe. *Marshall* was huge and because of his vast size, he seldom had to resort to violence whereas *Bruno* was a ball of utter curiosity, defenseless, affectionate and perpetually hungry Labrador. While *Marshall* was fond of water, *Bruno* hated it. Their escapades kept me engaged and we would often laugh at their antics.

> *I felt cheated and couldn't get it out of my mind that there were so many beautiful things around me and for more than twenty five years, I did not even stop to watch them or enjoy them.*

It is so easy to get caught in the drudgery of life. We are convinced that we are too busy to do things we really love. It was only in these few months, when forced to take it easy, to slow down and enjoy the beauty around me that I started appreciating and absorbing my surroundings.

Well! Something good was coming out from the grim realities of cancer treatment. I have no hesitation to admit that I did not notice the mystic sounds of nature, natural, habitat, chirping birds and rainbow like flowers which were in abundance around us . . . I did not see them . . . really see them . . . appreciate or enjoy their beauty. However, now these were the source of constant joy . . . physical and mental stability . . . peace. This awareness was almost like a spiritual experience and it kept me engaged, giving immense pleasure and helping me to forget my pains.

> *"See the world as if for the first time; see it through the eyes of a child, and you will suddenly find that you are free."*
>
> *Deepak Chopra*
> *Indian American Author, Holistic Health/New Age Guru*
> *and Alternative Medicine Practitioner*

Chapter 12

Fourth chemotherapy and my New Year resolution . . .

O_n *17ᵗʰ December 2010,* a month after my surgery, *Dr. Smruti* called me for the fourth cycle of chemotherapy. I was still weak and the stitches were still tender so my movement was slow and restricted. The abdominal belt was however very helpful while traveling. The first thing I did after reaching *Bombay Hospital* was to bow in front of Ganapati and pray as before. I told him, *"Gannu, take care, I have come for the fourth chemo."*

As we waited patiently for our turn, my father started talking to a patient who complained about the side-effects of chemotherapy and another lady who did not face any problem joined them. I decided to join them. Slowly everyone in the waiting room joined our group, sharing their experience.

> *I learnt—*
>
> - *It is a different experience for every cancer patient, undergoing chemotherapy.*
>
> - *Some cancer patients suffered from fatigue, severe pain and nausea. They found it difficult to cope with these side effects.*
>
> - *Some patients experienced these symptoms, but didn't find them as troublesome.*
>
> - *Some patients experienced these symptoms only minimally or did not experience them altogether.*
>
> - *However my experience was that with medicine, strong will power and positive attitude, these side effects could be managed.*

After an hour we were with *Dr. Smruti* in her chamber. Doctor was happy with my progress however, I complained, *"The tingling sensation has increased, doctor. I keep scratching my palm, sole of the foot, fingers and toes, there is no relief."*

Dr. Smruti promptly asked, *"How much weight did you lose after surgery?"*

I proudly told her, *"10-12 kg."*

She smiled and told me, *"Well, the tingling sensation is due the ratio of your body weight and Taxol administered."*

Oh! I thought, *"My weight, always the culprit!"*

Doctor explained that some chemo patients suffered numbness and tingling sensation in palms and feet (*called peripheral neuropathy*). She told me that the doctor determines the dose and the schedule of *Taxol* based on many factors such as height and weight, the general health of the patient etc. *She turned and showed her student, how Taxol dose was calculated in relation to the height and weight of a patient.* She saw our interest and immediately taught me, *Benu* and my father how the calculation was done. She reduced the dose for "*Taxol*" from 300 to 290 mg for the fourth cycle of chemotherapy and asked me to get admitted.

So *Taxol (290 mg)* was administered on *17*th *December* and the drip continued all day long. We searched the web and read about "*Hand and foot syndrome*" in which the patient suffers from the numbness and tingling sensation in fingers and toes. We read on the web that peripheral neuropathy could be temporary or permanent. I believed that in my case it would be a temporary symptom. It would disappear as soon as the chemo routine stopped.

If you ask me, why such a belief then I have no answer for that. Just a belief!

As the chemo progressed, every visit of the doctors became the high point and most anticipated moment. These visits brought a fresh breath of knowledge, love and compassion. Another important person who was eagerly awaited was the friendly helper in the hospital who served food, snacks, tea, etc. with a smile on his face.

As usual the chemotherapy cycle was rough and my endurance was put to test. The churning sensation and breathlessness started within half an hour. My father sat near me and kept patting my forehead. He gently and soothingly ran his hand over my head. By now my father, *Benu* and *Sonali* were well aware of the sequence of events so took turns to be with me.

Carboplatin (700 mg) was administered the next day. Positive mind-set helped me stay happy and interact with my doctors, nurses and visitors. I had a one point agenda—*kick cancer on its butt and become cancer free*.

I was discharged on *18*th *December* evening. *Dr. Smruti* advised us to report back after twenty one days for the next chemo.

Dr. Smruti said—

- *Cancer patients are particularly vulnerable to depression and anxiety, with fatigue as the most prevalent symptom, so take extra care.*

- *Avoid staying alone.*

- *Emotional support from family and friends helps to cope with psychological stress.*

As we were waiting for *Mr. Pansare* (*chauffeur*) to bring the car near the front gate of the lobby, we saw *Anil*, *Sudha* and *Ayushi* (*their daughter*) walking in. They had come to meet us all the way from *Vashi* (*New Bombay*). Though I was sitting on a wheel chair looking haggard after my chemo, *Ayushi* was absolutely *bindaas* (*cool and carefree*). She presented me with a bouquet of flowers, kept tinkering with the wheelchair and kept talking to me as any child would. This mindless chattering somehow cured me of my lethargy. Surprisingly, the return journey was not as daunting as it always was after a chemo.

At home, the side effects were there, but now I knew the ways and means to overcome them. Blood test was done at *Century Rayon hospital* after two days. The report showed that the *W.B.C. count* was low as usual. Precautionary measures were taken and later, the *W.B.C. count* returned to normal.

Dr. Smruti had reduced the *Taxol* dose but I noticed after few days, the numbness and the tingling sensation in my fingers and toes returned. Acupressure, hot water fermentation, massage etc. helped but only to a certain extent.

To be happy or miserable depended entirely on me. I visualized and held a mental picture of myself being hale and hearty. Though weak, I walked with support from one room to another, tended my kitchen garden or talked with friends from my balcony. We were growing *spinach*, *amaranthus*, *moong* and other green leafy vegetable which my mother used for preparation of soup. Picking and pruning these plants became a ritual for us.

I saw *Mrs. Swamy* who underwent surgery and six cycles of chemotherapy, looking fine. Her hair had grown and she was going for regular walks. She met *Benu* in *"Satyanarayan puja"* at *Mr. Pathak's* house and enquired about me. *Mr. Pathak*, who visited *Tirupati*

(*Andhra Pradesh*), offered prayers for my recovery and sent a photograph of *Balaji* with some *Prasad*.

Gargi in the meantime, successfully completed her project at *Hyderabad* in the month of *December* and was with us for fifteen days leave. Before leaving *Hyderabad*, she went to "*Śrī Veṅkaṭēśwara Swami temple*" to offer her prayers. She made a sañkalp, "*Śrī Veṅkaṭēśwara Swami, I will return with my mother to seek your blessings after she gets well.*"

She met the priest and told him that her project was over. She also told him, "*My mother has completed four cycles of chemo and only two more are left.*"

He blessed her and told her, "*Have faith, Śrī Veṅkaṭēśwara Swami will take care of your mother and your family.*"

> *Cancer not only affects your body, but it affects your emotions and feelings too and one day something happened for which I still feel ashamed.*

It was New Year Eve (*31st December 2010*), *Gargi* and *Nini* were at home and they were not ready to go to the colony club house to celebrate as we did every year. I requested them to go and enjoy. But they refused.

I implored, "*Go and enjoy the party with your friends.*"

They said, "*We will stay with you! We want to bring in the New Year with you!*"

They were not listening to me and their decision was depressing me. I felt suffocated and imprisoned in my present circumstances.

I pleaded with *Gargi*, "*Go out . . . go out and enjoy . . . . go to the party . . . . go and dance, I know you love dancing.*"

But *Gargi* refused, she said, "*I don't feel like dancing Mā, I would rather stay with you.*"

I knew *Nini* was crazy about dancing, I asked her, "*Will you go to the party?*"

She shook her head and sat beside me, reading a book. I sat quietly, brooding, silently getting worked up. I was depressed, angry and unhappy that my kids refused to listen to me. Why spoil their *New Year Eve* for me. The feeling of guilt and resentment started building up.

I became so desperate that in heat of the moment I murmured, "*I feel like hanging myself from the fan with my duppatta.*"

Nini sitting beside me was stunned.

I knew my folly the moment I saw her expression, "*Did I just utter that nonsense?*"

"*Oh, dear,*" feeling contrite and fighting back tears I hugged her. She hugged me tight as though she wanted to give me strength. Her silence was alarming. It scared me.

I was annoyed with myself, *"How could I have said such a thing? How stupid?*

A strong lady with a will power everyone admired, *what happened! How could I be so weak?*

I explained, *"Nini, I am not that stupid to commit suicide."*

She nodded but after sometime she quietly left the room. She must have told *Benu* and *Gargi* about my stupidity because the next thing I noticed was that both my daughters were getting dressed for the party. They told me that *Benu* would stay with me. *Gargi* would come back later so that *Benu* could go and meet his friends. I was happy that at least they were going for the party but was scared because the grilling would start as soon as *Gargi* returned.

Later much later, *Gargi* came back from the party and the cross-examination started, *"What happened, Ma? Why were you depressed? Why did you make such a foolish statement?"*

"A guilty conscience needs no accusers."

Late 14th century proverb, earlier in Latin

I made a baby face and told her, *"I didn't mean it."*

She scolded, *"Bad girl, never allow anybody to shake your belief in yourself."*

I told her, "*Don't worry! I am too strong a person to commit such stupidity. I feel foolish anyway I am ashamed to have even uttered those words.*"

Her stance was uncompromising, "*You better be,*" she categorically told me.

My life was in my hands. If I consciously tried to stay positive and believe that Yes, I will be cured . . . then it will bring in the change in my life, change for better as there was no such thing as a hopeless situation.

My dear friends were always with me for every occasion so how could they leave me alone this year? I found that after midnight, the party shifted to my place as all my friends and their children were with me to welcome the New Year. The years gone by showed me that I was blessed with a loving family and friends. I learnt a lot in just one year of my life and was happy to welcome the *New Year, 2011.*

My New Year Resolutions—

- *I would never be depressed again.*

- *Every day might not be special, but there would be something good in each day.*

- *With my positive attitude and strong will power, I would improve the quality of my life during cancer treatment and beyond.*

- *I would recognize and enjoy many blessings in my life and appreciate the little things in life to anticipate a glorious future.*

- *My goal was crystal clear, with faith in God and in myself, I would succeed no matter what.*

Chapter 13

Fifth chemotherapy and hyponatremia . . .

A New Year, a new beginning! With firm belief in my mind about my goal to root out cancer, I was in the *Century Rayon hospital* Path lab for the blood test. By now the usual ritual of finding a proper vein was time consuming but the smiling faces of *Ms. Jyoti Dhabak* and *Ms. Alka Suryavanshi* (*in Pathlab*), their efficiency and the love and concern of *Ms. Ratna Ningulkar(assistant)* always made me forget my pain. Blood test was done on *4*ᵗʰ *January* for *CBC* and the *W.B.C. count*, *platelets* and *S. creatinine* were normal. *CA125* reading was 5.5 U/ml.

Gargi was leaving for *Pilani* on 5ᵗʰ *January* and the fifth chemotherapy was scheduled on 7ᵗʰ *January*. She started grumbling, "*Mā, I will miss being with you during your chemo just by two days . . . . I want to be with you . . . I don't want to go.*"

Benu comforted her, "*Don't worry dear; I will take care of your mother.*" *Gargi* left for *Pilani* with a heavy heart.

On 7ᵗʰ *January* 2011, we reached *Bombay Hospital*. It was time for my interaction with Ganapati, a time for sharing what lay in my deepest heart, a simple request, "*Gannu, take care.*"

By now, *Bombay Hospital* was a second home for us. We were friends with the sisters, *ward-boys*, maids and the people who served food. They greeted us warmly. They were simple people who would sit and chat with us sharing their life stories and unknowingly making a difference in this difficult period of our life. The chemotherapy procedure was the same as before. On 7ᵗʰ *January* morning, *Taxol (290 mg)* and the next day *Carboplatin (700 mg)* was administered.

The chemo-sisters told me that with each passing chemo cycle it was becoming difficult to find a healthy vein through which the chemo medicines could be introduced. It became a routine as they would keep searching and tapping till they could find the appropriate vein. As always, my partners in my chemo journey—my parents, *Benu* and *Sonali* were with me to take care.

After discharge, Dr. Smruti repeated her advice—

- *Stay away from people who are sick.*

- *Do not latch or lock the door when you are in washroom.*

- *Don't hesitate to take support in case you feel weak.*

- *If you feel dizzy, don't keep standing, sit down immediately or you might hurt yourself if you fall.*

At home, I was suffering from the side effects associated with chemotherapy. This winter, the mornings and nights were turning out to be very cold. My legs were hurting and due to weakness, I could not walk without support. As advised, someone would stand outside while I used the washroom.

I hated this arrangement as it symbolized helplessness but I tried to change my attitude and accept help gracefully.

Later however, we understood why *Dr. Smruti* always insisted that we follow her advice meticulously. This arrangement turned out to be a *boon in disguise*.

On 9th *January*, I was feeling low and was not talking much. I was short tempered and started refusing food by late evening. My mother's effort to feed me was in vain. It worried and pained her to see me refusing food. *Benu, Nini* and my mother took turns to feed me but were unsuccessful. I was restless, irritated and bad tempered as I was finding it very difficult to lift my head and keep my eyes open.

On that fateful night, around 4:00 a.m., I visited the washroom and *Benu* stood out waiting for me.

I now write what happened from what I have heard later from Benu, my mother and Nini, because I was unconscious for the next two days.

As *Benu* patiently waited outside the washroom for me to finish, he heard a grunt and was startled.

He called out my name, *"Rina, Rina . . . what happened? Are you ok?"* When he did not get any reply, he knew something was horribly wrong.

He opened the door and what he saw scared him so much that he started yelling for help.

He found me unconscious, sitting on the western commode, my body lifeless with my head bent to a side. He ran inside to give me support. He called out my name. My mother and *Nini* were with us by then and they tried to get some response out of me but were unsuccessful. They decided to carry me out of the washroom to the bedroom. It was an uphill task for them to lift me, without hurting me, but they managed somehow.

Benu started to cry as I did not respond. My mother (*a lady with a dint of indomitable will and inflexible purpose*) however, believed that her daughter was a fighter, made of sterner stuff and would not give up so easily so she decided not to lose hope.

She started calling, *"Rina, Rina . . . Mamoni (darling) . . . Mamoni"* almost shouting so that I could hear.

My mother then started calling out for his divine intervention, *"Help Sāi, help."* She knew what the name of *God* could do; she passionately believed that if you cling to *God* through thick and thin, in midst of degradation and in desperation, if your yearning heart persists in your demand—*He responds.*

Once or twice I grunted and then kept quiet, my breathing was normal but my hands and feet were cold so they started massaging my hands and feet.

Prayer is powerful. To take the struggle out of your life, just ask God and when you ask, the wear and tear of life diminishes.

Nini, my wise little girl, ran to call *Dr. Leena* who stayed downstairs in the same building and *Benu* contacted *Dr. Smruti* on phone. Both the doctors were of the opinion that for immediate treatment, *Century Rayon hospital* was the best option. An ambulance was called to take me to the hospital. *Dr. Smruti* was monitoring and guiding from *Bombay Hospital.*

Benu told me later that I was mostly unconscious but once in a while I would wake up, look around in a trance, as though searching for someone but would not recognize anyone. When my friends heard the news, they came running to see if they could be of any help. My friends *Alka, Vandhana* and *Sarita* were disturbed, when they found that I was not recognizing anyone. When I remained confused, drowsy and irritable *Alka,* my dearest friend, started weeping, *"Rina is too young to face so much hardship . . . God, Why?"*

Dr. Smruti was on phone talking to *Benu* when she expressed her misgivings and enquired, *"Did she bang her head?"*

"Is she suffering from any head injuries?"

"Did you search carefully?"

To reassure herself, she told *Benu*, "*Hand over the phone to Moitreyee; I want to talk to her.*"

Benu had a tough time after that as he could not make me to hold the phone neither he could make me to speak to the doctor. Irritated with him, I would either express my displeasure or turn and go back to sleep. He cajoled me but I was not ready to budge. After lot of coaxing when he finally forced me, I showed my displeasure but agreed to speak to her. *Benu* held the phone and urged me to speak. I kept quite initially but after repeated coaxing I did talk.

> *"I don't remember what was asked and what my answer was."*

But the doctor was reassured. After I spoke to her, *Dr. Smruti* was sure that there was no head injury and that I was suffering from "*hyponatremia*" which is "*electrolyte imbalance caused by low blood sodium.*"

Dr. Leena, however, wanted to be sure that my brain was not affected as I was not responding. She sent me for *Brain MRI* to *Kalyan Scan Centre* since this facility was not available at *Century Rayon hospital*. This started a debate as my friends felt that if *Dr. Smruti* was satisfied why was I being sent for a *MRI*? Our family members however, were not ready to take any chances so they took me for the *MRI*.

My mother in the meantime had called *Ashish-Da* and my father. She asked them to come to *Shahad* as their help was required. My mother and *Benu* accompanied me in the ambulance and *Ashish-Da* directly came to the *Diagnostic Centre*. Till date, I don't remember what happened during that period, *what did I do? Who was with me? How did they manage? I have no recollection of this trip to the Diagnostic Centre. This episode remains a mystery for me!*

By afternoon, they brought me back to *Century Rayon hospital*. *MRI* report suggested that everything was normal. My treatment for "*hyponatremia*" was started. I remained unconscious but would respond when coaxed. Next day it was very quiet when I became conscious to two very dear voices (*Nini* and *Ashish-Da*) discussing something. I realized that I was in a hospital and the white curtains looked familiar, "*Oh right! It was the ICU of Century Rayon hospital.*"

I asked them, "*Why am I here?*"

The moment they heard my voice, they cried out loud for the doctor. *Dr. Leena* and *Dr. Meghana* were by my bedside at once. They started examining me and good-humoredly told me, "*It is high time you woke up, dear.*"

Dr. Leena asked me, "*How are you feeling?*"

I smiled, "*Fine, why doctor, what happened?*"

She smiled and said, "*You are suffering from hyponatremia.*"

Dr. Meghana later told me, "*Hyponatremia, is an electrolyte imbalance caused by low blood sodium.*"

The last couple of days were a mystery for me,
since I could not recollect what had transpired so
I wanted to know everything but first I scolded
Nini, Ashish-Da and Benu because they had
forgotten to cover my head with a scarf and now
all my friends and hospital staff had seen me bald.

Dr. Joshi had come for a visit. He told me that *hyponatremia* was a common side effect of chemotherapy. *Ashish-Da* asked him if I could be given coconut water. *Dr. Joshi* told us that coconut water was good as it contains important electrolytes like sodium, chloride and was rich in potassium.

Benu was worried that there were some serious cases around me in the *ICU* and it was very risky for me to stay there. Only few days were over since my fifth chemotherapy and blood test showed that the *W.B.C. count* was low so *Benu* requested *Dr. Leena* to shift me to a single room.

Patients undergoing chemotherapy need to be
very careful. They should not contract any sort of
infection.

We live in a close knit colony where news spreads like wildfire. So our well-wishers gathered in the hospital to see me. Initially they were allowed to visit. Eventually the room got crowded. *Dr. Leena* upset to see the crowd, asked everyone to leave.

She smiled and told me, "*Wear a mask; we don't want the risk of you picking up infections.*"

She told *Benu*, "*Restrict outsiders from coming near her bed*."

"*Better be safe than sorry.*"

Mid 19th century proverb

My friend *Vandhana*, standing at a distance from my bed heard what *Dr. Leena* said. She immediately left the room; I thought she must have felt insulted. But No! My friends were extraordinary . . . what she did next was that one little thing which made my friends very special. Well! She immediately went out and purchased a box of surgical mask and sent it to me.

My intravenous drip continued, blood was taken twice a day for various tests. Along with *Hyponatremia* blood test also showed magnesium was below range. Magnesium injections were prescribed by *Dr. Smruti*.

Mr. Mark, the male nurse (*also called brother*) was a jovial man and a good soul. He carried the injections like a trophy and with a huge smile on his face, told me, "*Only pin prick, madam*."

I was not aware that muscular administration of magnesium injections was so painful. The excruciating pain made me forget my age and I started screaming. Everyone in the room however started laughing when I kept yelling, "*Bums on fire . . . bums on fire*." *Mr. Mark* promised me an ice bag to counter the pain for the next injection.

So after every magnesium injections, *Mark* started giving me ice bags which to some extent reduced the burning sensation. I however started dreading his entry with the injection.

I asked *Nini,* "*Why me?*"

She immediately replied, "*God knows that you are the strongest, that's why.*"

I also heard that *Gargi* was calling repeatedly for the last two days. She wanted to hear my voice. Unconscious, it was not possible but after regaining consciousness, *Benu* asked me to talk to her.

It was a shock for me to hear *Benu* narrate the incident which followed after the ambulance was called. *Benu* told me that two men from hospital carried me in a stretcher all the way from second floor to the ambulance waiting downstairs. When the ambulance left for the hospital, *Nini* was left alone at home. She was terrified to see her mother in that state and the series of events that followed the night before were devastating. She called *Gargi* and started crying inconsolably.

Gargi was shocked to hear her crying, "*Gargi, Mummy will not survive . . . she will die, Gargi . . . she will die.*"

Gargi howled, "*Nini, what happened . . . stop crying . . . tell me what happened.*"

Nini howled louder, *"Mummy will die, Gargi, Mummy will die."*

Gargi wept, *"Is she alive, Nini? Is Mā alive?"*

Nini explained, *"Yes, she is breathing but unconscious."* *Nini* told her everything that had occurred since late night.

Gargi comforted her, *"Stop crying Nini, nothing will happen to her."*

Gargi, who was in *Pilani*, did not know what she could do other than comforting her little sister. It was around 6:00 a.m., the temperature was between 3.0-0.0°C in *Pilani*. She was going mad, so she did what we all do in moment of utter desperation . . . believe in *God*, have faith that every day of our life is due to the omnipresent guidance of the almighty . . . so in this bitter cold, she ran to the *Saraswati* temple in *BITS campus*. She prayed as in this moment of trail only *God* had the power to cure her mother. She had full faith that her mother would cross this hurdle.

Much later, her friend *Prerana* called as she was unable to locate *Gargi*. When *Prerana* realized what had happened, she dragged *Gargi* back to the college. It was the last date to fill the online resume for placements. *Gargi* sat in front of the computer but could not see the form, on the computer screen. Tears were blurring her vision; she could not see anything through her tears. She was clueless as to what to do . . .

but somehow with *Prerana's* help *Gargi* was able to fill the form.

Gargi felt lost and did not know why this was happening. Her friend *Sāi Neelesh*, who practiced *Reiki* (*Universal life force energy*), showed her how he was sending *Reiki energy* from there which he called was "*distant healing*", for my recovery. She found solace in his company and he taught her few "*mantras*" with which could she could help in healing me.

> *I called Gargi again to reassure her that I was recovering well and also to convey my thanks to her friend, Sāi Neelesh.*

Taking a cue from *Gargi*, I found comfort in *God* and in his love but in a passionate and mindless conversation with him I complained silently, *Why God*?

> *Why me and my family? What did we do to deserve this? This is the time when my daughter's need me the most . . . why are you doing this to us?*

After the last few days of struggle, slowly I came back to reality. I had not seen my mother after regaining my consciousness. *Where was she*?

I asked *Nini, "Where is Thamma?"*

She told me, "*Thamma accompanied you for the MRI in Kalyan and then she was with you in the ICU when the drip was started. She went home only after Mama (maternal uncle) and Dadu (Grandfather) were here to take over.*"

My mother entered my room late evening. There was a rumbling sound in my stomach and my appetite was back when I saw her carrying a huge bag. I was sure it was filled with some mouthwatering delicacies.

Happy to see her, I asked, "*Mā, I missed you. Where were you? What have you brought—fish curry or egg curry?*

My mother's reaction startled me, "*So! Now I am your Mā, is it?*"

Ouch! She was really cross . . . I smiled, "*Okay! Okay! What did I do?*"

My mother told me that in the last two days, I would regain consciousness periodically and search for someone. I would look around and softly utter only one word—"*Mā . . . Mā . . . Mā . . .*"

> "*Maybe in my subconscious mind I was calling out for help. Maybe in that world I had the child like trust only on my mother.*"

In tearful voice she recounted, "*I would stand in front of you, cuddle you and reassure you that your Mā was right in front but you would not recognize me and kept asking for . . . Mā.*"

Dr. Smruti called *Benu* with all the reports to *Bombay Hospital* on *14th January* and sent the MRI reports to *Dr. Inder Talwar* for his expert opinion. She was happy with my progress and unhappy with the way magnesium was administered in *Century Rayon hospital*. She advised to get the blood test done every week to check sodium and magnesium level and report for the sixth chemo on time.

I loved to have guests with me but their entry was restricted. I was amazed when *Juhi Shukla's* grandfather and grandmother came to the hospital to wish me well. I was basking in the love and affection showered by my friends, *Alka, Babji, Sarita, Manjul, Monica, Himanshu, Rashmi Zope, Rita Jain, Sujata Puranik, Rani, Vandhana, Varsha* and *Tiwariji*. I also loved to have the kids, *Priyam, Juhi, Nikita, Abhinav* and *Ankit* who came and erased all my negative thoughts by giggling, laughing and telling me about the *SMS* jokes they received. They were with me morning, afternoon and evening.

It was a good time for me to acknowledge their generosity so I thanked them repeatedly.

My hand was enflamed and sore. *Dr. Leena* instructed the nurse, "*See to it that the swelling subsides as she has to go for the next chemo after few days. There should not be any complain against us from Bombay hospital.*"

The nurse gave me an ointment (*Thrombophob*). There was some relief after rubbing the ointment.

I returned home after ten days and observed some changes in *Nini's* behaviour. In these few days, my playful, impish and ever smiling daughter had turned somber. She remained quiet and appeared frightened.

I looked at myself for the first time, through her eyes and thought there were few things in life that just sucks, doesn't it?

I cuddled her and asked, *"What is it dear?"*

She hugged me tight, her voice was nothing but an angry whisper, *"Mummy, I was scared that you would die."*

I wanted her to express her fears, I told her, *"Tell me from the beginning."*

A tear escaped her eye as she explained in a very low voice, *"Mummy, that night I woke up suddenly when I heard Dad cry out your name . . . I ran and found Grandma and Dad trying to revive you."*

Another tear dropped from her eye and she wiped it away quickly. She was silent, reliving the horror once again. I sat there holding her hand, gently prodding her, *"What did you see, dear?"*

She narrated each word through a torrent of tears, *"Your head was on one side and you were not responding. With great difficulty we could bring you out from the washroom. We tried everything but you did not respond so I ran and called Dr. Leena. When they carried you in a stretcher to the ambulance, I thought it's over, I had lost you."*

It was breaking my heart to see her cry. It was heart wrenching to see the fear, pain and the torment in her eyes. I had to break the ice.

I held her close and then softly asked her, *"Hey! Was my pyjama down?*

She burst out laughing and started teasing me, *"Your shirt was up and pyjama was down."*

I made a face and asked, *"Did you close your eyes?"*

She immediately started giggling and with that, my *Nini* was back. She started cracking jokes with glee. She described my antics, how I behaved like a small child, whenever I regained consciousness. She told me, *"You only uttered one word, Mā."*

I told her, *"I know."*

She said, *"I asked you, Gulli, Mā chai? (Goo-lee, you want mother?)"*

"What did I say?" I asked her.

Love shone in her eyes when she said, *"You looked at me and nodded your head like a baby."*

She started laughing and narrated that my behavior resembled that of a year old baby. There were few more jokes cracked as *Benu* and my mother joined her in teasing me. *Nini* in turn started teasing *Benu, "Bābā, should I tell mom what you did?"*

My curiosity arose I nudged her, *"Tell me, tell me."*

She recounted, *"While we were waiting for the ambulance, you revived for a minute and asked us, what has happen to me, what happened?"*

After that you were unconscious and did not respond to our calls. Dad ran out of the room. We thought that he had gone to make some enquiry. When he did not return for fifteen minutes, *thamma* sent me to look for him.

Nini asked me, *"Do you know where I found him?"*

When I shook my head she laughed, *"He was in the washroom, crying!"*

Benu told her, *"I was not crying!"*

She laughed louder, *"When I banged the door he told me that he was having loose motions."*

I told her it is true that nervousness starts all sorts of reaction in people. But she said, *"But Mā, he was sitting on the pot and crying."*

After that both of them started pulling each other's leg and my mother joined them. Healing with love and laughter worked as *Nini* was her normal self again.

Holding her close to me I crooned, *"You're My Heart, You're My Soul (our special song)."* And then I asked her softly, *"Are you scared now?"*

Nini shook her head and promised me to forget everything. There were some roadblocks no doubt but *Nini* had the courage to overcome them.

A few small but significant changes in the way
we think and a clear understanding of how to
create the life you want, can pave way to achieve
your goal.

In my cancer journey, this episode was eventful
and very close to my heart. In these few days, my
close encounter with death, life and hope taught me a
lesson . . . the lesson of my life . . . that cancer spares
no one. But I also learnt that cancer cannot silence
courage.

"Arise, awake and stop not till the goal is
reached."

Swami Vivekananda (1863-1902)
Indian Hindu Monk, orator, writer and founder of
Ramkrishna Math and Ramkrishna Mission

Chapter 14

Sixth and the last cycle of chemotherapy . . .

My sixth chemo was scheduled, two days after *Indian Republic day*. So on *28ᵗʰ January* 2011, it was *Bombay Hospital* once again! After we entered the hospital lobby, we stood with joined palms praying in front of *Ganapati*, *"Please accept my obeisance Gannu, my last chemo, remove all the obstacles. Please take care."*

We reached *Bombay Hospital* by 8:00 a.m. but there were many outstation patients who had reached the hospital much earlier. *Hmm . . . atrocious!* Thought the doctors timing was from 1:00 p.m. onwards, patients were in the queue from early morning.

Cancer journey is a learning process. Hours spent talking to the patients was often informative. My knack for listening helped me to understand their fight for survival. Every cancer patient had a unique story to tell.

We waited for hours for our turn to meet *Dr. Smruti*. You learn that patience is a virtue which every cancer patient and family members should possess in abundance. Your patience is tested at every instance in your cancer journey. It is tested when you wait for hours in doctor's consulting room . . . or when you are in a queue for a blood test, *USG* or *CT* scan . . . or even waiting for the reports.

Saburi (Patience) ferries you across to the distant goal.

Śrī Sāi Bābā of Shirdi (unknown-1918)
Spiritual Master, Saint, Sadguru, Fakir and Avatar

It is a progressive journey where you learn to deal with the physical and the emotional difficulties. It was necessary not to get depressed at the sight of blood, injections, smell of ether and the sufferings of the cancer patients in the waiting room.

Self-confidence and strong will power was the pre-requisite.

Cancer journey also teaches you to be efficient in managing a number of things such as collecting, organizing, filing and photocopying the reports and the bills after every chemo cycle. Managing the bulky files containing innumerable reports and bills was challenging but *Benu* managed well.

In her chamber, *Dr. Smruti* smiled and enquired, "*So, how do you feel now?*"

Before I could reply, my father told her, "*She is still weak and the tingling sensation in her fingers is irritating her.*"

Dr. Smruti nodded and said, "*It will go eventually.*"

She then told my father, "*Your daughter suffered from hyponatremia and hypo-magnesemia, I will keep your daughter under observation for an extra day, this time.*"

Benu asked what was foremost in his mind, "*Why did she suffer from hyponatremia and hypo-magnesemia?*"

He elaborated about the experience which had left a mark on our family. Doctor was sympathetic and told us that it was one of the side effects observed in cancer patients. She expressed her displeasure at the way magnesium injections were administered at *Century Rayon hospital*.

She asked me, "*It must be very painful for you?*"

I shuddered while recollecting and recounting my experience. Doctor told us that the magnesium injections should have been given intravenous as muscular administration was extremely painful.

She then told *Benu*, "*Don't worry, we will monitor her blood sodium and magnesium here and she will be discharged only when I am satisfied.*"

Doctor asked *Benu* to finish the formalities and get me admitted for the sixth chemo. As my father accompanied me to the 7th floor, he kept talking to me in his baby language making me laugh. I indicated him to stay quite as other people in the lift could hear him but he didn't care and continued with his baby talk.

Getting bored during chemo is normal but with *Sonali*, *Benu* and my dad around, there was round the clock activity. We watched live telecast of cricket match, comedy series and news on T.V. The hospital canteen "*Paritrupti*" was my relative's favorite haunt. I was in the hospital for four days, "*Taxol (290 mg)* and *Carboplatin (700 mg)*" were administered as before and blood sodium and magnesium were also monitored.

After discharge, *Dr. Smruti* called us to her chamber. She told us that I had responded well to chemotherapy and then uttered the magic words—

"Your treatment is over."

Joy filled the room as our prayers were miraculously answered. My father and *Benu* with tears in their eyes thanked the doctor.

Benu told *Dr. Smruti*, "*You are our fairy God mother; we thank you from the bottom of our hearts.*"

I was sitting quietly, paralyzed with fear because *Dr. Smruti's* statement surprisingly disturbed me.

Chemotherapy was far from enjoyable, but at least it offered some peace of mind. I felt protected and safe as long as it continued. Once chemotherapy stopped I wondered what was there to prevent cancer from returning. I was terrified to step outside, my comfort zone.

I was apprehensive, worried and somehow could not escape the empty feeling that I could no longer rely on drugs to keep cancer at bay. I shall not have medicine cover of *Taxol* and *Carboplatin* and this disturbed me. *What if any rogue cell was still floating around?* Dr. Smruti observed me intensely and told me with a compassionate smile, *"Your positive attitude and strong will power helped you through the treatment and it will also help you in future, so don't worry."*

I looked at my father, at *Benu* and then *Dr. Smruti.* Each one of them was so positive that there was no room for any negative thoughts I perked up and listened to what the doctor had to say. She said, *"Some cancer patients cannot tolerate chemotherapy. Fortunately you responded extremely well. Some patients are totally cured and in some recurrence occur like any other disease, so no one could predict or control the future."*

> *It is foolish to think we can accurately predict the future.*

Dr. Smruti spoke at length about her patients who successfully managed their lives as *cancer survivors.*

Then she asked us to get the blood tests done for *W.B.C., platelets, S. creatinine, blood sodium, magnesium* and *CA125* after 21 days and inform her about the reports on phone. She informed us to come for the follow-up after three months. She advised us to repeat all the tests and to get an *USG* of abdomen-pelvis with *TVS* (*transvaginal ultrasound*) before coming for the follow-up.

She stressed on the fact that a healthy mind and body was the mantra to stay fit. I enquired, *"Since I am gaining weight, can I start exercising?"*

She said, *"You can start with some light exercise or you can do yoga."*

I told her, *"After surgery, sitting on the floor for yoga is not possible. I do only deep breathing exercises and yoga which can be done sitting on a chair however it does not help in losing weight."*

She nodded and suggested, *"Go for walk, slowly get used to exposing yourself to crowded places such as a restaurant or a mall."*

She told *Benu* and my father, *"Take her for outings after few days, let her meet people, maybe your family friends, only take care that she stays away from sick people and avoid overexertion. Proper rest is mandatory."*

I liked the idea of going to a restaurant, visiting a mall, but was worried about my looks.

Then I consoled myself, *"Well for now, I will live for the present, take life easy, one day at a time."*

Dr. Smruti then asked us to meet *Dr. Pratima* and *Dr. Patil*. We went to meet *Dr. Pratima*. She was happy that my response to chemotherapy was excellent. She admired the way I stayed focused, marked my goal and finally achieved it with single minded devotion.

She enquired, "*Are you wearing the abdominal belt while travelling?*"

When she saw me nodding my head she asked, "*Are you following my instructions while climbing the stairs?*"

Again when she saw me nodding my head she said, "*Well, regarding your diet, remember the food which our ancestors usually had in villages, like whole grains, fresh fruits and vegetables, less of refined flour, more of brown rice, fish etc. are good for you.*"

Dr. Pratima's advice—

- *Body requires antioxidants and it is best to get the antioxidant from fruits and vegetables rather than supplements.*

- *She said that fiber intake is linked with improved bowel movement and good source of fibers are whole grains, nuts, vegetables and fruits.*

- *Eat multigrain chapatti or bhākṛī.*

- *Avoid eating refined flour (maida) as far as possible.*

- *Soy products are good.*

- *Mono unsaturated fats, found in olive oils, peanuts are helpful.*

- *Omega-3-fatty acids found in fish and walnuts are good.*

- *Yoga can be helpful in reducing anxiety, depression etc.*

My doubts started gnawing at me again, when I met *Dr. Patil*. I asked him, "*Doctor, the symptoms are so vague, what if cancer reoccurs and I ignore the symptoms again?*"

He advised, *"That's the reason why we insist, never be late for the follow-ups."*

Dr. Patil's advice—

- *Never be late for the follow-up.*
- *Before follow-ups get the tests done (as advised by the doctor).*
- *In case of emergency immediately call the doctor without any delay.*
- *No self-medication.*
- *Being over-weight or obese increases the recurrence of cancer.*
- *It is important to stay at a prescribed body weight.*

I was home after my sixth and the last chemotherapy. On *4*th *February* blood test showed the *W.B.C. count* was very low so two *Grafeel* injections were given. Blood test was done on *7*th *February* and everything was normal. My parents stayed back for few days and then left for *Nasik* reassured that I was stable.

A new learning dawned upon to me . . . I was suffering from the side effects associated with chemotherapy however it was not very difficult to overcome them because by now I knew how to deal with each one of the symptoms. I was amazed by the power of my mind over the body. I consciously developed an extraordinary ability to diffuse my physical pain by completely focusing on that part of my body and willing the pain to disappear. It was a kind of tussle between the mind and the body.

> ## *"Natural forces within us are the true healers of diseases."*
>
> *Hippocrates (CIRCA 460-CIRCA 370 BC)*
> *Ancient Greek Physician and Father of Western Medicine*

Now I had time to take care of my domestic responsibilities. *HSC examinations* were to start by *February* end and *Nini* was at home preparing for her examination. She appeared disturbed so I remained by her side to reassure her. We encouraged her to concentrate only on her studies. My presence had a soothing effect on her and she started studying in earnest. She received the examination schedule and was upset as her examination centre was in a school quite far from our residence.

I promised her that we would accompany her to the examination centre but my only concern was how people would react to my appearance. As I looked in the mirror, the view was scary. I would wear a scarf to hide my bald head, but what to do about my nails and teeth, they were still greyish black in colour and my skin was pigmented. My eyes were sunken and this gave me harsh and older look.

Surprisingly, my look was never an issue for *Nini* and *Benu* and they just overruled my misgivings.

Nini told me, "*You are coming there for me, I love you and want you there, don't give undue importance to unknown people.*"

I realized that day, *"Love is the most important thing in life. We should learn how to give it and also how to receive it."*

There was no point in caring what other people thought about my appearance as it was my daughters who really mattered. My family loved me . . . and no matter what the world thought of me . . . no matter if I looked like a joker in the eyes of world, the reality was that it was my daughter . . . who made me see life with a newer perspective.

> *We cannot change our circumstances however we can control what we think about them.*

Nini's examination started and we accompanied her every day. *Benu* and I would watch with pleasure as she entered the center with confidence. I would suffer from some anxiety and pray to *God* that she should do well. It was a relief when she completed her *HSC examination* and was free to prepare for her engineering entrance examinations (*IIT-JEE and BITSAT*).

On *18th February*, my blood test was done and as per *Dr. Smruti's* advice, she was informed about the report. *CA125* was 6.3 U/ml and rest of the tests was normal.

I still felt weak and needed support to walk but I made it a point to go for walks regularly. I did *Anulom* and *Vilom* (*alternative breathing*), as practiced in *Prāṇāyam* (*yogic breathing exercise*). Regular meditation, *Nām Smàraṇ* and chanting the sacred word

Om (*Auṁ*) helped me to harness my wayward emotions and strengthened my will power. A lady masseur came home daily to give me a whole body massage (*except abdomen*). However, sitting at home took its toll and my weight became a cause of concern.

Also it was noticed that during this period; whenever I got up from my bed or turn while walking, I felt dizzy . . . dizzy is a soft word . . . actually I felt the whole room swing. Initially it happened once or twice so we ignored it. But then the frequency increased so *Benu* called *Dr. Smruti* and apprised her about it.

She told him, "*We are meeting after few days, we will get it investigated.*"

He told her, "*We have searched the web; the symptoms are similar to that of vertigo.*"

Doctor advised, "*Ask Moitreyee, not to stand directly from sleeping position. First from sleeping position, let her sit on the bed for few minutes and only then stand up.*"

She told him, "*Also tell her, never to be in a hurry to get up from bed or a chair and not to turn with a jerk while walking or she will feel giddy and fall.*"

I followed *Dr. Smruti's* advice and took all the precautions, but the sensation persisted. Soon it was time for the first follow-up. The blood tests report was normal. *CA125* was 6.6 U/ml.

We asked for an appointment and were at *Bombay Hospital* for the follow-up. We bowed in front of Ganapati and then waited for about six hours for our turn. *Ms. Malati* told us that *Dr. Smruti* first attends to patients undergoing chemotherapy and only then the patients who are there for the follow-up.

After the check-up, *Dr. Smruti* sent us to *Dr. A. K. Shah* (*Otologist*) to check if the problem (*dizziness*) faced by me was indeed vertigo. Initially *Dr. Shah* did an interesting test (*pure tone audiometry*). I sat in a lighted room which had a glass partition and on the other side the operator sat (*in dark*) with her instruments. I could not see her but she could see me. My job was to listen carefully. Different sounds were presented through the headphones. My job was to raise my finger to indicate to the operator that I had indeed heard the sound. This was almost like the '*chidiya ud*' (*Bird fly*) game we played as kids. I enjoyed it immensely. After few more tests, the doctor concluded that I was not suffering from vertigo. He cleaned wax from my ears and advised me to improve my diet.

After that we went to meet *Dr. Patil*. In the waiting room *Ms. Jenny* and *Ms. Perry* (assistants) recounted in awe, the doctor's efforts to save cancer patients. *Dr. Patil* was very happy with my progress. He enquired, *"Have you put on weight?"*

I said, *"Yes doctor, my sedentary life style is the culprit."*

He was annoyed to hear my response, "*Well! I am a busy doctor, but I go for regular morning walks and if I don't exercise, I feel I won't be able to stand for hours in the operation theatre. What are you doing?*"

I felt chastised and was ashamed of myself. Losing weight was now my first priority. *Dr. Patil* then asked me to come for the next follow-up after three months.

Chapter 15

A hardship worse than chemotherapy . . .

Ten days after my visit to *Bombay Hospital*, mild cramps in my lower abdomen started troubling me. We were petrified because it reminded us of those early days in my cancer journey. By noon, the cramp was quite severe. *Benu* tried calling *Dr. Smruti* several times but she was not available. We knew that *Dr. Patil* was on leave, so *Benu* continued calling *Dr. Smruti*.

We believed in the strength of positive thinking
but our condition was such that it was easy to
panic and assume the worst.

By evening, my condition deteriorated as I developed high fever, started shivering and was delirious. Just when *Benu* decided to take me to *Bombay Hospital*, *Dr. Smruti* called back. Doctor heard about the cramps and told us that she suspected it to be *UTI*. The symptoms were of urine infection so she asked *Benu* to admit me in *Century Rayon Hospital* and get the urine test done.

Urine test showed that the infection was due to *Enterococcus faecalis.* The urine culture report suggested that this strain of bacteria was resistant to almost all the antibiotics tested except few which had to be injected intravenous. Hence the drip was started.

Dr. Leena wanted an expert's opinion so she decided to call urologist *Dr. Atul Mokashi. Dr. Mokashi* went through the reports carefully and recommended some medicines. He told us that cranberry was good however fresh cranberry was not available here so he recommended cranberry capsules.

He told *Benu*, *"She must have contracted UTI (Urinary tract infection) from a public urinal."*

Surprised, *Benu* told him, *"Other than hospitals, she does not visit any public places."*

Doctor smiled and said *"Hmm . . . she might have contracted it from there."*

So, my treatment for *UTI* started. In the hospital, for the rest of my stay, *Nini* occupied the twin bed in the room. She camped by my bed side with her books, preparing for her engineering entrance examinations.

The doctors, sisters and *ward-boys* of the hospital were known to us and were very friendly. *Dr. Meghna Bhalerao*, whenever on duty, would spend some quality time with me. She would discuss about my cancer journey. Once, we were talking about lifestyle diseases, yoga, stress management, etc. when she said something very interesting, *"There are two types of ladies, number one and number two."*

This was news to me. She said, "*The number one ladies are the ones who are caring and giving. They are ready to sacrifice their needs and dedicate their life to be a loving wife and a wonderful mother. They are always busy fulfilling their duties. If they are a working woman, then she is dedicated, hardworking and progressive. She would meet all the deadlines on time and would balance her personal and professional life by multitasking.*"

She then told me, "*The number two ladies are laidback and relaxed. Never in a hurry to complete task at home or in office. Their house would be in a mess, unorganized or unkept. Such working women would prefer to complete today's work tomorrow and tomorrow's work sometime later. They are caring and giving persons but some may find them casual mannered, lazy and easy going.*"

We were discussing that, the number one ladies were, "*Always busy, stressed out, caught up in endless multitasking and problem solving. These ladies have simply stopped enjoying life*" whereas the number two ladies were, "*Relaxed and stress free. Generally they are the one who are free from the lifestyle diseases.*"

Tongue in cheek, the doctor smiled and asked me, "*Where do you place yourself?*"

Working mothers! Could we categorize them into any type? Aren't they all the same?

After doctor left, as usual my brain started working overtime. There was a lot to think about.

I enquired, *"Am I the lazy type, Nini?"*

She smiled and chipped in with her phenomenal wisdom, *"No mummy, I can't imagine you as a lazy person."*

I quizzed, *"Are you sure?"*

She laughed, *"Mummy! Rest assured, you are not the number two type."*

So! I was definitely a number one person. *Good or Bad! God knows!* I only knew that my life was all about being a wife, mother, professor and researcher. This was me, my little world and I loved everything about it. My house was never in a mess; being systematic, meticulous and perfect took precedence over everything else. There were hundreds of things to be done and time was always short. Innumerable days and nights spent working late; helping my daughters complete their projects, doing college work, reading or simply writing some research papers was all about being perfect.

When you expect perfection, you are seldom lazy.

My stay in the hospital was for five days. These five days taught me the life's lesson, the lesson that there is no need to be perfect. It was important to accept the fact that life can never be perfect. The need to be perfect is an illusion.

Cannot change the past but could learn from it to improve the present.

My sincere pledge was that though it was hard to let go and completely change my nature, I would certainly make an attempt to change. It would be an uphill task, but *Hey! I could surely try.*

At *Pilani*, *Gargi* was tense as she started appearing for job interviews. *Nini* appeared for *IIT-JEE* entrance but did not fare well. She, however, did well in *BITSAT* and was sure that she would secure admission in *BITS*.

May 2011, *Gargi* was at home after successfully completing the last semester. She was fortunate to have two jobs offers and had the liberty to choose the one she liked. There was lot of activity at home as *Gargi* was back and *Nini* was free at last (free from coaching classes, lectures, examinations etc.). On *29th May* all four of us went to a restaurant and celebrated my marriage anniversary.

On *6th June 2011*, all of us were sitting and spending some leisure time together. We were making plans for a small family get-together to celebrate my birthday on *9th June*. Everything was fine till I felt cold and started shivering. Within no time my body temperature started rising, I developed high fever and was sweating profusely. My teeth started to chatter. It was a kind of uncontrolled chattering.

Gargi had never seen me like this. She was stunned, almost in tears to see me shivering violently. She straightaway bundled me in a blanket. However, when I still felt cold she put another blanket around me and held me tight. In the meantime, *Nini* who was by now well trained for such emergencies informed *Benu* and called the ambulance. I was admitted in *Century Rayon hospital* within half an hour.

> • *Life was full of challenges for our family but our ability to meet these challenges was growing.*
>
> • *It was a learning process for us too, but we had the faith that we could do anything, even when it seemed impossible.*
>
> • *It was this faith that always helped us to find the way out.*
>
> • *Positive thinking not only helped us to stay healthy but also added warmth and richness to our lives.*

Urine infection tested positive! Alas! The doctors had no choice but to start the intravenous drip again. So, down with *UTI* my birthday was celebrated in the hospital. In the evening, *Gargi, Nini, Snehal* and *Benu* were with me when *Nikita* (*Niku, my friend Alka's daughter*) and *Juhi* (*my friend Sarita's daughter*) visited me in my hospital room.

Niku was carrying a tiffin box. She told me, "*Happy birthday Auntie. I know, you don't eat outside stuff so I have baked a cake for you. Auntie, will you have some?*"

These words made my day and what made it special were the sentiments and the effort she took to bake a cake, especially for me.

I thanked her and said, *"Yes Niku, I would love to have some."*

In my lifetime, I have had cakes and pastries, quite a lot! But this cake was marvelous; I asked *Niku*, *"What have you put in this? It tastes divine."*

Niku told me, *"Auntie, it's a simple vanilla cake."* But I knew there was nothing simple about the cake, it was a very special cake, a cake made with lot of love and affection.

My room was filled with flowers presented by *Gargi's* friends. Our family friends made it a point to cheer me up. *Benu* brought sweets and we distributed it in the hospital. The doctors, nurses, ward-boys and my friends came together to celebrate my birthday. A month back I was admitted for five days for *UTI* and this was the second time and again I was in the hospital for five days.

Nini's results were out and she did extremely well in her *XII examination* and *BITSAT entrance*. As expected, she got calls for admission from all campuses of BITS *Pilani*. *Nini* decided to take admission in BITS *Pilani*. She was following her father and sister's footsteps.

We kept *Satyanarayan puja* at our place to thank the Lord, acknowledge his generosity and to request him to sustain our achievements. Our prayer to the lord was to preserve family harmony and bring success and enjoyment to all. The puja room was decorated with flower garlands by *Gargi* and a colourful rangoli made by *Nini*. All family members and friends joined us for the puja. They absolutely loved the ceremony.

Gargi decided to join "*Kony labs*" at *Hyderabad*. She was familiar with *Hyderabad* having stayed there earlier. *Benu* decided to accompany her as they wanted to search for a flat near her office. But before they left for *Hyderabad*, a *Nasik* trip was organized.

Nasik is three hour drive from our place but our trip took more than five hours as *Benu* took utmost care while driving. Moreover this was our family's first outing after a long time so the joy of simply being together for all four of us was a treat. We also enjoyed the scenic beauty of the hills of *Kasara Ghats* and the green fields of *Nasik*. It was planned that first we would visit "*Shirdi*" with my parents and then *Benu* and *Gargi* would leave for *Hyderabad*. *Nini* and I would stay back in *Nasik* till *Benu* returned.

We went to "*Shirdi*" with my parents, a spiritual trip to fulfill my mother's *saṅkalp* and were blessed with *Śrī Sāi's darshan*. Thousands of devotees thronged the same path we strode, to get only a few minutes *darshan* but in these few minutes, *Sāi* appeared to know our innermost thoughts. We were grateful for the blessings he showered on us. We thanked *Sāi Bābā* for *Gargi* and *Nini's* achievements and my recovery.

Immersed in my prayers, I could hear my mother softly placating *Gargi*. Through the rush I could locate them near the *Samadhi*. *Gargi* was crying . . . tears rolling down her eyes . . . and she was chanting . . . *Om Sāi! Śrī Sāi! Jai, Jai, Sāi!*

Mom spoke gently, *"Don't cry, Gargi."*

Gargi told her, *"Thamma, I am not crying. I am thanking Sāi, thanking for saving Mā."*

Tears rolling down her face, soaked her cheek, she wiped the tears from her cheek and looked up at *Sāi* and said, *"I want to say . . . Thank you Sāi."* She then prayed to the Divine Lord with a longing heart and that started fresh tears . . . tears running down her cheek . . . and she again started chanting . . . *Om Sāi! Śrī Sāi! Jai, Jai, Sāi!*

It was a memorable ten days outing for us. It was also the first time we met *Dr. Bhattacherjee*. We found him to be a very busy doctor who did not give any preferential treatment, to any of his patients. He had patients from far-away places, but everyone waited patiently for one's turn. We found *Dr. Bhattacharjee* to be extremely positive and highly motivated. He instilled confidence in his patients.

He went through my reports and told me, *"I was confident that you would be fine. I told your parents not to worry."*

I told him about the numerous side effects of chemotherapy which I was still facing. He listened to me patiently and addressed each symptom and gave me medicines to counter each one of them.

He told me to continue with the prescribed homeopathy medicines as it would cure the problem from the root. It was a pleasure to meet *Dr. Bhattacherjee* who gave us the statistics of cancer patients he cured with homeopathy. We read in awe, the board on display and which presented the statistics of the diseases cured by him. He told us that homeopathic medicines treat the root cause of illness. He showed us files with case history of patients he cured, patients who had lost hope and how homeopathy worked wonders in such problematic cases.

His view was that, "*Homeopathy cures with holistic, totalistic and individualistic approach. Homeopathy was extremely safe with no harmful side effects.*"

Dr. Bhattacherjee's advice—

- *Take his medicine regularly as prescribed.*
- *Avoid oily food, chilies and sour food.*
- *Avoid red meat and chicken.*
- *Avoid coffee, raw onion and raw garlic.*
- *Eat fish regularly.*
- *Drink plenty of water.*
- *He asked me to eat healthy, exercise regularly and reduce my weight.*

I did not think life would ever be same again. I thought of life differently now, my priorities changed and most importantly I changed beyond recognition.

Back home, I was happy to follow my doctor's advice. *Benu* and I went for morning and evening walk.

Not being very confident or stable, I took support and walked slowly, taking rest intermittently. This was also the time to upgrade myself (*a year's gossip which I missed due to illness*) to everything that happened and was happening in our colony. This time was devoted for gossiping (*my favourite time*).

Vandhana, the petite young friend of mine would support me though she was half my size, crack jokes to make things light and make me laugh. She would often boss over me and scold me, if necessary. In *Benu's* absence my friends told me that in the past year, *Benu* had lost his smile. Whenever they met him, he looked anxious, worried, and vulnerable. He had lost weight drastically.

My friends, *Alka*, *Sarita*, *Vandhana* and *Varsha* were of great help as they accompanied us for these walks and encouraged me to walk without fear. There were the usual hiccups such as suddenly feeling faint or dizzy. Walking short distances and frequently taking rest in between helped me to increase my stamina.

We were happy that most of the symptoms such as burning of eyes, mouth ulcer etc. had disappeared. My mantra to success was to push myself to be strong physically and mentally.

> *Personal efforts can bring about marvels, if the desire stems from the heart. My desire was strong and pure . . . so are you surprised that within a month, I could walk for an hour or more?*

It would be a lie if I said it wasn't tough. Yes! It was a difficult period and it would get me down sometimes. But when you have so many things going for you, you don't quit, do you? So I set a goal for myself which I firmly and unflinchingly believed I could attain.

"Let us rise up and be thankful, for if we didn't learn a lot today, at least we learned a little, and if we didn't learn a little, at least we didn't get sick, and if we got sick, at least we didn't die; so, let us all be thankful."

Gautama Buddha (CIRCA 563 BC-483 BC)
Founder of Buddhism

Chapter 16

Stopped struggling . . . started living . . .

Few days after returning from *Nasik*, there were cramps in my lower abdomen. I was shivering and though cold with the chills, I was also sweating profusely. Urine test confirmed it to be *UTI* and I was again admitted in *Century Rayon hospital*. I was put on intravenous drip and the urine culture report showed different bacteria this time.

E. coli (*Escherichia coli*) how it was possible! *Dr. Atul Mokashi*, as usual, enquired whether I used any public urinal. He also advised me to use the *Indian style toilet* as they are much safer. He then changed the medicines accordingly. He asked me to continue with cranberry capsules, drink cranberry juice, coconut water and sufficient water.

I asked the doctors that even after taking utmost care why did it re-occur? *Dr. Leena* sympathetically told me, "*Your immune-response has been suppressed due to chemotherapy.*"

I nodded, *Dr. Smruti* and *Dr. Patil* had discussed about it several times in *Bombay Hospital*.

Dr. Atul Mokashi further informed me, "*Your immune system is so weak that you can develop infections from bacteria, which are always around and are usually harmless.*"

This disturbed me, was my immune system so vulnerable that even harmless bacteria were capable of causing havoc in my body?

This was the third time I was in hospital. *UTI* was causing havoc. We understood that the relapse was due to suppression of my immune response and tried to find means to overcome the problem.

Urinary Tract Infection—

- *Most of the urine infection is caused by bacteria.*

- *Reason for recurrent UTI—Immune-response suppressed due to chemotherapy in my case.*

- *Symptoms—Pain while passing urine and frequent passing of urine. Pain in the lower abdomen and high temperature. Uncontrolled shivering and profuse sweating.*

- *Recommended—antibiotics course.*

- *Drink plenty of fluids to flush out the bladder.*

- *Drink cranberry juice or have capsules daily. Cranberry is not an antibiotic and it does not kill bacteria but reports state that it prevents urine infection*

- *Personal hygiene should not be compromised.*

By *July* end it was time for *Nini's* admission to *BITS Pilani*. I hit upon a plan and told *Benu*, "*If doctors give me permission, I want to accompany both of you to Pilani.*"

Benu knew that walking couple of yards was immensely taxing for me but he wholeheartedly supported my idea to accompany them. Our relatives, on the contrary were totally against it. We started receiving phone calls from them. My mother was nervous, she enquired, "*Will you be able to travel? Are you strong enough, Rina?*"

My dear father wanted to know, "*How will you travel?*"

Benu informed him, "*Two hours flight to New Delhi and five hours drive by road to Pilani.*"

He advised, "*See that she is comfortable and be with her throughout the trip.*"

Benu told my relatives, **"She deserved to stop struggling and start living."**

Our relatives were alarmed by our decision. They did not want us to take any risk. They chided us because they cared and we understood their concern. But, it was decision time and we did not want the hideous shadows of tomorrow spoiling our today.

Whenever admonished, I pulled the emotional string, "*Maybe I have survived to see Nini taking admission in a reputed professional college.*"

Or sometimes I would say, "*God has cured me in time and I can travel now.*"

There was some truth in what I said. I was diagnosed with ovarian cancer stage IV. My treatment started by September 2010 and by May 2011, six cycles of chemotherapy and a major surgery was over. Doctors felt that my recovery was excellent. Strange but true, I got well just in time, ready to see Nini take admission in a professional college.

Everyone remained quite after that but cautioned me, "*Go, only if doctors permit.*"

Nini usually doubled up laughing, whenever I made these dramatic statements. She would tease me, "*Nautanki (Drama queen) . . . Nautanki Mummy!*"

We were at *Bombay Hospital*, in the lobby I stood in front of Ganapati and requested him, "*Please let her say . . . Yes . . . I really want to go to Pilani.*"

In *Dr. Smruti's* chamber we told her about *Nini's* admission in *Pilani* and asked for her permission.

"*Can she go to Pilani, doctor? Can she travel?*" *Benu* asked.

Doctor smiled and told him, "*Yes, she can travel.*"

Benu informed her, that we would take flight from *Mumbai* to *New Delhi* and then travel by car to *Pilani*, five hour drive from *Delhi* airport.

Dr. Smruti was happy that I was ready to face crowd. But she cautioned, "*You can go but be careful about your diet and make the trip comfortable by taking lots of precautions."*

She warned, *"You still suffer from various side effects so pack enough medicines that will last the entire trip and store them properly."*

She suggested, *"Heed your inner voice, respect it, and use caution if you feel uneasy."*

When *Dr. Patil* heard about my proposed trip, he told me, *"Take utmost care, don't do anything foolish, if tired take rest, don't over exert. Also, take care of your diet. Do not take any chances with the food you eat and water you drink."*

When I nodded, he told me, *"You are weak due to repeated UTI but you will do fine. Don't worry your positive attitude and strong will power will help you."*

"Don't worry at all." He told *Benu,* *"And don't forget to take along photocopies of all the prescriptions."*

My doctor's belief in me was heartening. Their encouragement confirmed that our resolve to take the trip was indeed a good decision. Brimming with confidence, we made all the arrangements, as fear for the tomorrow, the forebodings had no right to rob us of our happiness today.

Needed the mental strength and determination to take action and push through the struggles.

A new lease of life began when draped in a gorgeous sāri, an attractive head scarf covering my head, with lot of guts and a prayer to *God* almighty . . . I ventured out . . . ready to enjoy freedom at last.

The airport was crowded. There were too many people around but facing crowd after a gap of almost a year was not as daunting as I thought it would be. The five hour's drive from *Delhi* to *Pilani* was enjoyable. *Nini* took admission in *BITS*. After her admission, there were three *BITSians* (*Benu*, *Gargi* and *Nini*) in my house. It was a remarkable ten days trip. Though exhausted, I was happy that my perseverance allowed me to overcome the hurdles.

> *"Strength does not come from physical capacity. It comes from an indomitable will."*
>
> *Mahatma Gandhi (1869-1948)*
> *Father of the Nation of India, Indian Political Leader and Freedom fighter*

Back home, I was lonely; when your children leave home, there is an emptiness which haunts you. Empty nest syndrome was indeed a fact, not a myth. For my emotional well-being, it was therefore essential to start living life, as I wanted.

> *As a kid my father encouraged me to read novels, short stories, poems and autobiographies. At a very young age, I inculcated the habit of reading as my father introduced me to the great works of Rabindranath Tagore, R. K. Narayan, Bankim Chandra Chattopadhyay, Charles Dickens, Premchand etc. He made me member of various libraries so that I could read different books of my choice. Starting from Enid Blyton, Nancy Drew, Hardy boys, to Sherlock Homes, Agatha Christie, Perry Mason to Mills and Boons, I read them all. This habit of mine was a boon in disguise. Everyone felt I should not stay alone, I would feel lonely but I started enjoying my own company. With plenty of time in hand my laptop and my books became my best friends. Yes, I missed my kids, but I started enjoying the silence. Yes! Silence was golden.*

As *Benu* was busy with his office work I stayed home. I started writing in earnest, played games on the internet, chatted with cancer patient worldwide, watched yoga and exercise routine on *YouTube* and practiced them. But most importantly I read plenty of books. So my life was packed with activities of my choice.

Dr. Jamdhade, my colleague who was more like my younger brother, was concerned and upset that I stayed alone at home. He would often call *Benu* to enquire about my progress. He knew about my reading habit so he sent books, journals and other reading materials for me. Finally one day he could no longer stay away so he came home to meet us. He expected me to be bedridden and was in for a pleasant surprise to see me moving around.

He told *Benu*, "*I am delighted to see madam so active. I did not expect this.*"

He brought with him lot of cheers and his visit was filled with so much positivity that it encouraged me to get well soon and join college at the earliest.

My daughters called regularly. We discussed books, music and food. We shared tit-bits which were mostly hilarious.

> *There were times when, distracted by wild and unpleasant thoughts, I would panic. My daughters, however, always shifted my way of thinking and directed my thoughts towards positive channels. I also sought to keep a rein on my wayward negative thoughts by concentrating and bringing my mind under control.*

By now my hair was growing and it was a mass of chemo-curls. Curls which filled my head were like springs. My chemo curls were of utmost interest and a hot topic amongst my family members and friends. One day, my nephew *Anjan* came for a visit. Out of curiosity he put a pencil in my curls to see if it would stay—*It did!*

Then he put some chalks in my curls—*again they stayed in place!*

By now everyone in my house started experimenting. We almost doubled up laughing when *Anjan* put a small pebble in my curls and it still stayed put. After this whenever *Anjan* came to meet me he would first put something in my curls or play with my curls and then talk to me.

Benu was very particular about the follow-ups. As it was again time to meet my doctors at *Bombay*

Hospital the blood tests were done on *9*th *September*. The *CBC* appeared normal and the *CA125* was 4.5 U/ml. The *USG* of abdomen and pelvis was done on *12*th *September*. *USG* report showed, "*No adnexal mass, liver, gall bladder, pancreas, spleen and kidney were normal.*" I also got bilateral mammography done and the report was normal.

This was my second follow-up. Seven months had passed since my last cycle of chemotherapy. The reports were encouraging and *Dr. Smruti* and *Dr. Patil* were happy to see my progress. They checked for lumps in my throat and breasts and were happy that my stitches were healed properly.

Dr. Patil questioned, "*Why did you get the mammography done?*"

Surprised I said, "*The earlier report stated to repeat after one year.*"

He laughed, "*They always write it . . . Business strategy, you know!*"

He then said, "*Rest assured for the next five years, don't get a mammography done.*"

He however, looked unhappy that my weight had increased. He recommended a dietitian's name and told me sternly, "*Please understand this—the cancer cells were located on the fat cells so stay fit, lose weight, go and meet the dietician.*"

I complained, "*Do you know how much I am trying doctor? But what should I do? I am not successful in reducing my weight.*"

Doctor scolded, "*You are not trying enough, are you?*"

I felt reprimanded so I took it as a challenge and promised him, "*I will lose weight and you will have no complaints regarding it.*"

Dr. Patil asked me to get the *CBC* and a *CT* scan for abdomen and pelvis done for the next follow up.

After few days, *Gargi* informed us that her convocation was to take place in *BITS Pilani* on *20*th *August, 2011.* She was getting her graduation degree, she wanted us to accompany her and attend the convocation. She asked me, "*Mā, will you come for my convocation?*"

I was dancing, "*Yes, yes, I will come.*"

But *Gargi* told me, "*Mā, first get doctor's permission.*"

So, we requested *Dr. Smruti* for permission to travel again. *Dr. Smruti* was happy to see my eagerness, she said, "*Go ahead, go and be with your daughter on her special day.*"

When my mother heard about it, she complained, "*Was once not enough, why do you want to go again?*"

I told her, "*Mā, I have survived because I wanted to see Gargi graduating.*"

Also I impishly told her, "*I also get to see Nini, your granddaughter, I have to see how she is managing in a hostel.*"

When *Nini* met me she held me tight as if we were meeting after a decade. *BITS Pilani* was special for us as *Nini*, *Gargi* and *Benu* were all from the same college. I am the only *non-BITSian* in my family. I did not follow the slang words used by them so I became the butt of all the *BITSian* jokes. The convocation was a grand affair. It was an emotional moment for us when we saw *Gargi* receiving her degree. *Remembered the day I cried in the hospital thinking that I would not be alive to see this day. It was this day I was crying for and here I was hale and hearty sitting and watching my daughter graduating!*

> *I was happy, immensely happy that I could witness this important event in my daughter's life because I had the faith and the willpower to overcome the difficulties.*

After I came back from *Pilani*, I found that the *UTI* was still persisting and I was in the hospital on and off, in the month of *September* and *October*. By now I was sick of hospital and intravenous drips but was grateful that *UTI* did not happen during chemo. If it would have happened during chemo then my story would be different . . . very different!

Festival time approached and it was *Diwali (festival of lights)*. We missed our daughters, more so during festivals. They called us regularly but their absence was deeply felt. We longed for their continuous babbling, chuckling and missed the beautiful rangoli they made. Their enthusiasm in decorating the house with decorative candle and lights was missing this year. However, by *God's* grace, we had many well-wishers. *Mr. G.D. Dharap*, our lab assistant in Botany department, was someone who shared my sorrow as his family member had travelled this path before. He was very sensitive since he knew what I was going through. He would sometime send a small note or a lengthy letter written with lots of love, praying for my early recovery or a beautiful get well card. He made attractive candles which he sent to me during Diwali and also some handmade flowers from colorful linen. These small gestures made a great difference in my life.

I wanted some change in my routine and the opportunity arose when on *3ʳᵈ November, 2011 Benu* was invited to attend a conference in *Pilani. Nini* was overjoyed, she hummed, "*Mummy, third time in a single semester! Wow!*"

After obtaining doctor's permission, I accompanied him and could meet *Nini* again. We celebrated *Nini's* birthday (*29ᵗʰ October*) on *4ᵗʰ November* in *Pilani*.

It was one year after my surgery and other than the persistent *UTI*, I was doing well. After returning from my *Pilani* trip, I was ready for the next follow-up. On 15ᵗʰ *December* blood test was done. The blood report was normal. *CA125* was 4.6 U/ml. As advised by *Dr. Patil CT* scan for abdomen and pelvis was done on *20th December* at *Bombay Hospital*. I detested the experience as usual I suffered from severe loose motion. My day was spoilt. *Benu* ran out to *Fashion Street* to purchase a new set of dress for me.

The *CT* scan report showed, "*Post-operative changes with no obvious residual/recurrent lesions.*"

Dr. Smruti checked for lumps in the neck and breasts. She was satisfied with my progress. We then went to meet *Dr. Patil*. I was scared to meet him because my weight had increased instead of being reduced. He checked for thyroid and breast lumps and was satisfied that there were no such growths. The *CT* scan and blood reports showed that I was cancer free. That was the good news, but doctor again lectured me on the drawbacks of obesity in a cancer patient. We could see that he was fed up with me. I was exercising, walking, eating proper diet and following doctor's advice meticulously. My only weakness was my sweet tooth, so now was the time to sacrifice that. Well that would be my next step to please the doctor.

Days passed by and I felt gloomy thinking about my life threatening experience. I missed people whom I met every day in college and would reminiscence those blissful days. When your life takes a downward turn, you get to know your friends. It was a fact that I was fortunate to have made so many good friends. *Dr. Mulgaonkar* called, few days after every chemotherapy cycle. She had cancer survivors in her family so she made it a point to tell me about them, the side effects they faced and encouraged me to counter the side effects. *Dr. Kalpana Phal* was one of my close associates. She would enquire about my wellbeing from time to time.

Dr. Darshna Patil, my colleague from Birla College sent me *prasad* after she visited *Ganapati* temple in *Titwala* and prayed for my recovery. *Dr. Meeta Bhot*, my best friend from Birla College called regularly. My colleagues, *Dr. (Mrs.) Behnaz B. Patel* from Ruia College (*Mumbai*) and *Prof. Shraddha Raut* from my college also made it a ritual to wish me on every important occasion. I always waited eagerly to hear from them.

My student *Upendra* (*Third year, Botany*), made it a habit to wish me with an SMS every morning. He also wished me on occasions such as *Holi, Diwali* and *New Year* or sent some interesting jokes or quotations which would either make me laugh or admire him for his consistency.

December is a month of joy and jubilation as our family members unite at one place and welcome the New Year together. *Nini* was home after completing her first semester and *Gargi* took leave to celebrate and the New Year with us. I was overjoyed to accompany them for the party and welcomed the *New Year, 2012* with friends and family members.

January, *February* and *March* were again troublesome for me, as the dreadful *UTI* returned. I was however, relieved when a relapse did not occur after that. I took care and was determined that I would not suffer from *UTI* ever again.

"Never, never, never, never ever give up!"

Winston Churchill (1874-1965)
British politician, British Army Officer, Historian, Writer,
Artist and Nobel Laureate

I was finally free from urine infection but in the process I learnt a lot about *UTI* and the precautions to be taken. I learnt that in *UTI*, relapse was common, cranberry was beneficial (*cranberry capsules and cranberry juice*) and *Indian style public urinal* helped to avoid *UTI*.

I suffered from urine infection from May to March, a period of eleven months and I was admitted in hospital eight times, each time for five to six days.

I was delighted to welcome *Ashrut* (*Shubho*), my nephew who had come for a short visit from *Glasgow* and wanted to meet me.

Arun-Da, *Anu-Di* and *Shubho* had only one thing to say, "*You looked superb.*"

Well! Always knew I could make heads turn but lately my looks had taken a beating so this gave a boost to my confidence . . . :)

They stayed with us for few days and we celebrated International Women's Day on 8th March. We cut a cake to celebrate womanhood and pray tribute to our indomitable spirit.

Life's lesson—

- *In this turbulent episode of my life, I learnt the hard way that . . . Health is wealth.*

- *Listen to what your body says. Do not ignore any symptoms and address all the symptoms without any delay.*

- *The past year was all about "Gir k sambhalna" (getting up and stabilizing after a fall). It was about hitting the rock bottom and then rising up from there.*

- *A journey where we stepped into the unknown without knowing the solution yet sensing that . . . victory is ahead.*

- *A journey where I was not alone; since cancer affects not just the person but it holds the entire family in its clutches. *

- *In the past year I learnt life's lesson. The lesson that misfortunes visits, knocking uninvited. So be prepared, be aware and be strong enough to face any such calamity.*

- *Know your goal. Mine was to get cured of cancer. It was our one point agenda.*

- *In cancer journey, life gets confined within the walls of the house, outings are confined to hospitals and clinics, so don't get depressed.*

- *The doctors, nurses, lab technicians, ward-boys, hospital staff and medical store salesman are the people of utmost importance in this journey; so store their phone number, in case of emergency.*

- *This journey reinforced my belief that we should treasure our family members. They are the ones who stand by you when you falter, cheer you when you lose heart and celebrate when you smile.*

- *This journey reinforced my belief that we should treasure our family members. They are the ones who stand by you when you falter, cheer you when you lose heart and celebrate when you smile.*

- *Friends are precious as they are the ones who pray for you when you suffer. As a teacher, I found that colleagues and students matter a lot.*

- *The most important lesson I learnt was that you should always have time to look around, enjoy nature, be aware of your surroundings and always believe that God is great!*

- *My journey included six cycles of chemotherapy and a major surgery (pan-hysterectomy, appendectomy and 4 layer of complete Omentectomy) and also homeopathy medicines.*

- *For UTI, I was admitted in hospital eight times in eleven months.*

- *It is vital to be aware of the medical facilities available and what are you entitled to, at your work place.*

- *Benu was complacent that his family was covered for all medical expenses. He thus did not invest in mediclaims. But what he did not know was that the medical reimbursement was only for medicines and not for the surgery. So learn from our mistake, know what the medical facility at your workplace excludes.*

- *We spent `50,000 for each cycle of chemotherapy, `3, 50,000 for the surgery and another `2, 00,000 for other expenses. A total of `9, 00,000 spent of which only the cost of medicines and hospital room charges were partially reimbursed.*

- *This was an important lesson we learnt, a costly one because though we had many policies, insurances . . . none covered for cancer. Read the fine prints of any investment done.*

- *We also learnt that most of the hospitals in general and few hospitals in particular have the provision for financial aid for afflicted patients hailing from poor families. These sources should be discovered in time and not after taking admission in hospitals which do not have these facilities.*

- *In esteemed and famous hospitals, there is a provision for lesser appreciable expenditure on various counts such as the type of room. The quantum of expenditure is based on the room rent and which in turn determines the visit and consultation charges of the doctor, surgery cost etc. This will make a sizeable difference in expenditure to cancer treatment.*

- *I had the opportunity to gather knowledge on alternative medicines. I met some patients who had opted for chemotherapy and homeopathy and some for chemotherapy and 'Ayurvedic' medicines to make sure that cancer is cured from the roots.*

Chapter 17

Life after surgery and chemotherapy . . .

A turbulent year had passed and my life was slowly moving back on track. Regular follow-ups at *Bombay Hospital* showed encouraging results and my doctors were happy with my progress.

For most patients, cancer is a tough and terrifying experience they have ever encountered. Cancer survivors usually go into a shell as they suffer from inferiority complex. At war with their own personal demons, they are always worried about their future and they keep brooding—*Why! Why did it happen?* I was no different, as I faced a variety of negative emotions and kept fretting about my future.

> *"Forget the past, for it is gone from your domain! Forget the future, for it is beyond your reach! Control the present! Live supremely well now! This is the way of the wise . . ."*

Paramahansa Yogananda (1893-1952)
Indian Yogi, Guru and Introducer of Meditation and kriya Yoga to Westerners

I told *Gargi* about my apprehensions. She said, "*Mā, Why worry unnecessarily? You have a strong will power; you can achieve whatever you set your mind on to.*"

I tried to analyze my attitude, harness my feelings. I was an independent lady, strong and steady.

What happened now? What was I scared of? What were the thoughts buried deep inside my heart? Why was I worried? Questions and more questions! I knew, worry never accomplished anything, what happened to my awesome attitude and my strong will power!

Something had to be done immediately to break the barriers of fear which persisted in my mind. To gain confidence, courage and strength, I made a decision to apply myself diligently to root out my deepest fear.

So the most important question, **"Did I fear death?"**

I accepted . . . **"Yes! I feared death."**

But why? Why did death strip me of my confidence?

Facing death . . . Changed it all? Yes, changed it all.

I focused on the essentials, looked death in the eye and considered, **"Why do I think of the worst?"** I squirmed, grappling with the tough questions about myself.

"What happened to me? Was I the problem?"

If so, it was best to concentrate on the solution rather than the problem itself. Everything suddenly made sense . . .

"What would I do . . . if I was not afraid?"

I sat alone for quite some time in silent contemplation and then answered . . . I would unplug . . . listen to my inner self . . . which was telling me, **"Don't allow cancer to ruin your life. Yes, don't allow cancer to ruin your life."**

"All the flowers of all the tomorrows are in the seeds of today."

Indian proverb

A creature of my own imagination, I recognized that the healing power lies within me . . . to free myself, I decided to let go of the fears . . . and . . . act fast so as to gain confidence. The power of mind is really astounding . . . *Yes! The healing power was within me.*

In my cancer journey, *Benu* was with me day in and day out. In my deepest moments of struggle, fear, frustration and confusion, I always found him by my side. Despondency came, but the tremendous love between us saw through this grueling period and I developed a childlike trust in him.

He became my strength and also my weakness.

I thought of the year spent, struggling to rationalize, fighting against all odds to remain steady in this cancer journey. However, the shadows of pain kept creeping. Blood rushing through my veins, a throbbing pain in my heart, arms and legs . . . a vacant feeling . . . when *Benu* was not with me was common.

He helped me eating, sitting or moving from place to place. He would bring my medicines and remind me to take them on time. He would take me for regular follow-ups. We would regularly go for walk together, holding hands (*like our honeymoon days*). His love and care was such that I gradually became totally dependent on him. He was my anchor to safety.

Why feel safe, only if Benu was with me? Why such a drastic change in me? What happened to the driven independent lady?

Time and again, I grappled with the big question of my survival. My worry was compounded with the belief that managing alone would be tough . . . together with *Benu* life seems so easy and so joyful.

So! The fear that built up in my mind was worse than the situation that actually existed! Yes! The unwelcome thoughts throughout the day were distressing and it was extremely challenging to control my wayward mind. Surprise! Surprise!

Why did a disciplined and organized person like me have such a muddled mind, filled with disruptive thoughts?

I discussed about my misgivings with my daughters. *Nini* dismissed my misgivings and *Gargi* told me, "*Mā, let go of your compulsive worrying.*"

My mother always advised, "*If you are presented with two choices in life . . . choose the difficult one . . . in the long run, it will help you.*"

The easy way out was to remain totally dependent on *Benu . . . But, was that my goal? Surely Not!*

So I took the tough decision and asked *Benu*, "*Will you start playing again? Will you start going to the club as before?*"

He was stunned because he knew that I was terrified to let him out of my sight. He asked me softly, "*Are you sure? Can you manage alone?*"

I answered with conviction, "*Yes, very sure, go to the club and start playing again.*"

Even if he was surprised by my answer, he didn't express it, but he certainly seemed reluctant to leave me alone at home.

Sensing his hesitation, I voiced my feeling to him, "*I want to be independent, my old real self again.*"

After that, he started going to the club regularly from 7:00 p.m. to 9:00 p.m. Sports being his great love, he started enjoying it as before. I stayed back but was never alone as my old friends i.e. books, music and my kitchen garden were always there for company.

My nurse realized that I was regaining my strength so she took up another job offer. Her absence initially rocked my comfort zone but I soon adjusted. I had maids to do the house work and cooking. With plenty of time in hand, I started giving direction to my thoughts and utilized my time in writing and compiling my book.

Life's lesson—

- *Life is full of decisions.*

- *It is never too late to begin thinking about your future.*

- *Set your goal.*

- *After setting your goal, acknowledge it, think about it and head for it.*

- *Things do not always go as planned.*

- *Have patience, stand firm, resolve to see through the distressing situations.*

- *See life with a newer perspective.*

Ashish-Da, Bipasha, Natasha and *Ankan* came for a visit. We were discussing about our life, the past year, when my niece, *Natasha* told us, *"Our family suffered a lot in the past year, no one was spared, there were near death situations, lots of pain and sorrow but I think we should actually thank our stars. Everyone survived in situations wherein people usually don't. So let's just consider ourselves blessed."* They say that inspiration comes in many forms and sometimes from a person you least expect. These few words of wisdom from my little niece stunned us. It now inspires me to think positively and put my chaotic thoughts into order whenever I felt low. It felt good meet them after a long gap.

In the meantime, *Sonali* invited us and my parents her place for a few days. She was leaving *Mumbai* soon for *New Delhi*. We spent ten action packed days filled with fun, laughter, good food and exhaustive shopping from the *Indian Naval Canteen* (*Gol Canteen*) at *Navy Nagar, Colaba*.

> *My limitations were in my mind. I tried to erase every thought of failure from my mind. I did my best to enjoy and left everything else to God.*

In my effort to live a normal existence, I started picking up my phone without any hesitation when it rang. I spoke to my students, friends and colleagues at length. In one such conversation with *Dr. Mulgaonkar*, she told me that *Mr. Sawant* (*field collector, Botany Department*), would be retiring soon and he wanted me to attend his send off. I decided to attend so *Benu* arranged for a driver to drive me to college.

I was excited throughout the drive but when my car entered the college gate I was surprised to find tears rolling down my face. I hurriedly wiped them away. *Yes! This is it! This is the place I missed the most . . . My College.* This place filled me with a nostalgic sense of belonging. Teaching was not just an occupation for me, it was my passion.

The send-off was a memorable occasion for us. My heart filled with unspeakable joy in response to the warm and cordial welcome accorded to me. I met *Dr. Mulgaonkar, Dr. Jamdhade, Prof. Shraddha Raut and Prof. Chetana Shetty*. I received a flower bouquet and lots of presents. Like a little child, I happily accepted the presents basking in their love and affection.

> *"One best book is equal to hundred good friends but one good friend is equal to a library."*
>
> Dr. A.P.J. Abdul Kalam
> *Missile man of India, Scientist and administrator who served as the 11th President of India*

And I did not have one; I had so many good friends. One such friend of mine was *Kalpana Phal* from Statistic department of my college. In the past year, *Kalpana* would call occasionally and enquire about my health and then start talking about my daughters. She would discuss about *Nini's* studies, talk about college and our colleagues. She would also tell me about her family. It was a pleasure talking to her and I would eagerly wait for her call because I, for some reason, felt very happy after speaking to her. Her innate goodness made a huge difference in my ongoing journey, the journey towards the holistic healing of mind, body and soul. I met her after a year; it was an emotional reunion for us.

The same day I also met *Prof. Francena Luiz* of English department. *Francena* was my close associate. We were of the same age and had joined college in the same year. So we shared many happy occasions together. When she came to know that I was suffering from cancer, she wanted to meet me. But as I would not meet anyone, she wrote a letter to me. It was a lengthy letter in which she had poured down all her feelings and belief that, "*I would fight and come back a winner.*" *Francena* knew about my fondness for cake so she took pains and baked one for me. It was not the gifts but the love which made her so dear to me.

I also met my Principal, *Dr. Madhuri Pejaver*. A lady with a human touch, she hugged me tight and congratulated me for my positive attitude. *Pejaver* madam was the one who inspired me when I was not able to reconcile about losing all my hair. She always quoted the example of her sister-in-law who was a cancer survivor. *Pejaver* madam kept a busy schedule as she was also the *Dean of Science, University of Mumbai*. But she always made time for me, guiding and advising me. There were many occasions when we would talk about the side effects of chemotherapy and how **yoga** and **reiki** could help and also how meditation would help me to harmonize naturally with everything around and within me.

She was positive that I would overcome the hurdles and join college which was the right place for me. Her very spirit of optimism to conquer all obstacles helped me in those times when depression knocked my door. The echoes of her kind words were truly endless.

The love and affection showered on me brought tears in my eyes. My throat was chocked and I was finding it very difficult to talk. I met *Dr. Kolet, Mrs. Meshram, Priyanka, Mamta* and *Shaymal* as I was leaving. Though climbing stairs was tough, *Francena, Kalpana* and *Mulgaonkar* madam held my hand and helped me. I left college buoyant and in high spirits, determined to return soon.

Advice to friends and colleagues supporting cancer patients—

- *When friends and colleagues suffer from cancer, do not shy away.*

- *Ask permission before visiting*

- *Make it clear that if the patient refuses then it is perfectly fine. There must be some reason.*

- *Call once to see if they pick up the phone. If they miss your call, they will call back. If not don't call back.*

- *Send a letter, email, card or SMS*

- *Call their close relatives once in a while to enquire if any help is required.*

- *Do not ramble, be a good listener.*

- *Let them know that you are with them in this journey.*

This experience made me realize that, "*If we want to do something in life, dream and desire for it. If we have the dedication, faith and belief in ourselves then our desires will materialize.*"

My dream was that I would be a cancer survivor.

Chapter 18

Cancer revisits . . .

A cancer detection camp was organized at *Century Rayon hospital, Shahad*, on *11ᵗʰ April 2012*. This was done with the help of "*Indian Cancer Society, Mobile Cancer Detection Centre*."

The camp was arranged specially for the members of *Cenray Mahila Pragati*. Being a member, my name was included in the list for the check-up. I felt lethargic and wanted to give this opportunity a miss. My excuse was, "*I am getting the follow-ups done regularly at Bombay Hospital, what is the use of another check-up?*"

Another reason was, "*Benu is busy on that particular day and I don't want to visit the hospital alone*."

When my friend *Sarita*, heard about my dilly-dallying, she laughed and said, "*Stop making excuses, I am going for the check-up, you will come with me*."

So we went to the hospital together. After we filled up some forms and our medical history was noted down, we were sent for the *pap-smear test*. Later, they sent me to the *ENT* doctor (*Ear, Nose and Throat doctor*). The doctor started examining me as well as cross-questioning me. He was probing my neck thoroughly. I gave him my medical history.

He asked, "*Are you on medication for hypothyroidism.*"

I nodded and replied, "*I am taking Thyronorm, 25mcg for the past five years.*"

He pressed a spot on my neck and told me softly, "*I can feel the presence of a nodule in the right lobe of your thyroid gland.*"

Nodule! What was the doctor talking about? Nodule! The word nodule made my heart beat faster as waves of fear rolled through me. Sweating profusely, I was frozen to the spot, Nodules! Tear in my eyes started blurring my vision. Nodules! My God! What was the doctor talking about? Was it benign or malignant! Oh God! Cancer! Again! Please . . . Please . . . Please God! Let it be benign . . . I prayed.

Life was queer with its twists and turns. Back to square one! Was I? I sat rooted in front of the doctor, unable to move. There was complete silence as he wrote his findings.

The silence was broken only when the doctor cleared his throat and said, "*Given your medical history, it is advisable to get it checked from Bombay Hospital . . . Get a USG of neck done immediately.*"

He advised, *"Also get a FNA and blood test done for T3, T4 and TSH."*

I wanted to know, *"What is FNA?"*

He smiled, *"Don't get frightened, FNA is Fine Needle Aspiration. A fine needle will be inserted to collect few cells from the nodule. Diagnosis (cytology or histology) will ascertain if the nodule is malignant or benign."*

Drawing in a deep breath, I shut my eyes and reasoned with myself, *"Why so worried . . . so desperate . . . so filled with despair? The nodule can be benign."*

Benu admired *Sāi Bābā's* cardinal principles of ***"Shraddha and Saburi"*** which translates to ***"Faith and Patience"***.

We tried to practice this in our daily life so why did I feel today that, patience is a virtue, I did not possess at all?

"Dear Sāi! What could I do to keep my faith intact?"

With a heavy heart, I came out of the chamber and met *Alka*. She realized that something had disturbed me. Instead of interrogating she started comforting me. *Sarita's* check-up was taking time so *Alka* called for a car and sent me home. After reaching home, my priority was to keep myself busy and wait for *Benu*.

Easy said than done, nothing was alleviating my circumstances. I remained listless and dissatisfied as I waited for him to return. In an effort to steady myself, I sat down, closed my eyes and started meditating.

But, the doctor's verdict cast a gloom.

It was possible to close my eyes and not see! But was it possible to close my heart and not feel? And what did I feel?

If I said I was not scared, that would be lying.

After *Benu* returned and heard about what the doctor had said, he was dumbstruck. We frantically tried to contact *Dr. Smruti* and *Dr. Patil*. *Dr. Smruti* was abroad so we could only reach *Dr. Patil*. He advised us to get the blood tests done from *Century Rayon hospital* and then take an appointment for *USG (abdomen-pelvis)* and *FNAC* at *Bombay Hospital*.

Next day, *12th April*, blood test was done for *CA125, W.B.C. count, S. creatinine* and *T3, T4, TSH* at *Century Rayon hospital*. The reports for blood test were normal and *CA125* was 5.1 U/ml, which was also normal.

The *USG (abdomen-pelvis)* and *FNAC* were done at *Bombay Hospital*. The report (*USG of abdomen and pelvis*) showed *tiny gall bladder polyp and post hysterectomy with no adnexal mass.*

The *FNAC* report showed words such as . . . *Nodule . . . papillary carcinoma* . . . I was disturbed to see these words in the report . . . *carcinoma meant cancer . . . doesn't it?*

Cancer revisits . . . the big question . . . could I survive, this time? I realized that one who losses courage . . . losses all . . . I am strong . . . master of my thoughts . . . I should not forget that.

So with the reports in hand, we sat patiently in the waiting room of *Dr. Patil's* chamber (*after taking an appointment on an urgency basis*). I sat quietly and started surfing the web, looking for information on polyps and thyroid cancer.

Did I just say, "*I am strong*?"

Laughable . . . gross exaggeration, because a shudder ran through my body as I surfed the web. The detailed information available on internet sent shivers down my spine so I switched off my laptop immediately.

This was the time when I missed my father's presence the most because merely holding his hands filled me with confidence. *Oh Daddy! I wish you were with me here today.* I looked around at other cancer patients in the waiting room. There was so much suffering etched on their faces. There was myriad of emotions which could be seen clearly and then I noticed *Benu*. He was sweating profusely, his shirt soaked in perspiration and his head hung low between his two hands, "*a sign of defeat*."

Oh God! Did he lose hope? Why was he looking
so lost? Did he not know that his wife is a
fighter? Then I decided time for getting scared
was over. Between us, I had to be strong . . . if
not for me . . . but for him.

My fear straightaway took a back seat because in the absence my parents, it was my responsibility to see to it that nothing untoward happened to *Benu*. I told him, *"You know dear, sometimes we give up hope even before we have reached our goal."*

He did not reply. I tried again, *"Together we crossed the hurdle once . . . and together we will cross it again."*

There was a blank look in his eyes. Realization struck that my words were not registering with him. *Benu* looked lost and dejected. Apprehensive about him, my goal was to make him understand that it was better to wait for the doctor's verdict before assuming the worst. I believed that no matter how hopeless the situation may seem we could always lift ourselves. *And this was not a hopeless situation.*

When tears welled up in his eyes, I frantically called *Gargi* and told her about her dad and made her aware of the recent developments. How defeated and lost her dad looked. I told her that he was behaving as though this was the dead end. *Dead end! No! There had to be a way out Gargi!* I complained, *"I am the one, who should be depressed, scared but Gargi, it is your dad who looks miserable and depressed. He is soaked in perspiration and looks dazed. He is finding it difficult to handle this shock. Can you do something about it?"*

She told me, *"Mā, don't worry, I will talk to him."*

She then asked me reproachfully, *"Mā why did you not tell me about it earlier? Why did you hide it from me? You under went so many tests but you did not disclose it to me."*

Caught! I wriggled out of the situation by telling her that we will talk about it later. Her priority now was that she should convince her dad to be stress free.

> *Gargi is her father's girl . . . loving daughter of a doting father . . . she adores her father . . . only she could bring him back on track . . . and instill confidence.*

Benu was lost in his thoughts, silent, morose when he received a call. It must have been from *Gargi* because he perked up immediately. What did they discuss? I don't know! But after sometime, *Benu* looked much better . . .

After sometime, *Dr. Patil* called us in and went through the reports. The *USG* report for neck showed, "Solitary well defined nodule within the right lobe of the thyroid gland." The *USG* report for abdomen-pelvis showed the status post hysterectomy with no adnexal mass, but the presence of "polyps in the gall bladder". The smear of *FNA* report showed, "The cytological findings were suspicious of papillary carcinoma in the right lobe of the thyroid."

He uttered the dreaded sentence, *"Yes, it is a suspected case of thyroid cancer."*

So the verdict was, *"Thyroid cancer."*

Thyroid cancer! Benu shouted, *"How could cancer of ovary spread? The CA125 and USG reports were always normal and we did regular follow-ups."*

Dr. Patil explained, *"No . . . no, please understand this . . . ovarian cancer has not spread. Your wife is completely cured of ovarian cancer. Thyroid cancer is totally different from ovarian cancer."*

I told him, *"Doctor, CA125 was always within limits after my surgery and six cycles of chemotherapy. How could I have thyroid cancer? Why it was not reflected in the blood test reports."*

He told me, *"For every cancer, there are different tumour markers and different tests. CA125 is the tumour marker for ovarian cancer. Understand this; you are cured of ovarian cancer."*

What good did it do! Here I am, struck with cancer again!

I realized that with all the advances made in the field of oncology . . . there were drawbacks . . . a major lacuna. A cancer patient could not be complacent after treatment. The follow-up may show everything normal and that she is completely cured, but cancer lurks . . . in another *avatār* (*form*). A cancer survivor should always stay alert because **cancer revisits**.

"*Which stage, doctor*", I asked softly.

He gently answered, "*Initial stages . . . I or II stage . . . and don't worry thyroid cancer is easiest to cure.*"

Benu cried, "*Why again doctor? She has undergone so much pain, why again?*"

He reassured *Benu*, "*Yes, I know that; Dr. Saha, but I also know that your wife is a fighter and she will fight this.*"

He explained, "*Thyroid is a small butterfly-shaped gland located in front of the neck just below the Adam's apple.*"

We touched and tried to find the thyroid gland as the doctor showed us its position, in front of our neck.

He continued, "*Thyroid gland produces three hormones T4, T3 and calcitonin. T3 and T4 are important for development and subsequent metabolism. Calcitonin regulates the concentration of calcium in our body. The production of T3 and T4 is regulated by the pituitary gland which releases TSH. Thyroid gland requires iodine to function properly.*"

Since the *FNA* report showed suspicious case of papillary carcinoma, *Dr. Patil* advised us to get the surgery done immediately and then to go for further treatment.

Benu was under extreme duress, he asked, "*Doctor, no doubt, she is strong but does she have to go through chemotherapy cycles again?*"

Dr. Patil said, *"Relax, relax . . . chemotherapy is not required in the treatment of thyroid cancer."*

This was good news! A cancer type, which did not require chemotherapy! Benu looked at me and smiled. His smile told me of his relief. We then listened to what the doctor had to say.

He said, *"The first line of treatment is surgery. An incision will be made to remove the right lobe of the thyroid (as the nodule is in the right lobe). While you are still on the operation table, the sample will be sent for freeze drying sectioning in pathology laboratory of Bombay hospital to find out if the sample is cancerous."*

Scared I asked, *"Well! What if it is cancer?"*

He said, *"If the result is in affirmative (nodule is malignant) then the left lobe of the thyroid will be removed. The entire surgery will be completed at one go, where as it takes two surgeries to remove the entire thyroid, elsewhere."*

I was scared because this surgery was in the neck. I asked him, *"What would happen to my voice?"*

But doctor convinced me that my voice would not be affected. *Dr. Patil* was the best *Cancer Surgeon, Specialist in Thoracic Onco-surgery in India*. I was happy that he was the one who would be operating me. I looked at him with admiration; how with practiced ease, he had made us comfortable, answered all our questions and cleared our doubts. He looked happy because he could soothe *Benu's* anxiety.

I did a double take when I saw him smiling angelically at something *Benu* had said. I looked at him again and transported back to the day, eighteen to nineteen months back when I first met him in *Bombay Hospital*, 10th floor. He was strict, glum and very serious. He had entered my room and had told me gravely, "*I am Dr. Prakash Patil.*" He had reminded me of my staid professor. Sorry to say this, but I felt in those days . . . the man never smiles.

Now I looked at him again and thought, "*You were wrong, Rina, you were wrong . . . He is great . . . God like . . . your savior.*"

He exuded energy, a force beyond mere charisma. I returned to the present when *Dr. Patil* told us, "*Surgery would be followed by treatment with nuclear medicines*"

"*Nuclear medicine that's new! That's News*"

Doctor explained, "*Nuclear medicine is a branch of medical science where radionuclides are used for diagnosis and treatment of diseases. These radionuclides are used for treating malignant and non-malignant conditions.*"

We were introduced to a new term "*Nuclear medicines.*" Cancer treatment, not involving chemotherapy or radiation was new to us. But it was music to our ears when the doctor informed us that unlike chemotherapy, Nuclear medicines have no side effects.

Doctor then asked me to stop taking my thyroid hormone tablets (*Thyronorm*), a procedure he called "*Thyroid withdrawal.*"

He said that the levels of *TSH* in my blood would gradually rise as soon as I stop taking the tablets. This would make me feel weak and dizzy. My head would feel heavy and I would face problem in standing or walking without help.

He said, "*During treatment with nuclear medicine the I-131(Radioiodine) would work best when the levels of TSH is high.*"

Regarding the polyps in gallbladder, doctor told that we could wait and watch for six months to see if surgery was required.

I wanted to tell him, "*Perish the thought.*" Instead, I told him, "*Ovarian cancer was in IV stage, Thyroid cancer is probably in second stage so I am scared to wait. I don't want cancer to spread to the gall bladder.*"

Already *Bipasha* and *Arun-Da* were operated for gall bladder so I knew about the procedure. There was no point waiting so I told, "*Finish both the surgeries, doctor. I will not wait for six month for cancer to spread and then to go for the third surgery.*"

It was decided that *Dr. Patil* would operate on 27th *April 2012*. He asked us to complete all the formalities. When *Gargi* was told about the operation, she informed us that she would like to bear the expenses of the surgery as she had the insurance which covered for her parents. Our finances were never stretched to such an extent that we required help from anyone during the past year, but it was with great joy that we surrendered to our daughter's wish . . . *"Even in our moment of fear and great sadness . . . this small incident filled our heart with great joy and pride."*

> *"I have become my own version of an optimist. If I can't make it through one door, I'll go through another door—or I'll make a door. Something terrific will come no matter how dark the present."*
>
> Rabindranath Tagore (1861-1941)
> Indian Poet, writer, composer, essayist, playwright, painter and Nobel laureate

Benu was busy looking into the formalities and I sat patiently in the waiting room writing on my laptop. Cancer being the most debilitating and deadly disease, there was plenty to write about my cancer journey. A journey which was now taking a new turn as . . . **CANCER REVISITS.**

Fear, anxiety is a normal reaction associated with cancer and like before I freaked out on hearing about cancer recurrence. But then it had become my second nature to make best of bad situations. My earlier experience, taught me to remain unruffled, stay optimistic and focus on positives. So even though my first reaction was of distress, my next move was to accept my present condition and then move on. My thoughts strangely were not negative. Yes! There was an ugly turn in my cancer journey, but somehow I was convinced in my mind that it was not the dead end.

It was not a fight, nor a battle against cancer. So what was it? Whatever it was, I was positive that my goal would be reached. A hurdle once crossed, will be crossed again.

> *"Never think there is anything impossible for the soul. It is the greatest hearsay to think so. If there is sin, this is the only sin to say that you are weak or others are weak."*
>
> *Swami Vivekananda (1863-1902)*
> *Indian Hindu Monk, Orator, Writer and Founder of Ramkrishna Math and Ramkrishna Mission*

Absorbed in listing the efforts to be taken to reach my goal, I looked up with a start as realization dawned upon me that I was being keenly observed. I found *Dr. Patil* watching me. He however, smiled pleasantly and told me to come with *Dr. Saha* to the chamber for further instructions when the formalities get over.

Later in his chamber, doctor asked me, *"What were you doing? You looked engrossed?"*

Well! It was time to tell him about my book, the book on my cancer journey.

He exclaimed, *"Writing about your cancer journey! Why? Why revisit the sufferings?"*

Benu told him, "*She is just jotting down the events and some thoughts regarding cancer treatment.*"

He said, "*Why recollect the painful happenings of the past year? Why not do better things so as not to get depressed?*"

It is not necessary that you agree with everything your doctor tells so I smiled and told him that writing was my passion and writing this book was my dream.

He said, "*Okay, just don't get depressed.*"

> *Revisit the sufferings . . . Yes, I was doing
> that . . . it was painful, depressing, disheartening,
> but . . . it was mostly cathartic to admire
> myself as a person who wanted to overcome the
> sufferings, struggle and disappointments.*

Yes, the doctor was right, I could get cured and go about my life; forget the pain and celebrate for surviving the scare.

But I was helpless. I could not shy away from my desire to write to reach the cancer patients, their family members, friends and colleagues. My thought was always dominated by a mighty purpose, stemmed from the bottom of my heart, it was pure and intense, an inner voice which insisted that this is the reality check, have the courage of conviction; spread the message that cancer is curable.

Pain did not stop me as I sat down to write after every chemo, surgery or a hospital visit. What started as mere jotting down of event was now taking shape into a full-fledged memoir. My experience . . . my cancer journey . . . a progressive journey . . . a true story was worth writing . . . re-living the struggle . . . discovering every nuance of my personality . . . was worth the pain.

Chapter 19

Double surgery . . .

*G*argi applied for leave and was with us before the surgery. My parents came from *Nasik*. *Nini* was in *Pilani,* busy with her comprehensive examinations (*second semester*).

Before leaving for *Bombay Hospital,* I bent to touch my mother's feet to seek her blessings. *My mother, who is just five feet tall, always appears taller because of her confidence, positive attitude and strong personality. She is our spiritual security. We shamelessly lean on her and always try to emulate her. She is a lady of substance and we always depend on her to solve every major and minor crisis in our life.*

I looked at my mother and was surprised to see tears, in her eyes. I closed my eyes and drew in a deep breath. My eyes started misting up, this was the first time I saw tears in her eyes and her tears disturbed me.

She realized it and immediately wiped them. She gently kissed my forehead and hugged me hard. Sometimes, the things that we feel deepest and that mean the most to us are also most difficult for us to express. I hugged her back, words were superfluous.

She smiled through her tearful, somewhat anxious eyes. Her smile filled me with warmth, I felt the love that surrounded me and thanked *God* for blessing me with such wonderful parents.

We reached *Bombay Hospital* and I stood in front of Gannu, bowed my head with respect and continued my ongoing conversation with him, "*Take care Gannu. My faith in you is unalterable; you gave me this . . . now you will look after me!*"

As proud parents, we watched *Gargi* organize everything efficiently to her liking in the hospital. The room she arranged was in a different wing and a special room. We reminded her that the hospital charges would go up. But she hugged me and said, "*You deserve the best, Mā.*"

Dr. Patil told us that he would first operate the thyroid and then *Dr. Jadliwala* would operate the gall bladder. We knew the best team of doctors would operate, so we were not worried unnecessarily.

Dr. Jadliwala sat down to explain that the surgery for removal of the gallbladder was done under general anesthesia. It could be removed either by laparoscopy or by open surgery but he preferred laparoscopy. He said that in laparoscopy, he would make three to four small cuts in my abdomen (*belly*). Gas, usually carbon-di-oxide, would be pumped into my belly to expand it (*like balloon*). This would give him more space to work. The laparoscope will be inserted through one of the cuts. Laparoscope is a thin, lighted tube that would allow him to see inside my belly. Other medical instruments will be inserted through the other cuts. First he would cut the bile duct and blood vessels that lead to the gallbladder and then the gallbladder would be removed using the laparoscope.

However, laparoscopy would be avoided if either my organs were fused due to earlier operation or the gallbladder was not seen properly. In such a case he would remove the gallbladder through one large incision in my abdomen. This technique was called open surgery. It was a more invasive operation than laparoscopy and it needed hospitalization for longer time as it took time for recovery. He said that open surgery would be performed only if *laparoscopic cholecystectomy* could not be safely performed.

Only I could follow doctor's detailed explanation because *Benu* and *Gargi* were from computer background and my father, a military man. I told doctor the same and he was then introduced to *Gargi* (*he already knew my father and Benu*). He was surprised to know that three members from our family were from *BITS Pilani*. He then disclosed to us that he wanted to know more about *BITS* as his son was preparing for *BITSAT* examination. So the discussion shifted to *BITS* and *BITSAT* entrance examination.

It was around 9:00 a.m. in morning of *27th April 2012*, I was wheeled to the operation theatre. My parents, keeping in mind their earlier experience with *Mumbai* traffic had started quite early. I sat with *Gargi, Benu* and my parents. *Gargi* looked nervous she was cuddling me and talking to me in her sweet and soft voice.

She asked me, *"Are you nervous Mā?"*

I thought about my previous surgery, my feelings then and asserted, *"Surprisingly there is absolutely no nervousness."*

Double surgery! So what? There was nothing to be scared off! I was strong, my family was with me, my doctors were the best and finally I had the blessings of God almighty. Nothing could go wrong. It's going to be alright. Everything is going to be alright.

"As I was taken to the operation theater, we stopped and offered our prayer to *"Lord Satyanarayan"*. This time I had a good look at him. Made of white stone maybe marble, he stood tall and blessed anyone who entered the operation theatre and the relatives who waited there.

I was in the waiting room of the operation theater when two more patients were wheeled in. As I waited, my thoughts could not be schooled, it went back to the day when I was in the same room and the atmosphere was the same. I was scared then, I was scared now and, as before, when I started reciting *"Hanumān Chalisa"*, I could feel the fear slowly seeping away.

I have lived through this horror once I could very well go through it again.

Dr. Jadliwala came to meet me. He said that *Dr. Patil* would be with me soon. They had just finished an operation and I would be the next. He stood talking to me and after he left, another doctor came and started talking to me. He told me that he read my case history and felt that I would do fine today. He asked me whether I was a professor. When I nodded he asked me about my specialization. When I told him that it was *Plant Tissue Culture* he started talking about *Organ culture*. After sometime he left.

My turn was taking time, I was left all alone so getting impatient I started reciting "*Gâyatrî Mantra*" and "*Hanumān Chalisa.*" This had a positive effect on me and I was quite calm by the time I was wheeled into the operation theatre.

There were some doctors and nurses standing in a circle around me. I looked up as I was shifted to the operation table and identified two faces very dear to me. *Dr. Patil* and *Dr. Jadliwala* were smiling and I smiled back at them. My earlier experience had taught me that looking around would scare me so I concentrated on the people around me.

Dr. Patil introduced me to all the doctors in the operation theatre. The doctors were trying to find a proper vein to start the drip. It was a very difficult task, one held my right arm and the other my left arm. They kept tapping till a healthy vein was located and almost like a trophy shown to everyone around. A pinprick and the IV was started.

Dr. Patil told them, "*She has undergone six cycles of chemotherapy so finding a vein will be problematic.*"

Dr. Patil was telling other doctors that I was writing a book on my experience with cancer. I could see different expressions, some were surprised, some enthusiastic but everyone wanted to know more about the book.

They realized that I was a professor and writing was my passion. Everyone started talking about their college life, remembering their teachers; they began smiling, laughing and chit chatting, all at once. I felt, I was in a class full of energetic bubbly students. I could feel the natural camaraderie between them and relaxed.

Dr. Patil smiled and told me, "*We doctors are not intelligent but you professors are real intelligent lot, teaching, research etc.,*" this struck a chord in me.

I told *Dr. Patil* with a break in my voice, "***We might be intelligent but doctor, you are . . . Next to God.***"

After sometime, I heard a voice coming from somewhere behind me, reminding everyone that they had an operation to start. The atmosphere changed, it was more dynamic. My sixth sense told me that they were raring to go.

Dr. Patil then introduced me to *Dr. Arora* (*anesthetist*). Yes, he was the same doctor who was there for my earlier operation too. *Dr. Arora* told me that he will administer the anesthesia. I remembered from the earlier operation, how soon I would lose consciousness and hurriedly prayed. "*Be with me Sāi, please be with me.*" After that . . .

When I was wheeled to my room, I was conscious. I learnt that my operation had taken about nine and half hours! The post-operative period was not as painful as the earlier operation. As before, there were tubes from different places in my body and I was not given water as usual. This time I behaved and thought it was better to listen to the nurses and the doctors.

The first thing *Benu* did was to proudly show me the photograph of the thyroid which the doctor had removed. He remembered to photograph it this time. I studied the photograph for a long time; it looked quite different from the photographs of thyroid we had seen on the internet. *Gargi* told me that she had seen both the thyroid and the gall bladder.

Ashish-Da had come from *Nasik*. My room was filled with my relatives. *Dr. Jadliwala* came for a visit and I asked him immediately, "*Did my organs behave? Could you perform laparoscopy?*"

He laughed and took my hands in his and told me, "*You behaved very nicely madam. You are a very strong lady and yes, open surgery was not required, operation was done by laparoscopy.*"

I told him, "*I can feel some pain in my abdomen.*"

He smiled and said, "*Don't worry you will be fine after sometime.*"

Ashish-Da came forward and told my doctor, *"I am sure, my sister will be fine. I can see the trust she has in her doctors."*

Ashish-Da decided to stay in the hospital with *Benu* and asked my family to come back the next morning. The room which *Gargi* had booked for me was very spacious. Both *Ashish-Da* and *Benu* could stay comfortably with me.

I was feeling hot and was sweating profusely. I could see the dressing in my abdomen and a huge dressing spanning the base of my neck. Due to local anesthesia they were not painful but were extremely uncomfortable. To relax myself, I kept moving my legs and arms, folded my pajama and shirt.

Ashish-Da saw this and told me to stay put and not to move so much. He scolded, *"You will hurt yourself."* This made me furious but he was my elder brother so I thought, *"Respect Rina! Respect for the brother you hero-worship."*

After some time, *Dr. Patil* came for a visit. He came late as he was busy with few more surgeries after mine. He told me, *"The frozen section report showed that in the right hemi-thyroidectomy the right lobe thyroid showed papillary carcinoma (follicular variant). Tumour diameter 2.5 cm, nine reactive lymph nodes were removed, all free of metastasis and the unremarkable parathyroid glands were also removed."*

Ashish-Da was surprised, *"Para thyroid glands were removed!"*

Doctor nodded, *"Yes, I have removed them."*

Dr. Patil told us the small pea-sized parathyroid glands located in the neck. It is found just behind the thyroid gland. He removed them as they were cancerous. He also told us that the parathyroid glands control the amount of calcium in our blood, bones and the normal conduction of the electric currents along nerves. Sometimes if the parathyroid glands were cancer free they are removed and inserted in the arm or any other area and they function normally. In my case however it was not so as the parathyroid glands were cancerous.

Ashish-Da asked, *"Will she have to take calcium supplement?"*

Doctor told my brother, *"Yes, she has to take calcium supplement lifelong."*

Dr. Patil then told us, *"The left lobe of the thyroid gland was free of malignancy."*

Benu asked, *"What about the gall bladder?*

Dr. Patil then told him, *"The gall bladder showed acute cholecystitis but no malignancy."*

He told me, *"Complete Thyroidectomy and cholecystectomy was done."*

He then informed me that he would remove the tubes for urine enabling me to go to the washroom by myself the next morning.

He saw that I remained quiet throughout the conversation so concerned he asked me, *"Why are you so quiet?"*

I complained to him *"Ashish-Da asked me to stay still and not to move much."*

It was a joyful moment when the doctor's serious face broke into a grin and he told me, *"I will certainly not come between a brother and a sister; you can quarrel as much as you want."*

As a peace offering *Ashish-Da*, gave me his laptop and connected me to Facebook so that I could play games on it. I played for few minutes but was too weak to continue.

I missed *Sonali*, who was posted to *New Delhi*. I missed her continuous chatter and bossing around but then, I was never alone, my parents were with me. As *Nini* was in *Pilani*, my mother was free to be with me throughout the day. *Gargi's* friend *Shreyas*, *Aaron* (*friends from BITS*) came to meet me. *Anjan* also turned up around the same time. So my room was filled with young engineers talking about work. As all of them were also professional musicians (*Shreyas and Aaron being a part of an Indie Rock Band-The Fringe Pop*), there was lot of discussion on music. We rejoiced when *Anjan* told us that his company would be sending him for two years to Cincinnati (*Ohio State*) and he would be leaving soon.

Dr. Jadliwala had come for a visit; he was introduced to my guests. Doctor found them interesting so he sat down to chat with these young Turks. He also wanted to know more about *BITS*.

The next day *Shreyas* came with his cousin. His cousin worked in the same hospital so in case of any emergency we could take his help. There was an *IPL* match going on in Wankhede Stadium. The discussion that day drifted towards Cricket, *Yuvraj Singh* and his battle with cancer. My room was buzzing with activity and the youthful energy helped me to mend fast from my double surgery.

Dr. Naresh Chandra called to enquire about me and was upset to hear about my double surgery. I was in the hospital for six days. *Dr. Patil* asked me to return after a week to get the stitches removed. He had already stopped my thyroid medicine and asked me to continue with my BP medicine. He recommended CCM as calcium supplement three tablets, a day (*CCM had calcium citrate Malate, Vitamin D3 and Folic Acid-250 mg*). We were talking about natural supplements for calcium and calcium rich food when he told me that *Ragi (finger millet), custard apple, banana* and *soyabean* were rich source of calcium. He told us that exposing ourselves to sunlight in the morning was also a good practice. We decided to study more on this subject (*Calcium from natural source*) and acquire more information from books and the internet.

Doctors told me, "*Monitor calcium and vitamin D3 whenever blood test is done. If required, the number of calcium tablets will be increased.*"

We already knew about the consequences of sodium and magnesium deficiency (*hyponatremia and hypomagnesaemia*), so scared out of our wits, we enquired about the symptoms of calcium deficiency. He told us that calcium deficiency may cause severe cramps in fingers and toes.

He said, "*One moment you will be fine, relaxing, completing your housework, enjoying watching television, talking to friends or reading books and the very next moment you will be withering with painful cramps in the finger and toes. These cramps may strike anytime; day or night, so take care.*"

So there were insurmountable problems ahead, but my ability to overcome hurdles and my indomitable spirit would see me through this hurdle as well. *Gargi* left for *Hyderabad* and my parents returned to *Nasik*. I sported a huge bandage across my neck. It was my new trophy which I had to sport for a week. The wound in my neck was painful; it felt as though I was carrying a huge weight in my neck. If I tried to speak it would be hoarse and rough so I preferred to stay quite. There was this strange silence in my house. Only when *Benu* was home we could hear some noise but that to only his voice.

Mr. Dharap called one day, on hearing my gruff voice he panicked. It took some time but finally he could understand what had happened. During this period whenever I received any phone calls from my friends and colleagues, I started sending messages instead of talking on the phone.

Chapter 20

Nuclear medicine . . .

On 8th *May 2012 Dr. Patil* removed the stitches. Nothing as elaborate as in my first surgery, this time it was simple. It took him just few seconds to remove the stitches, just a single pull and a blue coloured thread was out. Twelve days after my surgery my neck was still sore and stiff. The scar across my neck was still raw, there was swelling and bruising under the incision but *Dr. Patil* told me that it was healing nicely. My voice was hoarse and broken but the doctor assured me that it was temporary and I would soon be fine. He referred me to *Dr. B.A. Krishna (Consultant and Head of Department of Nuclear Medicines and PET imaging in Bombay Hospital)* for further treatment.

The Nuclear Medicine department of *Bombay Hospital* was a place where you get the essence of the advances made by modern medicines. We found that the area was somewhat secluded and the staff working here were wearing a kind of contraption in there hand. On asking, they told us that it indicated the radioactivity level. The Nuclear Medicine department appeared to be the epitome of modernization and as we looked around, it was of immense interest to see the advanced machineries housed in each room. Entry was restricted but what we could see filled us in awe.

Dr. Krishna asked us to meet him after two days. We were with him after two days. He had studied my case in detail. He started explaining the role of nuclear medicines in treating thyroid cancer. We were apprehensive about this new form of medicine but the doctor assured us that it was not new but was a relatively different approach in curing thyroid cancer.

It was called *"Iodine-131 ablation therapy"*. When *Dr. Krishna* realized that I taught Genetics in college, he started discussing about *oncogenes* and the research going on in this field.

He said, *"Only one or two patients in hundred suffered from thyroid cancer after being cured of ovarian cancer."*

I looked at *Benu* in agony and said, *"It had to be me!"*

Dr. Krishna understood my feelings. He patted gently on my shoulder and told me to stay positive as treatment with nuclear medicine was not as aggressive as chemotherapy.

He was pressing the scar on my neck gently but I kept flinching, as the cut was possibly still sore. There was a tautness and fullness in my neck. He sensed that my scar was still tender, he smiled and told me, *"Don't worry, it will mend in few days,"*

After my surgery, *Dr. Patil* had already stopped my thyroid hormone tablets and the blood report showed that my *TSH* level was high.

Dr. Krishna laughed and asked me, *"With TSH level this high, how can you sit so comfortably and talk so normally?*

I smiled and said, *"Trying to deal with it. Yes, I am weak but it is okay."*

"Yes, Yes." He then asked, *"Do you feel dizzy, have problem in standing or walking? Does your head feel heavy? Do you get headache?"*

Benu said, *"Yes, she has all these problems but somehow she makes conscious efforts to try and negate these adversities."*

"Believe me doctor" I said, *"These are trivial problems after what I faced during chemotherapy."*

Dr. Krishna said, *"They are not trivial, I can see, you have a strong will power."*

Doctor told me that isotopic iodine worked best when the level of *TSH* was high. He asked me to bear with weakness for few more days so that the nuclear medicines could be started.

He then stated that nuclear medicine (*radioactive iodine*) was used if residual thyroid cells remained after the surgery. We were surprised to hear that sometimes the cells of thyroid were also found in other organs (*by birth*), so again treatment with radioactive iodine was advised.

Dr. Krishna asked me to get the *T3*, *T4*, *TSH* and *Thyroglobulin* tests done again after 10 days and report to him by phone. If the *TSH* level was high as expected, he would arrange for *10 mCi isotopic Iodine* (I^{131}) from *BARC* (*Mumbai*) which would be in a capsule. This capsule was supposed to be swallowed with water. After two days, I had to report again for scanning. If the scan report showed the presence of residual thyroids cells then *Dr. Krishna* would advise me to proceed with *Iodine-131 ablation therapy*.

The very thought of swallowing radioactive substance scared me. I shut my eyes for a moment, to gather my equilibrium. These few minutes stabilized and prepared me to face the new challenge. If I said, I desperately wanted to exit the chamber, then it would be the truth . . . but I sat tight and spent the next hour with *Dr. Krishna*, discussing the *pros* and *cons* of nuclear medicines.

Knowledge has a beginning however it has no end . . .

There were so many misconceptions regarding nuclear medicines which were cleared. I was now in the right frame of mind, ready to receive treatment using radioactive iodine. Doctor advised me to take some precautions which were very simple ones but very important.

Dr. Krishna's advice—

- *Start eating a low iodine diet before the radioactive iodine treatment starts because too much iodine in our body can stop the treatment working properly.*

- *Avoid eating iodized table salt or sea salt.*

- *Avoid having cough medicine.*

- *Avoid having fish and seafood.*

- *Avoid having Vitamin supplements that contain iodine.*

- *Dairy products contain some iodine, so cut down on eggs, cheese, milk and milk products.*

I told *Dr. Krishna* about the book I was writing. A memoir written solely based on my encounter with cancer. How in these two years, my life journey had taught me an interesting lesson to be shared with cancer patients, cancer survivors, family members, friends and colleagues of cancer patients.

I told him that the important message in my memoir was, *"When things go wrong, have courage to go on. If you are with family and friends then failure cannot touch you and also that, success does not come from quitting but from the belief that you can get through anything if you set your mind onto it."*

Dr. Krishna was very happy; he asked me, *"Are you writing about nuclear medicines?"*

I shook my head, *"No, not yet. I don't know much about Nuclear medicine."*

I asked him, *"Will you write for me, doctor? It will be an important chapter . . . Will you write about Nuclear medicines and let people know how it cures, Thyroid cancer?"*

But he said, *"No . . . no . . . no . . . you write about your first-hand experience . . . there appears to be a major lacuna as far as nuclear medicines is concerned . . . misconceptions . . . people are scared . . . they fear the use of radioisotopes . . . let them know that nuclear medicines are safe."*

I reasoned, *"Don't you think, with your vast knowledge and experience, you are the right person to explain."*

He explained, *"No, if I write, it becomes a doctor's perspective, but if you write it becomes a true story. Nothing scientific but plain facts . . . from the patient's firsthand experience . . . people will relate to your story and believe you."*

He told me to write the chapter on nuclear medicines in such simple terms that people not really clued onto medical terms could grasp them without any trouble.

Dr. Krishna then told us that we would be informed when the capsules containing the radioactive iodine would arrive from *BARC*. We did not have to wait much as we were called to the hospital on *21ˢᵗ May 2012*. The waiting room was filled with patients but my name was called immediately. I was taken to a room and asked to gulp down a capsule containing *10mCi isotopic iodine-131 (I^{131})*, with a glass of water.

Earlier going anywhere near any radioactive substance would have terrified me but my cancer journey prepared me to literally tolerate anything and everything. Here, I was ingesting a capsule containing radioactive iodine and this did not scare me or make me wary. *Dr. Krishna* called us to his chamber and informed us that there would be no side effects but there were some precautions to be taken.

Effect of isotopic iodine-131—

When a patient consumes a radioactive substance, the discharges from the body like sweat, saliva, urine, faeces and discharge from nose and throat such as spit, cough etc. will also have radioactivity and if this comes in contact with children below the age of ten or pregnant women, it can be harmful for them.

Dr. Krishna asked me to stay in a separate room, in isolation for a week and then come back for a whole body nuclear scan. He said, "*Wear a sweater at the time of scanning since the room will be very cool.*"

At home, with both my kids away, it was possible to stay in a room and also restrict interaction with others. After a week we were at *Bombay Hospital*. There was a special isolated waiting room meant for the patients undergoing treatment with nuclear medicines. I knew that all of them waiting there must be emitting some kind of radiation, so I advised *Benu* to wait outside in a separate area away from this place, for his own good.

There were three patients who had come before me so I had to wait for at least two to three hours. By now I learnt from *Benu* and my father about how to keep myself engaged in a hospital waiting room. A small enquiry would land me with the life history of the patient. My, being a professor, made the patients comfortable; sharing our experience was always path breaking. We always learnt a lot from each other during these exchanges. I also made some good friends in these waiting rooms.

My experience during scanning was that it was very uncomfortable inside. The room was dark and scary. The big scanner was majestic but frightening. As per doctor's advice, I wore a sweater but it did not help. I still felt cold and was shivering so the technician covered me with a woolen blanket before the nuclear scan of whole body commenced.

My sentiments were . . . stay quiet, lay unobtrusively on the trolley . . . or you may get struck . . . machine after all. The technician punched few switches and the trolley slowly entered the scanner. The he switched off the lights and left the room. I was alone in a dark room, inside a scanner, with few tiny green and red lights for company. It appeared to be a room from *Nini's* television series on paranormal activity. So I immediately shut my eyes and started chanting "*Hanumān Chalisa*" which, as usual, helped me to remain calm and composed. The entire scanning procedure took an hour, it felt lonely in there. It was cold and dark with only mechanical sounds of the scanner for company. I wished that someone from hospital management would have the bright idea to put on some music, to make the patients comfortable.

Dr. Krishna asked us to return after two days. So we were at *Bombay Hospital* after two days. We did not have to wait as the report was ready.

Dr. Krishna told us that the report showed, *"Evidence of residual tissue in the right lobe of the thyroid region."*

He said that the report also showed, *"Evidence of a metastatic node in the right paratracheal region at the retrosternal level."*

Dr. Krishna's advice was that I required radioiodine treatment. Nuclear medicine was a good option for me.

"Hope for the best and prepare for the worst."

Mid 16th century proverb

We were praying, hoping against hope that I be spared. However, that did not happen. Another hurdle . . . we chinned up and started planning for the treatment.

> *When setbacks occur and we are devastated, we are usually open to learning new things and are ready to face the next challenge life throws at us. We realized that we had come a long way so we would not leave any stone unturned now.*

Bombay Hospital did not have the facility so *Dr. Krishna* referred me to *Inlaks and Budhrani hospital* at *Pune*. All the arrangements were made by *Dr. Krishna*. He called *Dr. Shefali Gokhale* (*Consultant, Nuclear medicine from Inlaks and Budhrani hospital, Pune*) and arranged that I would report to *Dr. Gokhale* on 2nd *June 2012*, morning and on the same day, I would be administered nuclear medicines.

Gargi, in the meantime, was offered a project in *Manila* (*Philippines*). She decided to refuse the offer because she wanted to be with me in Pune, during my treatment with Nuclear medicine.

Her decision disturbed us. We were not happy with her decision. He called and asked *Gargi* to come home before she let her office know about her decision.

Gargi was adamant because she wanted to be with us in *Pune*. *Benu* tried convincing her that such a sacrifice was not called for and she should immediately accept the offer. She was however, not convinced so it was my turn to persuade her.

I told her, "*If I so desired, you will stop whatever you are doing and be with me . . . but that is not what I want.*"

I told her emotionally, "*You go—I will be here, waiting for you.*"

She cried, "*But Mā, I don't want to go . . . I want to be with you.*"

I grumbled, *"Do you believe that I will not survive this time . . . is this the reason, why you are refusing to go?"*

Gargi started laughing, *"No emotional blackmail, Mā . . . I will go . . . but no emotional blackmail."*

So, she left for *Manila* but we had to work overtime to convince her. One day *Dr. Jadliwala* called and shared the good news that his son had scored well in *BITSAT* examination. He wanted *Benu's* guidance regarding the admission procedure to *BITS*. We rejoiced to have been recipient of good news, one after the other. We discussed about our kids, *BITS*, hostels, cancer patients, cancer survivors and about the book, I was writing. I requested him to write few lines for the chapter – *Reflections and Impressions*. I was elated when he promptly agreed to write his views.

Chapter 21

My experience with Nuclear medicine . . .

*A*shish-Da and *Benu* accompanied me to *Pune* (*Inlaks and Budhrani hospital*) and my parents stayed with *Nini* (*she was home for her semester break*). We reported to *Dr. Shefali Gokhale* who carefully went through the reports and sent me for an *ECG*. The *ECG* report worried her hence she sent me to *Dr. Mandora* (*Physician*) with the reports.

Dr. Mandora carefully went through the reports and asked, *"Why is your blood pressure high?"*

I shrugged and replied, *"Could be due to travelling."*

He asked about my medicines for hypertension and whether I had taken them in the morning. When I nodded he advised me to relax. I was then sent to a special section of the hospital. It appeared to be a separate area with an interesting entrance. The entrance had double doors; the outer door remained open during daytime, but was locked after dinner. The inner door was locked after sending the patients inside. This door had an open window with a wooden counter, which served as a small table.

There was a passage inside and on the left side wall of the passage, there was a big display screen which showed the radioactivity level of the patients. There was also a big book rack filled with books. On the right side of the passage, there were two independent rooms each with an attached bathroom and balcony. These rooms were furnished with a cot, phone, television and an arm chair. It looked really impressive.

It was told to us that any personal item taken inside should be left behind after the treatment. They asked us to take some chewable candy but food, medicines and other necessary items would be provided by the hospital.

A lady from *Kerala* was put in the second room. She spoke only in *Malayalam (her mother tongue).* We were told that after we were given the nuclear medicines, the door in the passage would remain closed. We could not come out till the radiation level reduced to an acceptable level. If we needed anything or wished to talk to our relatives, we could come near the door and talk or we could use the intercom. Though we could not make outstation calls, we could receive them. There was a waiting room furnished with cots, intercom and attached bathroom for relatives to stay.

After an hour, we were called in and asked to sip *150 mCi, iodine-131 (I^{131})* with the help of a straw. My vision of it being something dramatic was sadly shattered. It was like sipping plain water. Isotopic iodine was tasteless and odourless.

The doors were locked after that and we were asked to stay inside. Our movement was restricted, we could not come out and slowly the novelty of the situation wore off. Other than watching *TV*, there was nothing else to do there. So, it now felt as if we were in a jail.

I desperately wanted to keep myself engaged so I tried communicating with my neighbour using sign language and then stood in front of the door to see *Benu* and *Ashish-Da* waiting for me, curious to know what was happening inside.

It was interesting to note that food and medicines were left on the counter and a calling bell, alerted us. Happy to hear the bell, I would run like a child to see who had called or which one of us had received a parcel.

I was not allowed to carry my cellphone but could talk to *Benu* on the intercom. There were phone calls from *Nini* and my relatives who encouraged me to stay positive. *Gargi* called me from *Manila*. Though confined in a room, I spoke to all my relatives.

Sitting idle was painful; I did not watch *TV* much so I was drawn to the book rack. I decided to investigate. There were some magazines, few religious books and *Surprise! Surprise!* There were twelve books which took me back to those lovely, carefree days of my teens. As a teenager, I used to guzzle down on these books, the king of romance, *Mills and Boons*. Fantasizing about the "*Tall dark and handsome*" heroes, living in my own world of romance, making friends with those who eat, sleep and breathe *Mills and Boons*, exchanging books and discussing the plot used to be my favorite pass time as a teenager.

I ran to the front door and called *Benu* and *Ashish-Da*, "*Can you believe, of all the places, there are around twelve Mills and Boons here.*"

Benu and *Ashish-Da* had smiles on their faces when I told them, "*I will read all of them.*"

Ashish-Da raised an eyebrow, "*All of them?*"

"*Yes, yes all of them!*" I smiled.

After lunch *Ashish-Da* left for *Nasik*. *Benu* told me that he was going out to explore the surroundings. So after a gap of almost twenty five years, I started reading a *Mills and Boon*, once again.

As I was reading the book, half way through I asked myself, "*Why did I stop reading them?*" Romancing a tall dark and handsome hero was fun. Was it just a fantasy . . . or . . . did it happen in real life?

Because here I was in my real life! What was I doing . . . romancing? Romancing what or should I say whom? CANCER!

What crazy thought! Only a scatterbrain like me could have such a thought! Romancing Cancer! Nevertheless, I certainly liked the coincidence of having Mills and Boons, in this isolated room.

Well! Why not? Scatterbrain or not, it did
indicate something. Let me try to get something
good come out of it. Let the fascinating episode
of my life story—the romance of achievements
in difficulties, trials and tribulations, be my date
with cancer and not my fight with cancer.

The title of my book was decided, **"My date with cancer."**

This place was certainly lucky for me . . . I thanked the person who had left the books here wholeheartedly, called *Benu* and announced, "*I decided the title for my book—It is—My date with cancer.*"

Benu asked, "*Date or fight?*"

I told him happily, "*It is date, date, date . . . My date with cancer.*"

A wonderful feeling enveloped me and my happiness knew no bounds when the same happiness reflected on *Benu's* face. So I went back to my room and concentrated on finishing the *Mills and Boon* I was reading.

On the first day, the doctors did not enter the room. They stood in the passage and wore padded coats to protect themselves from radiation. The radioactivity level was checked periodically by technicians. The nurses kept watch, checking us every hour. I got into a habit of observing them, asking them questions and talking to them. It was interesting to see them working. They were extremely knowledgeable and efficient in their respective fields. They were also exceptionally warm and friendly.

By evening, my neighbour stopped coming to the passage. This worried me . . . I felt a stab of anxiety. *What was the matter with her? Why was she not coming out of her room?*

I gingerly entered her room and asked her whether she needed any help or should her family members be informed. When she nodded, I informed her relatives. The doctors were with her after sometime but she remained in her bed for rest of the day.

I was taking all the prescribed medicines and the sugar candies as advised by *Dr. Gokhale*, but found that by evening, there was a kind of sensation in my tonsils. Slight heaviness in my head made me uncomfortable.

Dr. Mandora found that my blood pressure had not normalized. He recommended that I take *50 mg Tenoclor* instead of *25 mg (once a day)*.

I tried to keep myself engaged with books, meditation and some light exercise but nothing worked. *Dr. Gokhale* said these symptoms are expected because the *TSH* level is very high. After treatment, she would prescribe the thyroid hormone tablets which would normalize things.

On *5th June 2012*, the radioactivity level came down to normal. I was given discharge. There was a feeling of joy and relief because it felt as though I was being released after a life imprisonment.

Dr. Gokhale called us in her chamber. She made us comfortable and then explained about the treatment and the precautions to be taken for the next few days. A very sweet and friendly lady, the doctor told *Benu* that she had worked under *Dr. Krishna* for many years. *Benu* told her that the hospital was very good and the non-medico staff was extremely friendly. Our four days stay in the hospital was exceptionally good.

Dr. Gokhale gave us a list of instructions to be followed. She advised me to take one tablet of *Eltroxine* (*100 mg*), empty stomach, early morning, daily. She also asked me to report to *Dr. Krishna* for the regularization of the medicine. She then advised that my *BP* should be monitored and medicine should be prescribed accordingly.

Instructions given by Dr. Gokhale—(to be followed for the next few days)

- *Avoid close contact with pregnant woman and children below 10 years.*

- *If possible stay in a separate room.*

- *Should refrain from physical contact with spouses for 15 days.*

- *Keep personal utility articles such as dresses, bed sheet, pillow cover, towels, napkins, handkerchief, toothbrush, toothpaste, comb, shampoo, hair oil and utensils such as plates, glass, cup, spoons etc. separate.*

- *Flush the toilet twice after use or have a separate one, if not then ask the others to pour a bucket of water before use.*

- *Avoid contact with other people and do not allow children to enter the room.*

- *Avoid moving around the house and cooking food in kitchen.*

- *Wash your own clothes and utensils for 15 days post therapy.*

My father arranged a car for our return journey. *Benu* told me that a day back *Babji* had informed him that my mother was not well. *Nini* informed *Babji* and he had called *Dr. Joshi*. *Dr. Joshi* had prescribed some medicines and asked my mother to meet her family doctor at the earliest.

After we returned *Nini* told us, *"Thamma was not feeling well so I told her to go and meet her doctor in Nasik. They have left just an hour back."*

At home, as my parents had left for *Nasik* just *Nini* and *Benu* were with me. This time it was not hard to completely isolate myself for fifteen days as I followed all the instructions given by the doctor meticulously.

Nini aware of the repercussion of being exposed to radioactive substances did not come near me. She however, kept me in splits with her antics from the next room.

Dr. Krishna called me for post therapy Iodine scan on 9th *June 2012* (*my birthday*). The scan took about an hour and the report collected after two days showed, *"Evidence of significant radioactive intake in the residual thyroid tissue and metastasis in the right para-tracheal region favouring adequate radioblastic effect."*

Dr. Krishna was not available on both the days as he was attending a conference.

At home, I started suffering from some side effects. This troubled me because doctor had assured me that there would be no side effects. I felt dizzy, couldn't keep my head up nor walk a short distance without feeling faint. There were cramps in my toes and fingers as *Dr. Patil* had predicted in case of calcium deficiency. I found my taste buds were affected as my food appeared salt less even though normal salt was added to it. We called *Dr. Krishna* and told him about the symptoms.

Dr. Krishna asked us to meet him immediately. When I met him and complained about my weakness, he was exasperated, *"Why did you not come earlier?"*

He told us that though I was taking *Eltroxine (100 mg)* it was not the appropriate dose. All the side effects were as a result of this. *Dr. Krishna* increased the *Eltroxine* dose from 100 mg to 200 mg. He told us to keep him informed if the dizziness persisted. He then called me for consultation after a month with the blood test done for *T3, T4, TSH* and *Thyroglobulin*.

We were with *Dr. Krishna* in his chamber for the follow-up after a month. The test for *TSH* and *Thyroglobulin* was done. *Dr. Krishna* was happy to see the report. My throat was still sore and my voice raspy but the doctor pressed the scar on my neck and told me that he was impressed to see the improvement. He smiled and told us that I responded well to nuclear medicine and there was complete ablation of the disease.

However, we were stunned when he told us that since my treatment was over, he would see me next in *May 2013*, a year later.

A year later!

We thought, probably we heard him wrong but he reiterated, *"Yes, you will meet me after a year."*

A cold wave swept in and I started shivering. The very thought that my treatment was over, brought back memories which haunted me in the past.

I asked *Dr. Krishna*, *"Now that the treatment was over, what next?"*

Emotionally, I described how after being treated for ovarian cancer, I had suffered from thyroid cancer and polyps in gall bladder. *Dr. Krishna* pacified me, *"You are a lady with a strong will power and a positive attitude . . . you should not worry."*

It was only I who knew that sometimes, I was a coward and I let the tears flow in my moment of loneliness. Sometimes, I was not as brave as everyone thought and sometimes, even I had some misgivings about my survival but I chinned up, kept my loneliness aside and lapped up the praises doctor was showering on me.

He told me, *"Join College after a month."*

The doctor was dropping bombshells, one after the other.

Join College Indeed! The doctor must be joking. I patiently explained to him that teaching undergraduates required stamina and a commanding voice. My voice was a pitiable hoarse whisper which cracked if I tried to talk loud. *What would I do after joining college?* Doctor laughed and advised me to give my throat a month's time to heal.

He said, "*After that you will be your old self.*"

I realized that this was not the only issue which disturbed me. There were number of other issues that ate me up. It bothered me that my hair was still short, my teeth and nails were stained black, my skin was pigmented with dark patches under eyes and now my neck had an ugly scar across it. I did not feel like facing my students and colleagues yet. My aversion to loud noise and crowded places was a major problem.

Lame excuses no doubt and somewhere down the line these souvenirs of cancer treatment had to be shed. Becoming an introvert and suffering from inferiority complex was not me.

Self-check—

- *After six cycles of chemotherapy I was completely bald . . . but now my hair had grown into a wild, curly spread across my head (also called chemo-curls).*

- *My eyebrows and eyelashes had still not grown.*

- *There were dark circles under eyes and my skin had dark patches.*

- *My teeth turned blackish grey in colour.*

- *My nails had also turned grey.*

- *After my three surgeries, I was not as agile as before, I was weak and needed support to walk.*

- *After the thyroid operation, I had an ugly scar across my neck.*

- *I had lost my commanding voice. Now it was gruff, hoarse and gravelly, almost like a whisper.*

- *It was challenging to withstand noisy and crowded places. I felt dizzy.*

Dr. Krishna was very patient. He told me that physical discomforts would disappear within a month but what I needed to do was to school myself mentally. Overcoming my inadequacies, despite all odds acclimatizing to the change was the challenge for me. I thanked *Dr. Krishna* for his advice though I perceived it to be unattainable at that point of time.

He told me, ***"Your health exactly follows your subconscious expectations"*** . . . so let all doubts go and focus on getting better.

> *If I wanted to conquer my fear, I should not sit at home and worry, but go out and get busy, the future would take care of itself. Success does not come from giving up and quitting, it comes from the belief that you can get through anything if you set your mind to it.*

He then sent me to *Dr. Patil*, with all the reports for reference. *Dr. Patil* as usual was very happy to see us and we were very happy to meet him. I told him about my experience and soon he was sharing his experiences with other patients. He then asked me to get *USG (abdomen, pelvis and neck)* and complete blood tests by *September* and come for the follow-up.

I told him about the cramps in my fingers and toes. He told me that he would increase the number of CCM tablets *(calcium tablets)* from three to four. He also advised me to take cholecalciferol granules *(1 G)* once in a week. He then advised me to get the blood calcium and D3 tests done after two weeks and to inform him on phone about the status. He also asked me to start exposing myself to sunlight. He asked me to visit crowded malls, attend public functions and meet friends. *Dr. Patil* told me to remember the past only to learn from it.

Life is a ceaseless change.
The only certainty is today.

I introspected that in the past I worried unnecessarily, thinking about what the future held for me . . . and today, is the future . . . I was worried about . . . so anxious about and . . . look I am fine today and my doctor was encouraging me to walk tall and leave my worries behind.

"Bondage is of the mind; freedom too is of the mind. If you say 'I am a free soul. I am a son of God who can bind me free you shall be."

Ramakrishna Paramahamsa (1836-1886)
Hindu Sage and Priest of the Dakshineswar Kali temple

My family and friends rejoiced when they came to know about my doctor's verdict. I was certainly blessed when I heard that our neighbor, *Bhatta-Ji*, made a *sankalp* in front of *Ganapati* at *Titwala*, *"God bless Rina, I'll walk bare foot all the way from my house to offer you prayers here, when the doctors pronounce her, cancer free."*

Bhattaji walked barefoot almost thirteen kilometers to *Titwala* and offered prayers and thanked Ganapati for his *Kripa Druśti* when he heard about my doctor's verdict.

Gargi was back from *Manila* (*Philippines*). She filled the house with presents and my fridge with dark chocolates (*my weakness*). She was happy that she had taken heed of our advice because this trip turned out to be very informative professionally.

In the meantime, I came to know that Mrs. Swamy (*living upstairs in the same building*) treated for cancer had succumbed to the disease and expired in *March*. She was taken directly to her native place from the hospital so I was not aware of this fact. It was only now that I came to know about her sad demise. I was surprised because everyone from our colony (*be it my family members, friends, even Mrs. Swamy's daughters, and my maid servants*), conspired to keep me out of the loop because they were worried that this news would depress me. I was indeed disheartened to learn about it but my family and friends helped me regain my confidence.

My mother was seriously ill. After a battery of tests she was diagnosed with *aneurysm*. Four doctors were consulted from four different hospitals but all of them were of the opinion that since my mother was now seventy three years old, surgery was not advisable. Other than her medication she now had to take extra care and lead a peaceful life, devoid of any stress. I remembered the day, I distinctly heard *Śrī Sāi's* forecast, "*You will be fine but take care of your mother*". I recalled my chagrin to see my father's skepticism, that day. *Dad . . . Oh dad! Will you believe me now?*

As a second time cancer survivor, I am quite often approached by colleagues, friends and family members for counseling patients diagnosed with cancer and giving them the address of the hospitals, names and phone numbers of my doctors who helped me in my cancer journey. *Dr. Meghana Bhalerao* from *Century Rayon hospital* called me for counseling patients suffering from cancer as my experience made me sense their anguish as my own. *Yes*! And drawn towards their grief, I try to lead them towards holistic healing of cancer.

I am a good listener and this serves me well in my efforts to help my cancer friends. My counseling is just that I sit quietly with the cancer patients and listen to them. I encourage them to express their feelings and always make it a point to tell them about my cancer journey.

Yes, my cancer journey has taught me to feel closer to those who are traversing the path I once walked.

I considered it my duty to answer all their queries, share their concerns and be of some help so that they could benefit from my experience. My counseling works wonder with patients who are from different age groups and in return, I get the satisfaction of not only helping them but also helping myself.

Chapter 22

The journey continues . . .

*T*he very thought that soon I will have to rejoin college was scary.

Scary . . . Why? What was the cause for this panic?

The reasons eluded me and I remained concerned and nervous.

I was teaching in my college since 1986 and was away only for two years!

"A gap of only two years, Rina, harnesses your wayward feelings immediately," I rebuked.

But I remained disturbed. I could not comprehend, why a confident and self-assured person like me, felt unsettled, apprehensive and nervous.

Fortunately, we still had few days to prepare ourselves mentally. *Benu* proposed that a change of place, an outing, a holiday of sort was what we really required.

When *Gargi* heard about it, she enquired, "*Mā, why don't you and Bābā come to Hyderabad?*"

She reminded us about her *sañkalp*, her promise to *Śrī Veṅkaṭēśwara Swami* that she would return with me (*after my treatment*) to seek his blessings. So to fulfil her wish, we decided to visit *Hyderabad*.

Once there, we first went to the temple and offered our prayers. We met the priest and expressed our gratitude for the kind words he spoke to *Gargi*. As *Benu* and *Gargi* were busy talking to him, I sat down with bowed head and folded hand in front of the Lord. Shutting out distractions and focusing on the emotions churning inside me, I thanked the lord repeatedly for shielding *Gargi* and protecting her faith in him. My eyes welled up with tears, remembering how, when she was going through a rough patch, she was all alone and lonely, he stood tall protecting her, giving her hope and courage.

Hyderabad is a beautiful historical city famous for its *Hyderabadi* cuisine-a princely legacy of the *Nizams*, amazing *biryani* and *kebabs.* The change of place was indeed, invigorating for us. Our stay was action packed as we went for a movie and then to the famous *Birla Mandir* in *Hyderabad*.

One day *Gargi* said, "*Mā, let us try experimenting with your hair. Let's go and get a bit of hair styling done, what say?*"

This was definitely a very good suggestion. We enjoyed immensely getting a head spa, hair cutting and styling done. Though the stylist had taken a long time to decide what he could do with my chemo-curls, the end result was indeed beautiful.

After returning from *Hyderabad*, we started preparing for the changes we were expecting in our lifestyle in the near future.

First, *Benu* presented me a new car as he did not want me to travel by a *local train* or an *auto-rickshaw*, anymore. Then he employed a chauffeur.

"*You need not drive,*" He said.

Our next step was to expose myself to people, noise and traffic. So we started visiting restaurants, malls, attending get together, anniversaries, marriages and birthdays. On one such trip to *In-Orbit Mall*, we bumped into my colleague *Francena Luiz*. She was stunned to see me there. I told her about my doctor's advice. We also met *Sudha*, *Aman* and *Ayushi*, as planned and had a wale of time together spent window shopping, chit-chatting and catching up with each other's life. We certainly rejoiced when *Dr. Jadliwala* informed us that his son had taken admission in *BITS Goa*. That day we realized that the renowned doctor was also a very proud father.

These few days were action packed and soon it was time for the follow-up. As instructed, blood test, *USG* for abdomen pelvis and neck were done. A chest X-ray was also done. The blood report showed everything was normal except calcium. *CA125* was 5.4 U/ml (*normal*).

After taking appointment, we reported to *Dr. Patil* on *27*th *September 2012*. He went through the reports meticulously and asked me whether I was taking the *calcium tablets* and *chole-calciferol*, as advised.

When I nodded, he told me to concentrate on eating calcium rich food as my calcium count was lower than normal. I told him that *boiled eggs (after discarding the yolk), nachani (finger millet, Ragi)* and *custard apples* were included in my diet schedule and then enquired, "*Why did you ask me to stay away from dairy products? As per my knowledge, milk and cheese are rich sources of calcium.*"

He told me, "*Why depend on milk and cheese? There are so many calcium rich fruits and vegetables . . . have them. Your cancer cells had spread, so that is the reason why I asked you to stay away from dairy products and oily food.*"

Dr. Patil was however, very happy to see that my weight had reduced. There was a smile on his face when he said, "*I can see that you have heeded my advice and lost weight, what is your weight now?*"

Smiling like a Cheshire cat that had just licked cream, I announced proudly, "*58 kg.*"

He laughed and asked, "*What did you do to reduce your weight?*"

I smiled, "*Just followed your advice, doctor.*"

He told me, "*I advise all my patients but no one listens to me . . . all of them are obese.*" Then he surprised me by asking, "*Why don't you start counseling my patients, take lectures on how to lose weight and stay fit?"*

> *I had tears in my eyes when he said that. Tears of happiness . . . Praise, at last! I was very sensitive about my being over-weight. When the doctor complemented me, I was overjoyed. And . . .*
> *Yes . . . What a complement!*

Dr. Patil meticulously went through the reports again and then repeated what *Dr. Krishna* had proposed earlier, *"You are fine, you should join college."*

Join College!

"When, doctor," I muttered, my voice hardly audible.

"Let's say, tomorrow," He told me.

Tomorrow . . . tomorrow! I exclaimed. *"But, I have one year and three months sick leave on hand . . . Don't you think I should wait, recuperate and then join."*

"No . . . join your college, tomorrow," He said.

We were sort of expecting *Dr. Patil's* advice to join college and were prepared for it. But for reasons unknown, I muttered about my pending leave and was unhappy to hear him talk about my rejoining college with immediate effect . . . *immediate effect! What was he telling?*

Dr. Patil realized that I was unhappy so he spoke gently, *"You are fortunate that you are working in a college. Books, colleagues and students are the best medicines for you. Go and join your college from tomorrow."*

I informed him, *"Once I join, doctor, I will not get leave again. I have one year and three months sick leave on hand if . . ."*

Before I could complete, doctor smiled and told me, *"There are no ifs. Go and join. I will call the College Management or your Principal and tell them to take special care, don't worry."*

The man was bribing me and that made me laugh, *"Thanks, that's not necessary."*

It was only that my voice troubled me. Crowded place and people made me nervous. My cancer journey had probably turned me into an introvert. There were these strong sentiments that troubled me. I did not like the feeling of being helpless and abhorred it when people said that they felt sorry for me. I did not want to be an object of empathy. Though I looked sick, weak and unattractive, I did not want pity.

But the doctor was firm, he told me, *"Your voice is not as bad as you think. No doubt, it is hoarse but with time it will improve. You have a strong personality and you are not an introvert."*

Then he added, *"Don't worry, everyone will admire your guts."*

I sat digesting his views about my personality. It felt good to hear them, it spread positivity. Well! It was not that I did not know about my personality but it helped to hear about it once in a while.

However troubled thoughts, the expected question arose inevitably, *"Doctor, I was diagnosed with cancer not once but twice . . . so . . . What should I expect next . . . or should I say . . . when I should, expect it again?"*

There is an uncertainty of my existence . . . what is the solution?

Doctor briskly brushed aside my doubts and asked me to let go of anxiety and ask myself what was I afraid of? Do I know for sure that because it has happened twice, it will happen again?

Good thoughts but, "Dil hai ki manta nahi (my heart did not agree)."

Why did my heart not listen to all the good thoughts? Why the palpitation? Was my anxiety because I believed in my fear of what might happen, not in what might not happen.

Why mar the beauty of today for a future that no one can possibly foretell.

He said, *"You remained in a positive frame of mind throughout the treatment. Now is the time to live life. Do not allow any doubt or fear stop the flow of positive energy that you always had in abundance."*

Doctor was talking to *Benu*. His words convinced me . . . *Yes, I can and I will.* I am *Moitreyee,* my parent's courageous daughter, *Ashish-Da's* pretty sister, *Sonali's* spirited sister-in-law, *Anu-Di's* strong *Bhabhi, Benu's* loving wife and my daughter's robust mother.

Whatever happens, I would move on with confidence. Yes, I was not scared . . . just the opposite, I was now raring to start my journey . . . a joyous journey towards progress.

> *Dr. Patil issued the certificate stating that I would join college on 28th September 2012 as my treatment for cancer was over.*

He suggested that I should avoid local trains, rush hours and take it easy for the first few months. I informed him about my new car. He congratulated me and said this was definitely a positive start for my journey ahead. He called me again for the follow-up with complete blood report and *CT* scan of abdomen and pelvis in the month of *November, 2012.*

I believe, *"The road towards progress is always under construction . . . the journey continues."* This is the firm belief I always carry with me.

> *So true . . . What if my life took an ugly turn . . . here I am, ready to walk the path again . . . continue with the journey . . . the life's journey . . . as a cancer survivor.*

I also realize that it is time to conclude the story about, "*My date with cancer*," a journey I ventured for the unknown two years ago. In those days of uncertainty and disillusionment, my whole life was overwhelmed by forces beyond my control but now I know that I hit the rock bottom and bounced back.

I learnt a lesson the hard way and have emerged a reformed person. I don't brood over my recent past, an important episode of my life story, but try to draw strength from my experience. The foundation of my success was my positive attitude, the support from my loving family, friends, doctors, modern medicines and *God almighty*.

> *Life is too precious I want to live life with*
> *dignity, to build it again and now I don't pray*
> *to God to take my problems away but to give me*
> *strength to face them.*

I am now ready to embark on another leg of my journey, it will be a lot like the life I experienced before, but in many ways, it will be different. It will be all about adjusting to life as a cancer survivor who lived the cancer scare not once but twice.

*28*th *September 2012* is an important date in my cancer journey. This is the day when with the doctor's certificate in my hand, I am travelling to rejoin college . . . I am apprehensive, nervous yet excited and eager to start again . . .

REFLECTIONS AND IMPRESSIONS

"At times our own light goes out and is rekindled by a spark from another person. Each one of us has cause to think with deep gratitude of those who have lighted the flame within us."

Albert Schweitzer (1875-1965)
German French theologian, Organist, Physician, Medical missionary, Philosopher and Nobel Laureate

WON THE BATTLE

Dr. Madhuri Pejaver
Principal (B.N. Bandodkar College of Science, Thane)
Dean of Science (University Of Mumbai)
(Colleague)

It was shocking news, when I heard that Moitreyee has been attacked by the scary disease "Cancer". It was unbelievable because I had seen her laughing around and climbing stairs just a few days back. Hence I could not believe my ears. But that was authentic news, because Moitreyee herself had asked me the meaning of some words used by doctor. I was worried about how she will take it.

Still hoping against hope, I was feeling that Moitreyee need not have to take chemo, because now days with all good new medicines in market, she may be able to escape the horrifying chemo. But No! It was told to me that she will have to undergo chemo that too of higher does. Rather chemo first then surgery and again chemo. And then I knew no one else other than God Almighty can save her. I was praying that miracles do occur and miracle must occur to save Moitreyee . . . I cried.

Most of the time Mulgaonkar madam used to update me, but getting the news of progress of any work is always a pleasure but not the news of this deadly disease. Moitreyee rang me and we discussed about effect of chemo mainly reduction of W.B.C. Count and after third chemo she rang me again telling about the hair loss.

I remembered Dr. Borgaonkar madam, who is not in this world any more. I also remembered my sister-in-law. I had seen both of them suffering from cancer and had suffered along with them. But I never uttered a single word about Borgaonkar madam. I only spoke about my sister-in-law who is totally cured after five years. I even advised her to make a wig and keep ready to avoid further embarrassment. But Moitreyee decided not to go for it.

Then the news came that she was to be immediately operated because Cancer has spread to a great extent which was beyond the 4ᵗʰ stage and later when actual operation took *place it was found that one after the other many organs had got affected.*

We went on talking about all positive patients and how Moitreyee was 100% positive in her attitude and also about full support of family and friends. I consoled her that I was very sure that she is going to win the battle because of her attitude. In a way I was happy being at the other end of telephone because Moitreyee could not see tears from my eyes.

After the multiple organs getting affected in abdomen, the cancer hit thyroid and it was a further shock to all of us. Basically thyroid operation is risky and that too with carcinoma. But Moitreyee was Moitreyee and non-else.

Whenever we spoke, I told her about Reiki and Yoga. We had talked about it before but I insisted you must do this and must continue it. I also insisted about the meditation. Moitreyee listened and the miracle is in front of us.

She not only went through all these risks but got completely cured. And once she knew she is out of danger she called me for another reason. She wanted to join college. My God! I could not believe it. Only two years and one month had passed and she wanted to be back! With a very doubtful mind I agreed with her decision and Moitreyee joined the college on 29ᵗʰ September 2012.

Through this entire journey her family was behind her with a solid rock support. Hats off to Moitreyee and her beloved and of course the doctors who treated her.

—X—

AUTHOR WITH HER DOCTORS

MY PATIENT, A CANCER SURVIVOR

Dr. Mannan K. Jadliwala
M.N.A.M.S. (Gen Surgery)
Hon. Surgeon, Bombay Hospital

I met Dr. (Mrs.) Moitreyee Saha at Bombay hospital after she completed three cycles of chemotherapy for ovarian cancer and was now planned for the surgery. She was inquisitive about the role of a gastro-intestinal surgeon in the surgery. A year later when thyroid cancer and gall bladder polyps were detected, for which she was operated again. I operated her for the gall bladder by laparoscopy. By then I knew the family well, as the Dr. Saha and his daughters were from BITS and my son was preparing for BITSAT. I found a special bond in the family, each member taking care of others need and staying positive throughout the treatment.

Uncontrolled and senseless proliferation of cells with a tendency to invade and disseminate is what defines a cancer. Substantial genetic damage to the cell is central to all the environmental, dietary, infectious and hereditary causes of the cancer. The interaction of genetic predisposition for the cancerous kind of genetic damage with the environmental exposures such as infections, ionizing radiations, smoking, alcohol etc. results in cancer. By manipulating environmental arm of the interaction a substantial proportion of cancers can be prevented though, at present, it is almost impossible to trim off the genetic predisposition of a person. By avoiding smoking/tobacco, alcohol, obesity, sedentary life style and promoting personal hygiene and a fresh diet rich in green leafy vegetables cancer of lung, oral cavity, liver, stomach, food pipe, colon and breast can be *prevented. Healthy sexual practices to avoid infections with Human papilloma (HPV) and immune deficiency virus (HIV) can prevent cervical, vaginal, penile, anal and certain lymphoid and hematological (Leukemia) cancers.*

Cancer particularly of skin, thyroid, breast, colon, oral cavity, rectum, cervix, vagina and penis, if detected early can be cured. The treatment modalities for a cancer are surgery, chemotherapy, biological therapy and radiotherapy. Most of the cancers are treated with a various combinations of these individual modalities. My patient, a cancer survivor underwent three operations, received six cycles of chemotherapy and a radio-nuclear ablation.

—X—

I WILL FIGHT IT, DOCTOR

Dr. P.G. Joshi
M.B.B.S., A.F.I.H.
Industrial Physician

Dr. (Mrs.) Moitreyee Saha consulted me for cramps in the abdomen, after basic investigation she was advised for USG of abdomen—pelvis. The results reveled that there was ovarian tumour and further investigations showed that it was malignant. I was sorry to know the result and was saddened to know that one of my family patients will have to fight this deadly disease at such an early age and at the prime time of her career.

I have known them since last twenty five or more years as their family doctor and it was my painful responsibility to disclose to them gently, that Moitreyee madam was indeed suffering from ovarian cancer. Dr. B.G. Saha, her husband was almost in tears however, I was astonished by her reaction. She was quite for some time and then she told me "I will fight it, Doctor." I knew then that, apparently she took the challenge very sportingly and she would fight the disease with courage. I found her reaction very encouraging.

Subsequently she underwent the ordeal associated with the disease not once but twice in next two years. She had the excellent emotional support from her husband and both daughters. I also think that she could fight this disease because of the inherent virtue which she might have received from her father. I met him once and found him very energetic, full of life even at the age of seventy seven. I think her parents were her source of inspiration for fighting this calamity.

Her fighting spirit was inspiring and knowing this example of Dr. (Mrs.) Moitreyee Saha, I always feel that patients who are suffering from malignancy, if they face the challenge without losing their heart, then they can certainly get over the disease with the help of newer drugs and other therapeutic measures but the most important thing is to have a will to fight the disease. By writing the memoir "My date with cancer", a true story of how she fought cancer, Dr. Moitreyee sets an admirable example of how to handle adversity with positive attitude . . . is something I like my other patients to understand and follow.

—*X*—

CANCER SURVIVOR

Dr. Leena Sonekar
Physician
MD Medicine

It was one fine evening, I was returning from hospital when I met Dr. Moitreyee Saha who was returning from her college. As usual we greeted each other and started casually discussing about "Menopause" because she said, "I have some dragging sensation in lower abdomen, I have mood swings and get tired easily." Frankly I never thought, it would be such a dreadful cause, but somehow I took the symptoms very seriously and told her to get it investigated.

When she reported to me and I could feel the presence of lumps on examination I asked her to get the CA125 and USG abdomen-pelvis done. The next day it was shocking to all when the USG report showed malignancy. It showed the presence of multiple cystic heterogeneous lesion and moderate free fluid in abdomen and pelvis . . . Very very shocking!!!

Then we confirmed the malignancy with CT-abdomen, which showed hepatomegaly with hypo-dense area in the VI right lobe of the liver, a large solid cystic lesion in the pelvis, possibility of ovarian neoplasm and moderate amount of free fluid in abdomen and pelvis. The CA125 report supported our findings.

Dr. Moitreyee was then referred to Dr. (Mrs.) Pratima Chipalkatti from Bombay hospital. I was meeting Dr. Benu Gopal Saha and he use to update me regarding Moitreyee's clinical status. I could feel the sorrow he felt from within, would pray to God, that everything should be fine. I just couldn't imagine a family without a 'mother'. Nini was in XII, a crucial year ahead, I just could feel it (having been in the same situation in my own life), but I was helpless—in front of God's destiny.

When Moitreyee was back home after her fifth chemo-cycle the same night Nini had come running to my place to tell me that her mother had collapsed in the washroom. She was immediately rushed to the Century Rayon hospital ICU and was later diagnosed and treated for hyponatremia. Moitreyee underwent six chemo-cycles and a surgery and the treatment was nicely completed. God was very kind and I thank him . . . everything was fine.

Life was not easy because she was admitted repeatedly for UTI which was a post chemo complication but she went through it smiling all through this agony with great courage.

Co-incidentally after almost a year a cancer camp was organized by "Cenray Mahila Pragati" at Century Rayon hospital, Shahad. This was done with the help of "Indian Cancer Society, mobile cancer detection centre" and Moitreyee was again detected with thyroid cancer. This time she had to face the trauma again as she passed through repeated investigations, surgeries and nuclear medicines.

But again she did not lose heart, she fought bravely and defeated the disease, I see her everyday as a "CANCER SURVIVOR," and rejoice.

—X—

CANCER CURE WITH HOMEOPATHY

Dr. Satya Prakash Bhattacherjee
MD Homeopathy
Nasik

Sqd. Ldr. Chittaranjan Saha and Mrs. Chitra Saha were in my chamber one evening looking extremely worried. They told me that their daughter Dr. Moitreyee Saha was diagnosed with ovarian cancer, IV stage. They showed me the reports, the sonography report showed the presence of multiple cystic heterogeneous lesion measuring 136x110 mm and moderate free fluid in abdomen and pelvis.

The CT scan reports showed hepatomegaly with 2.3x3.0 cm sized hypo-dense area in the VI right lobe of the liver, a large solid cystic lesion in the pelvis, possibility of ovarian neoplasm and moderate amount of free fluid in abdomen and pelvis and the CA125 was "394.0 U/ml, normal being <2.0-35.0 U/ml.

They were worried because doctors were apprehensive about peritoneal fluid and hepatomegaly. They told me that the doctors were concerned about the hypo-dense area in the VI right lobe of the liver as it was very near to the diaphragm and could not be operated without causing damage to the diaphragm. Dr. Moitreyee Saha was advised three cycles of chemotherapy to bring about the reduction of the cysts followed by surgery and then again three cycles of chemotherapy. Dr. Moitreyee's parents had come to me for their faith in Homeopathy and me because earlier (a decade back) I could help in curing their niece from leukemia.

Homeopathy is an alternative medical system that was developed in Germany at the end of 18th century. It involves treating patients with highly diluted substances and it is a medical philosophy and practice based on the idea that the body has the ability to heal itself. Homeopathic medicine views symptoms of illness as normal responses of the body as it attempts to regain health. Homeopathy is based on the principle that you can treat 'like with like', that is, a substance which causes symptoms when taken in large quantity, can be used as a cure for the same symptoms when used in minute quantity.

The term "homeopathy" was coined by Hahnemann. He formulated the principles of homeopathy based on Law of Similar (like cures like), Law of the Infinitesimal dose (The more diluted a remedy is, the more potent it is.) and illness is specific to the individual.

That is, substances that in healthy persons would produce the symptoms from which the patient suffers are used to treat the patient. Hahnemann further stated that the potency of a curative agent increases as the substance is diluted. Homeopathic physicians seek to cure their patients on the physical, mental and emotional levels, and each treatment is tailored to a patient's individual needs. Homeopathy is generally a safe treatment, as it uses medicines in extremely diluted quantities, and there are usually minimal side effects.

Homeopathy is a good treatment to explore for acute and chronic illnesses and can be used to assist the healing process after surgery or chemotherapy. I asked Dr. Moitreyee to continue with the homeopathy medicines I had given simultaneously with chemotherapy.

The entire family was in for a pleasant surprise when they saw the results after twenty one days, when they reported for the second cycle of chemotherapy at Bombay Hospital. After the clinical check-up, the doctor asked Dr. Moitreyee if the peritoneal fluid had been aspirated in between because there was no sign of any abdominal fluid, the peritoneal fluid had completely disappeared.

Dr. Moitreyee and her family's belief in homeopathy were further strengthened when I told them that I would give them the medicine to completely remove the hepatomegaly (2.3x3.0 cm sized hypo-dense area in the VI right lobe of the liver). Dr. Moitreyee was sincerely taking the medicines given to her and before her surgery she got a CT scan done and there was complete disbelief when the CT scan report showed that Yes, the cyst in the liver had disappeared completely.

I met Dr. Moitreyee only after her six cycles of chemotherapy and surgery was over. She was suffering from repeated UTI, antibiotics were not helping so she started with my medicines and was soon on the road of recovery.

However, Dr. Moitreyee was again struck with thyroid cancer and polyps in Gall bladder and after double surgery and her treatment with nuclear medicine she faced multitude of side effects but each one of these symptoms were addressed and now she stands completely cured. She is still continuing with her medicines to stop spreading of cancer cells but most of all she carries a positive attitude which helps in her cure.

I told Dr. Moitreyee that the study tells that the incidents of cancer are more in vegetarians. She and her husband were surprised and they refused to believe me. I told them that fish fat retards the growth of cancer cells and can possibly help in preventing the dreaded disease. This was according to a study at University of Oslo in Norway (Homeopathy Preventive medicine by Fredrick L. Compton).

—X—

ANNEX IN MEMOIR OF MY DAUGHTER, DR MOITREYEE SAHA

Sqn. Ldr. C. R. Saha (Retd)
(Father)

9*th* June 1963, a beautiful and lovely day! The day, Almighty poured down blessings onto our family; we, the proudest parents ever to be blessed with a daughter, an Angel to be nurtured and fathered; named instantly as 'Rina' ringing the bell of musical chord 'R' (Re) with Rana (Ashish) and Raja (Ujjal), brothers. "Moitreyee," the name came automatically later from the ancient treatises and philosophical literature of Yester-years. My sweet baby, Rina has been dancing, singing, laughing, and crying (scarcely though) in musical notes. Everything is musical about her. She is so special to us that even a fallen leaf on her cheek used to be an agony and pain to us all. She used to be a real diva; talk about music, dancing, fine-arts or studies, my Moitreyee" was in the forefront due to her pleasant attachment and regards with books and quality of perseverance. The thresholds of school/ college/ Universities were crossed by her with distinction and she oriented herself on her journey forward as an enlightened personality while being a well-disciplined learner all the way. She attained M.Phil soon, took just the time to become a Doctor in Botany like her husband, our beloved Son-in-law Dr B.G Saha, a Doctor in Chemistry. Dr. Moitreyee, my sweet little doll, now an Associate. Professor is obviously happy beyond bounds with her chosen career and due to her professed acumen to teach and learn under Mumbai University; so far so excellent!

Then a devastating storm came in our life. We came to know that our dearest daughter had become a victim of cancer.

It was a burning bolt from the blue which shattered our life. Pronouncement of the Medical Team confirmed the disease. I for one though a retired Service Officer, could perceive only darkness around and did not know how to face the truth. Family appeared to be totally lost and did not know what to do at least for some time.

Two years went past like two decades nurturing my poor child while uplifting her mental strength in particular, for her recovery. Doctors were no less than the Angels sent by the Lord, for the rescue of my child. In spite of assurance of the Doctors of Bombay Hospital we had been feeling some kind of vacuum within us and unsure of the future. A thought came sometimes to her poor parents that our pure, simple and religious child was possibly suffering only due to some sin committed by us. Why otherwise my dearest one had to suffer the way she was suffering.

During these years of sufferings of my dear child, one truth was established. My little Rina is a brave-heart and is in a position take on any adversary in her stride. We did know that my dearest one had the natural attribute of determination right from her childhood. Which used to be natural to her as observed throughout her life's journey. What we did not know that no adversity can beat her; a factor that nothing could beat my daughter as far as winning the goal is concerned. I have observed during these days of sufferings that my little one was full of determination to win the battle against Cancer but father has to be around. That she decided to come back and I wanted her to come back fully unscathed, was loud and clear to her and she achieved our goal.

I appeal to all who are fighting against this disease to be real Brave-hearts and wish them to win the battle.

We have really no words to extend our thanks to the doctors for their golden touch to bring back my little one safe and sound as a fully-recovered Dr. Moitreyee.

It was a scene to see when she went smiling and going around to meet the Doctors, Sisters and all staff who had been with her during sickness and partaking with her happiness now to bid 'Good bye'. Thanks to God almighty and to all those wonderful Hearts who were with us during those two years to make her stand on her two feet and start anew her professional life with the same vigor as before. God bless!

—X—

CROSSED THE HURDLES TOGETHER

Dr. Benu Gopal Saha
(Husband)

When my wife, Rina asked me to pen down my feelings it was like bringing back those horrifying memories which haunt me even today. To be honest I was a little hesitant, as writing about my feelings was like reliving the traumatic event. My hesitation was however momentary, Rina's positivity encouraged me to sit down to write from my heart.

When Rina decided to fulfil her dream to write a book we were overjoyed. When she disclosed that the book was on her cancer journey, we were taken aback. However when she explained that she would write every episode as it actually happened from the beginning to the day, she walked out of the hospital completely cured and also about holistic healing, we were proud of her.

Married to Rina was twenty five golden years of togetherness. With an all-rounder wife and two beautiful, meritorious, god gifted daughters, life was going pretty smoothly. When we celebrated our silver wedding anniversary on 29th May 2010, I complemented her, "Looks like we married just yesterday, how time flew by." Twenty five years of happy married life and our next goal was celebrating our Golden wedding anniversary.

And then all of a sudden it hit us. It hit us so bad that it shook us to the core. Horrendous Mumbai rain was drowning the city and it was also stopping Rina from going to the hospital for a check-up. She was suffering from severe abdominal cramps and at last when she did go the hospital, she was detected with the dreaded disease.

When I heard the cancer diagnosis, my heart sank; there was total chaos in my mind. I was devastated, how could this be? My thoughts were Ovarian Cancer! There must be some mistake in the preliminary reports. A healthy, sturdy lady with no major health problem diagnosed with Ovarian Cancer! It zapped me, how could such a dynamic person like her suffer from cancer? What about the symptoms. My mom suffered from cervical cancer and she showed plenty of symptoms.

A battery of test confirmed Ovarian Cancer! Remembering those days gives me the goose bumps. So the cancer journey started. Every cancer journey is unique. However, we decided to never leave Rina alone in her cancer journey. Every member of our family traversed the path ridden with hurdles trying to support her. She had her parents, our daughters Gargi and Nini and me always by her side. We felt her pain and she bore the pain stoically.

Rina was admitted in Bombay hospital for her treatment under Dr. Pratima Chipalkatti. The doctor decided to consult Dr. Prakash Patil and Dr. B.K. Smruti. When the doctors told me that Ovarian Cancer was at stage IV, I felt it was the dead end. How could I save my wife? I could see darkness, only darkness ahead. But then I heard Dr. Prakash Patil softly telling me not to worry, "Your wife will be alright." This one sentence gave me a ray of hope, strength and the belief that my beloved will be cured of cancer. I promised to give all my efforts to make Rina healthy again. All the time I was constantly praying to the Almighty God to help us to fight this difficult situation in our life. I thank my father-in-law and mother-in-law for their constant support. They helped me whether the storm. We had full faith in holistic healing, homeopathic medicine and felt that friends and colleagues helped her in this cancer journey.

Rina underwent 3 cycles of chemotherapy, a surgery and again 3 cycles of chemotherapy. I saw the independent smart dynamic lady turning her weakness into her strength as she tried innovative methods to overcome the side effect. She suffered her pain in silence and we admired her capacity to tolerate pain.

For a lady who rarely visited a hospital in the last 47 years, her life was now only about blood counts, medicines, chemotherapy, doctors and hospitals. Her positive attitude, strong will power and a determination to conquer all saw her through these tiring times. She was also highly disciplined and sensible throughout the treatment.

Her surgery lasted for a massive 5-6 hours. Later doctor told us due to metastasis of cancer "pan-hysterectomy, appendectomy and 4 layer of complete Omentectomy" was done. There was a time after the fifth chemo when we thought that we have lost her. There are nights when I wake up in cold sweat, the nightmares are troublesome but things are slowly returning to normal.

When recurrent UTI played havoc with her health, she was determined to not let UTI ruin her chances to get well. She decided to stop struggling and start living. She visited Pilani thrice and also her college once. She was progressing well when a chance checkup showed the presence of a nodule in the thyroid gland and polyp in Gall bladder. The cancer diagnosis this time was most disheartening. Thyroid Cancer! I lost hope but Gargi helped me to recover from the shock. Rina, the plucky lady underwent double surgery. Dr. Prakash Patil and Dr. M. K. Jadliwala took 9 and half hours and the operations were successful. She was then referred to Dr. B.A. Krishna who advised her for nuclear medicines. Rina joined college as doctor said that it was the best medicine for her. Rina, my brave wife is back to her old self, happy and confident to be a cancer survivor.

At this point I would like to thank all the people who have helped me directly and indirectly to overcome the difficult situation we faced.

—X—

LITTLE SISTER . . . RINA

Ashish Kumar Saha (Ashish-Da)
(Brother)

I thought I knew you for decades . . . but life has proved me wrong. I am fortunate to closely appreciate the new "Rina" after your date with Cancer. You were always an easy going, decent normal girl, beautiful, educated, well-bred and from a good family, married off to a nice guy. You developed to have good interpersonal skills thus building good relationships with one and all. You were honing up with age to be a good teacher with very high value systems.

Yes, you have been one whom the family was always proud of. This was the past. Your date with Cancer changed everything. Your date with cancer has taken you to through an experience which changed the basic fabric of your persona. The initial anxiety, pains, fear, non-stop thoughts and finally ecstasy you went through were telling on you.

Today in addition to love and affection, we look at you with awe and respect. I always knew you were a strong person, but frankly you zapped us. In times of pain the strength of silence was beyond my imagination. I remember watching your calm face when chemotherapy was administered. The small twitch of the vein on your temple could not hide the pains you were under. You have trespassed into the dark silent alleys of hallucination.

Self-confidence and courage had always been your forte. After six doses of chemotherapy and a major operation, you were telling the doctor . . . **Come on doctor, finish both the** *operations together* . . . *was like putting all brave men to shame. Benu and I objected to this, but you insisted. You were stronger than us. Bugs me, this is not the "Rina" I knew.*

When you suddenly see a rattlesnake near you, for sure your heart skips a beat. I shudder to think what must have been your mental status for that fraction of second when doctors told you the C—word. When I received your first call on this, I recollect I had said. **"It's a false call; we need to get other checks done."** *But your tone told it all. Internally you had already absorbed the initial hit. And you endured this all alone.*

Then started the two years turmoil, day after day, the mental agony of hospitals, tests, operations and medicines took its toll. But surprisingly you were still a bundle of confidence. Possibly it was the cool strength we got from our mother which took you through the toughest of times.

I must confess, even our mother gained from you, big time. She has also become stronger and firm. Good you rubbed against each other for quite some time. Your belief in God, confidence on family, will power, childlike exuberance, face book games etc. possibly made you stronger and positive.

I often wonder how you could be strong, soft, naïve, loving, pious, face book addict, a thinker, a good mother, wife . . . . all together at one time when you were fighting the battle for your life. You could not change what shall happen, but changed how you act on the face of it.

Yes your date with Cancer had made you a . . . Woman of Steel . . . Steel has got grit, character, is strong willed, and sure of itself. You have added tons of emotions to it. Your tone changed. Dada became Dadaa. You started looking at life better, and for a change you started feeling healthy. Reaching out lovingly, with very good sense of humor . . . Sister the transformation was magical.

You have become a stronger with a lot more emotions. The next generation shall look to you to emulate. "Deserving daughter to deserving parents . . . Steel of mother and Emotions of dad . . . Not bad."

Winston Churchill said . . . **"Attitude is a little thing which makes a big difference."**

Little sister . . . . Do you understand . . . You challenged Cancer . . . And you won hands off, coming out as a winner . . . a stronger person physically and mentally. Your hair is prettier than before. You look better, healthy and more beautiful than ever. I always loved you and shall love you always . . . Today I also respect you after your date with cancer.

Happy days are back again . . . Rise and Shine little sister . . . . And yes, write one more book . . . "A Date with Life."

—X—

A LIFE OF COURAGE AND INSPIRATION

Col. Sonali Ghosal Saha
(Sister-in-Law)

I am serving with Indian Army in the rank of Colonel. I was transferred from Guawahati (Assam) and was gearing myself for Mumbai . . . I joined my unit INHS ASVINI Colaba

Mumbai on 2nd September, 2010. After office hours on the same day, I got a call from my dearest sister-in-law that she felt a dull pain in her abdomen while taking lecture in college and had approached family physician for treatment. She was investigated which showed peritoneal fluid accumulated in peritoneal cavity. Little did I realize that this unusual occurrence would totally alter the course of her life? A series of tests confirmed that she is suffering from ovarian cancer.

The word cancer generally evokes a host of tumultuous feelings in us, the foremost being fear, panic and despair. Cancer is indiscriminate and is a life changing event for any victim, rich or poor. And here was my sister-in-law, she had faith, courage and confidence. She learnt to face life with optimism and a strong will.

Dr. Moitreyee Saha, my sister-in-law is associate professor in University of Mumbai. She is daughter of an officer in the Indian Air Force and wife of Dr. Benugopal Saha. They have two jewel daughters Gargi and Nini, doing excellent in their field. My sister-in-law was admitted in Bombay hospital and was diagnosed as ovarian cancer stage IV. Faith in God gave her the strength and confidence to face the crisis with will power. As per the protocol she had to undergo three cycle of chemotherapy then followed by surgery and again three cycle of chemo. During her treatment, her parents, husband and brothers bore the greatest brunt of the disease as it shattered them emotionally but they kept a brave front to give her the morale support. Her daughters were amazing. The younger one who had to appear for the HSC board exam had transformed into a mature girl. She handled her father's emotion and mother physical stress remarkably.

Our family and friends were always by her side with prayers and comforting words. This experience of her life made her realize the good will she had gathered throughout her life. The energy of the prayers of her well wishers played a great role in tiding over the trauma. It was clear in her mind that there is no point in running away from the situation. She had to face it and get over it. This was her mantra throughout her treatment. There were times when she asked me why it happened to her? But she always felt that God knew the best and he would help her tide over this period. She had unshakable faith in "Shirdi's Sāi Bābā" and had left everything on his hand. This gave her a strange confidence to battle the trauma.

She was fortunate to get the best treatment. She had full faith and confidence in the doctors who treated her. They were always ready with a cheerful response to her queries. Going through the chemotherapy was trying. The stark reality of the disease hits when she started losing her hair but slowly she got used to it. Problem comes in everyone's life. No one is without problem; if one had to be happy all the time then we would not value happiness.

Today, she has left the disease behind. But this disease has an uncanny knack of rearing its ugly head so she goes for her follow up without fail because however reluctant and confident, she cannot compromise there. In addition she has proper diet, goes for regular walks and Yoga has helped her considerably. Our life has now become a new normal again. It is just faith, hope and optimism in our family that has ferried us for better tomorrow. Above all the realization that nothing is in our hand, our life is moved by a destiny, over which we have no control.

My sister-in-law is the example of a brave heart. I salute my sister-in-law for her tremendous willpower and deep faith in God.

—X—

A NEW DAWN

Mr. Arun Saha
(Brother-in-law)

Dr. Benu Gopal Saha (Benu) is my wife Anupama's (Anu) brother. My introduction with my sister-in-law (Rina) started through a matrimonial correspondence for my brother-in-law, about three decades ago. With the responsibility solely lying on me, I and Anu met Rina and her family at Nasik and that set the foundation for a beautiful relationship. Three families A.K. Saha (Powai), Benu-Da (Shahad) and Sqd.Ldr. C.R. Saha (Nasik) were unified by the sacred thread of matrimony. I believe that—Marriages don't just happen, they are made in heaven and we are blessed to witness the union here. For us Benu-Da and Rina's marriage was a wonderful memorable event in our life and we cherish several unforgettable occasions we spent together thereafter.

Everything was going fine when suddenly a storm swept out all our happiness. There was a small hint from the doctor, she suggested that Rina might have been attacked by the dreaded disease. Initially like other family members, we could not accept the doctors diagnosis of cancer, however when series of tests confirmed it, we were heartbroken.

However there is this saying in Bengali—No one can be destroyed, if they have the will power, determination, and strength and over and above God's hand on her head.

Rina fought and won the battle over all odds, eventualities and pain. The tremendous mental agony by passed any bad dreams one has. I might be wrong but I want to say that there are very few fighters like Rina I have ever seen in my life. From her first to the last chemo she stayed positive.

Let me confess that after such a major surgery, when she was wheeled out of the operation theater in a stretcher, I expected her to be unconscious. But to my surprise I not only found her conscious with a pleasant smile on her face but she raised her hand to acknowledge my presence, when I wished her and indicated that all was well, the surgery was successful. After this incidence I understood the braveness of this brave lady and I was sure that one day she will surely come out of this mess.

I knew that the surgery was successful as the doctor has stressed that he had completely removed all the cancer cells. I had full faith on Dr. Patil and wanted to covey the same to Rina. Got the opportunity after few hours when I met her in the ICU.

During the two years of her cancer treatment we met several times. We rejoiced to see the positive attitude, strong will power the family possessed, as they united to face the calamity.

After two long year of cancer treatment we rejoiced to hear the doctor's verdict that Rina was cured of cancer. We met occasionally and today a year after her nuclear medicine treatment we have again gathered here in our house. Benu and Rina have come all the way from Shahad to Powai. No more pain, no after thoughts, no agony. Life has given all of us a reason to smile again.

—X—

MY RINKI

Ujjal K Saha
(Brother)

I saw you open your eyes in awe to this world and swore to protect you always . . .

Going back down memory lanes, meandering through the hazy bits and pieces, faces of my loved ones shine crisp and clear. Time fleets and lest I don't get a chance to say grace again, I take this moment to thank those beautiful souls, my Mom, Dad, Dada and my ever so beloved sis Rinki, for being everything for me, back there where it all started. Ashish-da was the sombre dark cumulonimbus that rained good times on us and our Rinki has been the sunshine of our growing years and although younger, she would always pull off the sensible and righteous, in every of the many predicaments I would find myself in. She always has been daddy's little girl and like him has been the gentle caring soul who made life so easy for us. Having said that I must however concede that I have no doubts that she is my mom personified when it comes to the strength of character, grit and focused determination that I have seen nowhere in any other human being.

I got the sordid mail one day in Johannesburg (S.A), which stated that Rinki was diagnosed with cancer and is under treatment. I felt a cold gloom spread across my chest slowly covering my entire being and a heart wrenching sadness paralyzing my innards. Those were the darkest moments of utter helplessness in my life and words fail to describe the desolation aptly. I closed my eyes and prayed looking for a divine intervention within this sordid mess in my head as the magnitude of the predicament slowly sunk in.

It was then that I felt a tingle in my heart and sublime warmth return deep inside and I knew in an instant that the gloom was am misbelieve and a blatant hoax, because Rinki would be fine, I believed it and knew that for sure. I called mom and told her, not to worry because Rinki would be fine and I so really believed it.

I called Rinki and said the same thing and told her that I would be taking the next flight out to her. She asked me not to come yet, because she was losing hair and did not want me to see her like that, my answer to her then was that "No matter what, Rinki you shall always be the prettiest girl to me". That statement shall always remain true to the best of my belief and understanding.

I had assigned myself the task of protecting Rinki, from the day that she was born and getting the news of her life threatening ailment had put my beliefs in the rationale and the logical order of things in a tizz, because Rinki equals life and she has everything to live for, because life rejoices in her and one has to meet her once to see and feel it.

I had whispered my silent "Savitannam" which in Armenian means "I take away your pain", and waited upon the divine intervention that absolved me of all worries because I knew for certain that tomorrow shall be hers. She would own the future and show us all that no odds can ever keep a good soul down.

The best part is that I knew for certain that she would overcome this ailment and given that, the rest was to undergo the very difficult phases of physical and psychological mandatory negotiations of the process of the cure.

Rinki is a beautiful soul, who has so much love and care to give in so many ways, to everyone who comes in touch with her. It was a dark cloud for sure, but I clearly saw the sun and her smile shine through even when the chips were down and I have never worried a single moment fearing the worst, because this ailment was much too sundry for Rinki to give in to. She has a long life to live and oodles of love to give and I wish her every good thing that life can bring about, because she truly deserves it.

You are a role model and a beacon hope for the many unfortunate who fight cancer, and may everyone emulate you and come out a winner.

—X—

KISS YOU BETTER

Gargi
(Daughter)

People have always called me my Father's girl and probably I am to a certain extent. However, people fail to realize that I actually am more like my Mother. Not only do I resemble the younger version of her but we also possess an astonishingly similar personality. But lately I have come to realize that I am nowhere close to her when it comes to the strength and courage that she embodies.

I idolize her in every way possible. Since childhood, I wanted to work like her, sing like her, dance like her, paint like her. I basically wanted to be like my mother . . . the woman, who juggled her career and her kids with utmost ease, poise and love. She was the star professor of her college and the star mom at home. God couldn't have blessed me and my sister with a better Ma (as we lovingly called her). But all of a sudden, our whole life came crashing down when we heard of her illness. The news left me shattered, in tears and pain which I still feel whenever I recall that moment.

Ma has always been an inspiration to me and she continues to inspire me every day. I have seen two versions of her. The Ma I knew before the illness and the one after recovery. I see a different version of her today. It's different because the pain and torment that she underwent somehow changed her for good. She became optimistic, determined and a brave lady who could face anything that came her way. I am not saying she wasn't positive before but suddenly for her life made more sense as she had to fight for hers, twice.

As a kid whenever I fell sick or got hurt, Ma used to tell me lovingly "KISS YOU BETTER" baby and give me a peck on the forehead or on the hurt and somehow all the pain would vanish. I felt amazing and wonderful after hearing those magically words and receiving the pure love's kiss. (Being a fan of fairytales while growing up, I knew only pure love's kiss could break any curse!).

Seeing her undergo chemo again and again was the toughest task, I had to do. And when it is your own mother, it's harder, because you don't want her to suffer. I used to say to myself, she is the one who has sacrificed her whole life for us. She doesn't deserve this pain. Then why would such a horrible thing happen to her. I felt her pain and agony. However, I couldn't do anything but pray for her wellbeing.

It was my turn to kiss her better. I knew in my heart that medicines were working. Nevertheless, I wanted to heal her with my thoughts and love. So, I took the help of my kind friend, Neelesh who taught me how I could do that. Sitting alone in my room in Hyderabad or at the temple, I used to often drift away in my thoughts where I imagined her hale and hearty, laughing and giggling, doing things that she loved. I used to imagine healing her. I thanked God a million times during the day, for her recovery. I realized the power of the phrase "Thank You". With gratitude and love in my heart, I sent her positive and healing thoughts. I kissed her better, everyday.

She overcame every hurdle of this illness with flying colors. Major one was the emotional trauma of hair loss. It's easy to say it's just hair. It will grow back! But only a woman knows how important her locks are to her. But there she was looking all cute in the yellow scarf I got her and those big beautiful eyes gleaming with high spirit. Even when her hands were sore with the injection piercings, she donned a big smile, giving us hope that everything is going to be alright. And I believed her. The way she interacted with the doctors immediately after gaining consciousness, asking about technical details of the surgery left me astounded. Only a woman with immense strength and faith could pull this off. My admiration for her grew every day of her struggle.

She had to make several life changing, mind boggling alterations in her lifestyle. To start with losing more than 12 kg of weight, I know how much she loves to eat and for a foodie like her to survive on bland food for the rest of her life was a herculean task. Ma has a sweet tooth and to think about quitting sweets forever especially for a hardcore Bengali, is just beyond difficult. Nevertheless, she was pretty successful in achieving all her goals. And I am extremely proud of her.

She has been my constant support system from kindergarten, till date. She is my greatest critique and my biggest fan. We both have this mysterious cosmic connection that is inexplicable and brings us close to each other. No one can take her place in my heart for she is one person I'll idolize till eternity.

In the end, I just want her to be happy and live a wholesome, positive and healthy life.

To my mother, my ultimate hero, I love you . . . always!

—X—

MY GULLI

Nini ☺
(Daughter)

My mother and I share a bond which is beyond comprehension to anyone possible. I always share each and every piece of information of my life with her. She listens to all of them painstakingly and laughs at all my antics. We talk in a language that nobody will dare to decipher. Often my sister gets furious, unable to understand this baby language. She is my biggest fan and loves to see me dance. She makes sure that whenever she's feeling low, I should entertain her with my chitchats and funny dances. My mother can recognize my happiness with just one look on my face. **Often I get scolded by others for disclosing everything to her which sometimes becomes stressful for her.** But then, I just can't stop narrating things to her . . .

Honestly, I don't remember my mother before cancer because the scarred memories are etched in my mind and fail to fade away. Before cancer, she was my mother. After cancer, she became my child. She was smart, stylish and beautiful before. She became cute and adorable later. Her wavy locks of hair got replaced by tiny unruly curls which made her even more childlike. Earlier, she used to juggle with her personal and professional life and still manage to smile; now she's learnt to take it easy and worry less. She used to take responsibility and teach me a lot of things. Now, she expects me to take care of her.

People say that I am a very strong person but whenever I see my mother, I melt and the feelings are mutual. I follow whatever she requests me to do, and if I beg to differ in some circumstances, I eventually end up doing what she wants, authoritative but yes, that's how it works!

The day she told me that she was detected with cancer, the whole world came crashing down for me. I cried my heart out thinking that she'll leave me forever. Yes, I know cancer is curable but at the age of 17, things like these don't register especially when it's your own mother. For days, I looked at her and tears welled up in my eyes. Later, I realized that my mom derives happiness from me and if I breakdown, she'll lose hope as well. And in no way I was going to let that happen. That was the last day I cried. A few came later when she was completely cured and they were definitely tears of joy.

She battled cancer not once, but twice. Those months of torment, felt as if they would never end. But eventually, she fought cancer with high spirits and emerged as a true winner of life. She is a true inspiration for me and my sister. I have seen her in the best and worst moments of her life and I am glad that I was there for my mom. Not many children in this world are lucky to get a chance to take care of their parents.

My mommy is the strongest! There's no doubt about it . . . . 6 chemotherapies, 3 major operations and, innumerable numbers of injections taken, countless visits to the hospital and the list goes on. She is the most important person in my life and she'll always be. I have been staying away from her for the past three years and I always make it a point to call her five times a day. Writing this piece is making me cry because I can see flashes of memories in front of my eyes.

To my mother, the most important part of my life . . . I love you and I am proud of you.

—X—

AUTHOR WITH HER FRIENDS

LADY WITH A GOLDEN HEART

Dr. V. M. Jamdhade
Asst. Proffessor
B.N. Bandodkar College, Thane
(Colleague)

You are a beautiful human being with a golden heart. Your life is a precious gift for all those who are associated with you and will be. So take care of your valuable life for your near and dear ones. You have always been there and will, always be needed in development of the younger generation.

—X—

VICTORY OVER CANCER

Mrs. Francena Luiz
Teacher
B.N. Bandodkar College, Thane
(Colleague)

Moitreyee, after the shock and turmoil of your encounter with cancer, I have had friends and family either succumbing to the disease or surviving the ordeal. Though I could empathize with their pain and plight, I found it easier to take the situation in my stride after the life shattering experience of your battle with cancer. The stunned disbelief when I first heard the bad news followed by sleepless nights of dread and despair was a nightmare. I shudder to think of. Those days, I could really bond with Dr. (Mrs.) Mulgaoankar and Dr. (Mrs.) Kalpana Phal, as we shared the same sentiment. Every time I met them my heart would skip a beat with apprehension. Both of them were my only link to you and talking to them and sharing our concern gave me a lot of solace.

Prayer is often our best and only refuge when faced with life's grim reality and Moitreyee I can honestly say that every word of prayer I uttered for you was wrung from the depths of my heart. I am very sure the experience must have been no different for all those near and dear to you. And Yes! . . . Your victory over cancer has only reinforced my belief in the miracle of prayer.

I was stunned as to how someone as active and exuberant could fall a victim of cancer. My shock turned to awe and wonder at the courage and fortitude you displayed to emerge the victor.

I remember anxiously waiting to see you when you came to the college in the month of April, 2012. As I watched you trudge up the stairs, your legs seems a bit weak but the spark f determination glittered in your eyes. I was convinced then of my gut feeling that cancer cannot kill your fighting spirit and you will catch the crab by its claws . . . so to speak . . . . and you did . . . . twice over . . .

Your grit and positive attitude impresses me no end Moitreyee. When I saw you at the IN-Orbit Mall, Vashi, I was choked for the want of words, when you spoke about another tryst with cancer and showed me the scar on your neck, I was dumbstruck . . . . you were so sportingly defiant . . . to such spirit . . . no wonder cancer took a bow.

The battle won, you bounced back to resume duty calm, confident and cheerful. You were perhaps a little frail physically but emotionally stronger and unscathed. Kudos to you Moitreyee—you are truly a women of substance and your cancer survival story is a testimony to your unshakable faith, invincible hope and extraordinary courage—truly a triumph of the human spirit.

—X—

A STANDING OVATION

Dr. Kalpana Phal
Associate Professor
B.N. Bandodkar College Thane
(Colleague)

A Sanskrit verse "समान शीले व्यसनेषु मैत्री" means those with similar nature, character and passion usually hang out together. Moitreyee and I have many things in common. We both have kids of similar age. We both joined the college in the same year. We have interest in good quality research. And apart from being caring and proud mothers, we still share many things in common.

One day, while discussing randomly about the health problems,—just one of our usual conversations, I asked Moitreyee to undergo thyroid test as she was showing similar symptoms as mine. Unfortunately, the reports confirmed hypothyroidism—which, yet again, became a common subject of discussion. Moitreyee was always one step ahead, updating herself with the information regarding different aliments, obtained from the internet. She used to surprise me with her all new facts and stories about which diet has how much iodine content and which is not good for hypothyroid patients and so on.

In the month of August 2010, as I was recovering from a shock of my close relative's fatal accident, Moitreyee's cancer news hit me. News was shocking and equally threatening. If a strong woman like Moitreyee becomes a victim of destiny, anyone and everyone in this world is vulnerable. By that time I had also started taking my Eltroxin, which I had never touched, although my thyroid was detected 15 years back.

Initially she was in a 'den', having cut the communication with the outside world. We used to get her health reports via Mrs. Mulgaonkar. I, Rachel and Francena felt bad for her and prayed to lord to see our colleague and a dear friend back with us. Whenever any of us got to know any minuscule news about Moitreyee's health, we used to exchange texts and emails. One day, after having waited for a very long time, Moitreyee called me up on my phone. I was glad to hear her voice and the tone of confidence in her. Even in that situation, she had a positive approach about life. She showed us a ray of hope, that she will soon join us for a cup of tea. From that moment on, I decided to talk about everything she was enthusiastic about, but about her health. We liked to discuss about new research. Apart from that, I became her "news person." We used to share all the activities right from University to the College department. But our main topic of discussion was 'the kids'. Although Moitreyee had a positive approach toward life, she was a bit depressed. Depressed, not because of cancer, but because Gauravi was in XII, a crucial year in one's career. But both daughters stood by her and became her motivation. And in addition to Moitreyee's determination though her health was not in good condition she had an urge to publish papers, doing something for which she always longed for. Looking at her confidence level, I was pretty sure that she will recover soon. With the will power, ever ending determination, love for the research and the power of the motherhood had *given her tremendous strength to ward off the evil. The reality had shaped up much better than the reel. For me Moitreyee is a modern Savitri, send to fight the destiny and the manner in which she fought surely deserves a standing ovation. The manner in which she fought would always be an inspiration for me.*

—X—

THE STRONGEST WOMAN I EVER MET

Ms. Snehal S. Phirke
(Research Student)

I am closely associated with Saha madam from 2007 when I did a M. Sc. Project under her since then I have worked under her guidance for a major research project.

Madam encouraged me to join for Ph.D. and we visited various institutes in Hyderabad for literature survey. After returning from Hyderabad, Madam and I were sitting and compiling the literature survey for my research work, it was monsoon period so it used to rain heavily but we spent almost six to ten hours together every day, working, I never found madam having any health related issues. Just the day before she got the investigations done, she complained of backache and told me that she will take leave for few days.

I was shocked when on teachers day I called to wish her and she told me, "Snehal, I have been diagnosed with ovarian cancer and now I am admitted in Bombay Hospital."

I was shaken, I could not believe it . . . I did not want to believe her but she told me, "Don't worry, I will be cured."

Her chemotherapy had started and when I used to visit her place to complete some pending college work or few formalities, she would not meet me as the W.B.C. count was low and she was prone to infection. I would talk to Dr. Saha Sir or Nini. It was only after her third chemo that she met me, she looked so pretty, her usual self, only that she wore a scarf, no one could make out that she was undergoing chemo and I felt that nothing will happen to her, she will be fine and come back strong as ever.

She started telling me that I should not waste time and first started coaxing me and then insisting that I should register for Ph.D. under some other guide but I refused because I wanted only her to be my guide and no one else. I was convinced that she will be fine.

Due to chemo effect madam was suffering from UTI and was admitted repeatedly in Century Rayon Hospital. I was the only person whom she would meet and was a source of information to college people. She was a voracious reader so I used to give her lots and lots of scientific papers to read.

I was getting married so I invited her for the marriage however she could not attend my marriage as she was diagnosed with cancer the second time. Madam got well and after two months I met her again and we started our work right from the first day she joined the college. I have almost finished my work. I am her first research student for Ph.D. I pray that our association continues for life and our bond stays strong as ever.

—X—

VIEWS ON RINA'S FIGHT AGAINST CANCER

Mr. Babji Choudhary
Senior Manager (Safety Dept.)
Century Rayon
(Friend)

It is always felt that an accident or untoward incident happens only to others. But, when it happens to someone close to you, the world shatters and you get into a phase of depression, frustration and grief. I went through this phase when suddenly we heard the news that our dear friend Rina has got cancer. The initial indicators were waived off with disbelief, doubting the integrity of the reports, of the tests carried out. But never-the-less, fear of the worst crept into us. Finally, when further diagnosis confirmed the news of the existence of ovarian cancer, our world turned upside down.

Talking to one another in whispering tones within our friends circle, it was clearly visible that everyone was in a state of shock. Finally, realization dawned on us that if such is our predicament then what could be the state through which Dr. Saha and Rina might be undergoing. Gathering courage, we started facing this lovely couple, consoling them in our own way and deciding on the future course of action. On meeting the couple after this news, though Dr. Saha was very tense as is obvious in such situations, it was observed that Rina was unbelievably cool, calm and composed.

The two yearlong battle with cancer started when we went to Bombay Hospital where she was admitted on 5ᵗʰ September, 2010 under the supervision of renowned Doctor, Dr. Pratima Chipalkatti and her numerous chemotherapy sessions began under the astute guidance of Oncologist Dr. B.K. Smruti after which she underwent her surgery under Dr. Prakash Patil and Dr. M. K. Jadliwala. Recalling this period, the chemotherapy sessions started showing signs of its side effects. The sweet natured, very charming Rina had lost her hairs and it was very sad to see her in this state, which was pretty unbelievable as I used to often tell her that she always reminded me of one of my favorite film actress—Shilpa Shetty (No jokes). Alka, my wife and I made it a ritual to visit them every Saturday. We were inspired by the strong will power of Nini and Rina's parents. The atmosphere there was always positive. Rina would meet us from distance and was always cheerful.

Later, after a year, it started again with a chance discovery. During a medical camp organized at Century Rayon Hospital for detection of Cancer, Rina was unfortunately again diagnosed with cancer, further investigation confirmed that it was thyroid cancer. The cycle of tension began all over again and Rina again underwent two surgeries at Bombay hospital and later was rushed to Pune for treatment of thyroid cancer with Nuclear medicines. The ordeal started all over again, grief and depression crept in the friend circle. Anguish due to helplessness was clearly seen in all of us.

It is said that . . . . **dava se jayada dua kam karti hai** (prayers work more than medicines) . . . though Rina was fighting this disease medically, all others were rendering their prayers in their own ways continuously. Rina's popularity could be seen by the large number of well-wishers, be it her students, her relatives or her friends with their continuous visits / messages and good wishes for early recovery.

When Dr. Krishna and Dr. Patil pronounced her cancer free, some of our colleagues Mr. G.D. Bhatta and close associates walked bare footed to Titwala temple (a distance of 13 Kms from Century Colony), to offer their prayers, to Lord Ganesha, for Rina's recovery.

Rina's zeal, courage, determination, willpower, dietary control and disciplined life during her recuperating period saw her beating all odds and coming out of it as a winner. It seemed like Rina was not fighting cancer but cancer was fighting her. Her insurmountable positive attitude and cool and calm temperament saw her coming out of her two year ordeal, defeating cancer successfully.

Rivers never reverses, so Rina try to live like a river, forget your past and focus on your future . . . .

With this, I on behalf of self and my wife Alka wish you a long, healthy, robust and energetic life, here on . . . .

—X—

MUSINGS : CANCER IS CURABLE

Mr. Ratanlal Sharma
Personal Manager
(Labour Office and Time Office)
Century Rayon

I served in Century Rayon for nearly forty years and now I have retired for more than thirteen years. I knew Dr. Benu Gopal Saha for more than two decades but I personally met Dr. Rina Saha in November 2013. That was the time I was diagnosed with cancer and I had finished my first cycle of chemotherapy. My daughter-in-law Vandhana Sharma is a close friend of Rina as they are active in social services and as members of Cenray Mahila Pragati. Vandhana is also a committee member and vice-chairman of Century Rayon club.

Rina would come to meet me and spend some time with me. She counseled me and explained about those little things which only a cancer patient knows. Rina explained how she was treated for cancer not once but twice and how she is fully cured now. She told me, "Uncle, you will be cured all you need is confidence and proper precautions during chemotherapy."

She told me that I have a strong will power, good doctors, love and support of my family members, what else did I need? I am almost cured and very soon will recover fully.

I liked her way of explaining things which has given me full strength and confidence. I am motivated. I feel that I will be cured of the disease. Yes, "Cancer is curable" I thank Dr. Rina Saha for her good wishes and bless her for a happy future and prosperous life.

—X—

INSPIRATIONAL QUOTES

Śrī Sāi Bābā of Shirdi (unknown-1918) Spiritual Master, Saint, Sadguru, Fakir and Avatar

- **"Why fear when I am here."**
- **"My eyes are ever on those who love me."**
- **"Saburi (Patience) ferries you across to the distant goal."**

Gautama Buddha (CIRCA 563 BC-483 BC) Founder of Buddhism

- **"All that we are is the result of what we have thought. The mind is everything. What we think, we become."**
- **"Let us rise up and be thankful, for if we didn't learn a lot today, at least we learned a little, and if we didn't learn a little, at least we didn't get sick, and if we got sick, at least we didn't die; so, let us all be thankful."**

Ramakrishna Paramahamsa (1836-1886) Hindu Sage and Priest of the Dakshineswar Kali temple

"Bondage is of the mind; freedom too is of the mind. If you say 'I am a free soul. I am a son of God who can bind me free you shall be."

Swami Vivekananda (1863-1902) Indian Hindu Monk, orator, writer and founder of Ramkrishna Math and Ramkrishna Mission

- **"Arise, awake and stop not till the goal is reached."**
- **"Never think there is anything impossible for the soul. It is the greatest hearsay to think so. If there is sin, this is the only sin to say that you are weak or others are weak."**

Mahatma Gandhi (1869-1948) Father of the Nation of India, Indian Political Leader and Freedom fighter

"Strength does not come from physical capacity. It comes from an indomitable will."

Rabindranath Tagore (1861-1941) Indian Poet, Writer, Composer, Essayist, Playwright, Painter and Nobel laureate

- **"Let us not pray to be sheltered from dangers but to be fearless when facing them."**
- **"I have become my own version of an optimist. If I can't make it through one door, I'll go through another door—or I'll make a door. Something terrific will come no matter how dark the present."**

Mother Teresa (1910-1997) Sister, Social worker and Nobel Laureate.

"I know God will not give me anything I can't handle. I just wish, He didn't trust me so much."

Jawaharlal Nehru (1889-1964) Political leader, Freedom fighter and First Prime Minister of India

- **"Facts are facts and will not disappear on account of your likes."**
- **"There is perhaps nothing so bad and so dangerous in life as fear."**

Paramahansa Yogananda (1893-1952) Indian Yogi, Guru and Introducer of Meditation and kriya Yoga to Westerners

"Forget the past, for it is gone from your domain! Forget the future, for it is beyond your reach! Control the present! Live supremely well now! This is the way of the wise . . ."

Hippocrates (CIRCA 460-CIRCA 370 BC) Ancient Greek Physician and Father of Western Medicine

"Let food be thy medicine and medicine be thy food."

"Natural forces within us are the true healers of diseases."

William Shakespeare (1564-1616) English Poet, Dramatist and Playwright

"To weep is to make less the depth of grief."

Charles Dickens (1812-1870) Writer

"We need never be ashamed of our tears."

Charles Darwin (1809-1882) English Naturalist and Geologist

"It is not the strongest of the species that survive or the most intelligent, but the one most responsive to change."

Bill Cosby American comedian, Television producer, Veteran stand-up performer, Author and Activist

"Through humor, you can soften some of the worst blows that life delivers. And once you find laughter, no matter how painful your situation might be, you can survive it."

Winston Churchill (1874-1965) British politicion, British Army Officer, Historian, Writer, Artist and Nobel Laureate

"Never, never, never, never ever give up!"

Albert Schweitzer (1875-1965) German French theologian, Organist, Physician, Medical missonary, Philosopher and Nobel Laureate

"At times our own light goes out and is rekindled by a spark from another person. Each one of us has cause to think with deep gratitude of those who have lighted the flame within us."

Dr. A.P.J. Abdul Kalam Missile man of India, Scientist and administrator who served as the 11th President of India

"One best book is equal to hundred good friends but one good friend is equal to a library."

Deepak Chopra Indian American Author, Holistic Health/ New Age Guru and Alternative Medicine Practitioner

- **"Every time you are tempted to react in the same old way, ask if you want to be a prisoner of past or a pioneer of the future."**

- **"See the world as if for the first time; see it through the eyes of a child, and you will suddenly find that you are free."**

Mid 13th century proverb
"If it were not for hope, the heart would break."

Late 14th century proverb, earlier in Latin
"A guilty conscience needs no accusers."

Mid 16th century proverb
"Hope for the best and prepare for the worst."
"The best doctors are Dr Diet, Dr Quiet, and Dr Merryman."

Early 19th century proverb
"Better be safe than sorry."
"Coming events casts their shadow before."

Indian proverb
"All the flowers of all the tomorrows are in the seeds of today."

POSTSCRIPT

A year has passed since I joined my college. The best thing in my cancer journey was to listen to the advice given by Dr. Prakash Patil and Dr. B.A. Krishna . . . "Join College." After joining college, there were few complications, usually faced by cancer survivors, but what Dr. Patil said, was indeed true . . . students and books were definitely the best medicine, for my progress towards good health. In the past year, fulfilling my duties in my personal and professional life kept me busy but I was never late for the follow-ups and I continued taking homeopathy medicines, prescribed by Dr. S.P. Bhattacherjee. Sorting all the notes written during my cancer journey and compiling it, took a year.

I lost weight and maintained myself at 58 kg. I carry my scars with dignity and pride as it reminds me that I am a cancer survivor. I have seen admiration, heard praise and words of encouragement from people, I met. Delivered lectures on holistic healing of cancer and to do my bit, counseled cancer patients there by trying to fulfil the dreams I dared to dream . . . slowly and steadily. I am ready to write few more books, a book on life, as my brother suggested or maybe a book on Genetics or Biotechnology.

I made many new friends . . . in hospital . . . Facebook and . . . anyone connected anyway with cancer . . . found a friend in me. For most patients, cancer is the most difficult and frightening experience. There is nothing fair about cancer and no one deserves to have it. I lost friends to cancer, Mrs. Jhunjhunwala, Mrs. Philipose (Principal, Century School), Mrs. Swamy (stayed in same building as mine), I also lost Sharma Uncle (who has written his musings in my book), my Facebook friend Dianne Clark . . . they were fighters, may their soul rest in peace. There are many, who are winners all the way . . . my friends . . . who in cancer journey . . . survived the scare. There are many who are still walking the path, I walked. I would like each one of my friends . . . to see the bright light in the end of the tunnel . . . have a strong will power, positive attitude and the tenacity to . . . get there.

OM SĀI RAM

GLOSSARY

2-D Echo	Two-directional Echocardiogram

A

Abdominal bloating	Abdomen (*belly*) feels full and tight. The abdomen may be visibly swollen.
Abdominal distention	Visible outward expansion beyond the normal girth of the stomach and waist.
Ablation	Removal of material from the surface of an object by vaporization, chipping or other erosive process.
Alopecia	Partial or complete absence of hair from the areas of the body where it normally grows. Baldness.
Anti-Emetic	A drug that is effective against vomiting and nausea.
Anulom Vilom	Alternative nostril breathing.
Appendectomy	Surgical removal of the appendix.
Ārati	A form of ceremonial adoration of a deity or a person with lamp, flowers and incense which may be accompanied with chants or music.
Ascites	Accumulation of fluid in the peritoneal cavity.
Aspiration	To draw in or out using a sucking motion.
Asthothram	A form of worship offered to the deity by reciting 108 names of a deity.
Aum	Same as Om
Auto-Rickshaws	Three wheeler public transport in many countries.
Avatār	Incarnation, appearance or manifestation of God.

B

Bābā	The Bengali word for Father
Balaji	Name for the Hindu deity Venkateswara, a form of Vishnu.

Bal-Gopāl	Baby Krishna. Childhood of Lord Krishna.
BARC	Bhabha Atomic Research Centre.
Bazaar	Market.
Bengali	Bengali or Bangla is an Eastern Indo-Aryan language native to the region of Eastern South Asia known as Bengal which comprises of West Bengal, parts of the Indian states of Tripura and Assam and present day Bangladesh.
Benign	In medical sense, not harmful in effect. A benign tumour lacks the ability to invade neighbouring tissues or metastasize.
Betā	Son.
Bhabhi	Brother's wife.
Bhagya	Fate, fortune or luck.
Bhākrī	Round flat unleavened bread coarser than roti prepared from the flour of Jowar, Bajri, Nachani etc.
Bhākta	A devotee
Bharata Natyam	A classical Indian dance form.
Bhog	Food offered to God before serving the devotees
Biotechnology	A branch of science which uses living systems or organisms to develop or make a useful product.
Birla Mandir	A Hindu temple constructed by Birla foundation.
Biryani	A rice based dish made with mutton, chicken, eggs, fish or vegetables and flavoured with different spices.
BITS	Birla Institute of Technology and Science.
BITSAT	Birla Institute of Technology and Science admission test.
Bitter-Gourd	Extremely bitter edible fruit called Karavella in Sanskrit.
Bloating	Become swollen.

C

CA125	CA125 is a protein that is a potential tumour marker or biomarker. CA stands for cancer antigen.

Cancer	A broad group of diseases involving unregulated cell growth. Cancer cells are able to invade other tissues and spread.
Cancer Antigen	Antigenic substances (*protein*) produced in the tumour cells and it triggers an immune response in the host.
Cannula	A thin tube inserted in the vein or body cavity to administer medicines or to drain off fluids to insert a surgical instrument.
Carboplatin	Cancer medicine that interferes with the growth and spread of cancer cells.
CBC	Complete blood count.
Cenray Mahila Pragati	A ladies club for the staff of Century Rayon Company.
Chaas	Buttermilk preparation from India.
Chapatti	Unleavened round flatbread also called Roti.
Chemo	Short form of Chemotherapy.
Chemotherapy	Any drug to treat any disease but to most it refers to the use of drugs for cancer treatment.
Chidiya Ud	Bird fly.
Cholecystectomy	Surgical removal of the gall bladder.
Cholecystitis	Inflammation of the gall bladder.
Chor	Thief
Communicable disease	Transmissible disease.
Cramps	Painful involuntary contraction of muscles.
S. creatinine	Produced by the metabolism of creatine and excreted in urine.
Crochet	Needlework using a hooked needle and a crochet thread.
CT Scan	Computerized tomography. Computer takes data from several X-ray images of structures inside the body and converts them into pictures on a monitor.
Cyst or Cystic lesion	A closed cavity or sac, having a definite membrane. It may contain gaseous, liquid or semisolid material.

Cytology	A branch of biology that deals with formation, structure and function of cells.

D

Dada	Respectful addressing of elder brother in Bengali.
Dahi-Handi	A joyous occasion in which youngsters make a human pyramid to reach an earthen pot containing butter, dry fruits and milk hung at a height and breaks it.
Dal	Split pulses, in particular lentils. A soup made from lentils.
Dalia	Broken wheat. Breakfast cereal made of whole wheat.
Dandiya	Traditional folk dance form of Vrindavan, India.
Darshan	An opportunity to see a holy person or the image of a diety.
Dhuni	Sacred fire
Dhyana	Meditation
Diaphragm	A dome-shaped muscular partition separating the thorax from the abdomen in mammals.
Dil	Heart
Diwali	Festival of light.
Durgā	Hindu Goddess of supreme power.
Durgā Puja	The worship of Durgā
Dwarkamai	Baba lived in his physical body for 60 years in a dilapidated old mosque in Shirdi which he called Dwarakamai.

E

ECG	Electrocardiography
Endophytic	A bacteria or fungus that lives within a plant for at least part of its life without causing any apparent disease.

F

Fakir	A religious ascetic who lives solely on alms
FNA	Fine needle aspiration.

FNAC	Fine needle aspiration cytology

G

Gall Bladder	A small organ which stores bile. It sits just beneath the liver.
Ganapati	A Hindu deity widely revered as God of wisdom and the remover of all obstacles. He is also called Ganesh, Vinayak or Vigneshwara.
Ganesh	A Hindu deity widely revered as God of wisdom and the remover of all obstacles. He is also called Ganapati, Vinayak or Vigneshwara. God with elephant's head.
Ganesh Chaturthi	Hindu festival to celebrate the birthday of lord Ganesha.
Gāyātri Mantra	A highly revered mantra, based on Vedic Sanskrit verse from a hymn of Rig Veda.
Genetics	The study of inheritance and the variation of inherited characteristics.
Gir Ke Sambhalna	Falling and to be on your feet again.
Guru	A Hindu spiritual teacher. An influential teacher.

H

Handi	Round vessel
Hanumān Chālīsā	Devotional hymn addressed to Hindu deity Hanumān.
Havan	Also called Yagna. It is a Vedic ritual in which people put on a fire in the center (*Havan Kund*) and make offerings along with chanting of mantras, mostly to please the lord and to achieve a certain objective.
Hemato-Oncologist	A doctor proficient in the diagnosis and management of blood disease, blood cancer and solid tumours etc.
Hepatomegaly	Abnormal enlargement of the liver.
Heterogeneous lesion	An abnormal area in which the texture or composition isn't the same throughout.
Histology	Study of the microscopic anatomy of cells and tissues of plants and animals.
Holi	A Hindu festival of colours celebrated in honour of Lord Krishna.

Holistic healing	It recognizes and heals the emotional, mental, spiritual and physical elements of the patient. It seeks to treat the imbalances and propagates to live a balanced life style.
Homeopathy	A system of complementary medicine which treats the patients with highly diluted substances with the aim of triggering the body's natural system of healing.
HSC	Higher Secondary School Certificate. Class XII.
Hypodense area	An area of tissue that is markedly different (*more black*) from the normal tissue when looked at on a computerized tomography (CT).
Hypomagnesaemia	Deficiency of magnesium in blood.
Hyponatremia	Low level of sodium in blood.
Hypothyroidism	Abnormally low activity of the thyroid gland.

I

I^{131}	Radioiodine, an important radioisotope of iodine.
ICU	Intensive Care Unit.
IIT—JEE	Indian Institute of Technology—Joint Entrance Examination.
Immune-response	The reaction of the cells and fluids of the body to the presence of a substance which is not recognized as a constituent of the body.
Isotopic	Variants of a particular chemical element.

J

Jowari	Sorghum or millet. It is grown for grains and also as fodder plant.
Jai	Victory

K

Karela	Bitter gourd
Kartikeya	Son of Goddess Durga
Kebabs	Meat, fish or vegetables roasted or grilled on a skewer or spit.

Kismat	Fate or destiny
Kripa Drishti	To favour
Kumkum	Vermillion

L

Langars	Common kitchen, the food served given to all regardless of caste or religion as a gesture of equality.
Laparoscopic	Minimum invasive surgery, keyhole surgery. A modern surgery technique in which the operation in the abdomen is performed through a small incision.
Lassi	A yogurt based savory drink
Laxmi	Hindu Goddess of wealth, prosperity, fortune and the embodiment of beauty.
Lesion	Any abnormality in the tissue of an organism usually caused by disease or a trauma.
Leukemia	A type of cancer of the blood or bone marrow.

M

Mā	Mother.
Mahārāja	King.
Malayalam	A language spoken in India, predominantly in the state of Kerala.
Malignancy	Often refers to cancer cells which have an ability to spread to other sites in the body.
Mammography	A diagnostic or screening tool using low energy X-ray to examine human breast.
Mandir	Temple.
Manipuri dance form	A classical dance form originating from Manipur, a North-Eastern state of India.
Mantra	Sacred verse or text from Vedas
Marker (*tumour*)	A substance that can be found in the body, usually in urine or blood for cancer diagnosis
Mataji	Mother.
Maya	The invisible, illusory or un-manifested and material world.

Memoir	A historical account written based on personal knowledge.
Menopause	The ceasing of menstruation.
Metastatic	The spread of cancer from one organ to another non-adjacent organ or part.
Moh	Love and affection to worldly things and relations.
Moong-Dal	Moong or mung bean also called green or golden gram native to India subcontinent.
Moushi	Aunty
MRI	Magnetic Resonance Imaging

N

Nachani	Finger millet or Ragi widely grown cereal grown in arid regions.
Nahi	No
Nām Smàraṇ	Chanting the name of God.
Navratri	A festival (*nine nights and ten days*) dedicated to the worship of the Hindu deity Durga.
Neoplasm	A new and abnormal growth of the tissue in a part of the body.
Nizams	Nizam-ul-Mulk of Hyderabad, popularly known as Nizam of Hyderabad was a former monarch of Hyderabad.
Nuclear Medicine	Application of radioactive substance in the diagnosis and treatment of disease.

O

Obesity	The state of being grossly fat or overweight
Om	The most sacred word of the Vedas also written as Aum.
Omentectomy	A procedure in which part or all of the abdominal lining (*omentum*) is removed
Onco	Relating to tumours
Oncogenes	A gene which under certain conditions can transform a cell into a tumour cell.

Oncologist	A medical doctor who specializes in diagnosis and treatment of cancer.
Oncology	The branch of Science that deals with tumours and cancer.
Onco-Surgeon (Surgical oncology)	A specialized area of oncology that engages surgeons in cure and management of cancer
Ovary	The female gonad, a pair of the reproductive glands in women.

P

Pan-Hysterectomy	Surgical removal of ovaries, uterus, oviduct, cervix and related lymph nodes.
Pap-Smear	Papanicolaou test for cervical screening to detect potential pre-cancerous and cancerous processes in the endo-cervical canal of the female reproductive system.
Paratracheal	Adjacent to the trachea.
Paya	Trotters or hoofs of goat or lamb
Peritoneal cavity	The fluid filled gap between the wall of the abdomen and the organs contained within the abdomen. A potential space between parietal and visceral peritoneum.
Peritoneal fluid	A liquid made in the abdominal cavity.
Prasad	Material substances such as food is given as religious offerings to God and then distribution of the same to the worshippers as Prasad.
Prophetess	Women who speaks by divine inspiration, interpreter through whom the will of God is expressed.
Puja	Worship

R

Radioiodine	I131 an important radioisotope of Iodine
Rāmāyana	A famous Hindu epic.
Ramleela	A Hindu religious festival depicting Rāma's life
Rangoli	Design drawn with lines and filled with coloured powder.

Reiki	Developed in 1922 by Japanese Buddhist Mikao Usui. It uses technique commonly called Palm-healing or hands-on-healing as a form of alternative medicine.
Retrosternal	Behind the breast bone
Rig Veda	An ancient Indian sacred collection of Vedic Sanskrit hymns.

S

Saburi	Patience and perseverance
Sadguru	Realized teacher and avatar, an incarnation. True teacher. One who dispels darkness called ignorance and lights the lamp od wisdom.
Sage	A person of profound wisdom.
Sāi	A protector, father or a religious teacher.
Sāi Bābā	A great spiritual leader
Sāi Bhakt	Sāi devotee
Sāi Mandir	Sāi temple
Sāi-astha-shatnamani (Asthothram)	A form of worship (*archana*) offered to Sāi Bābā by chanting his 108 names.
Sainath	God
Sañkalp	Dedicates, promises
Saraswati	The Hindu Goddess of Knowledge
Sari	Dress worn by Indian women
Sat	Truth/real
Savdhan	Attention
Seer	A person who can supposedly see into the future, prophet.
Shirdi	A small village in Kopargaon Taluka, in Ahmednagar district, Maharashtra.
Shraddha	Faith
SMS	Short message service
Śrī Satyanarayan puja	Worship of Lord Satyanarayan
Śrī Veṅkaṭēśwara (Veṅkaṭēśvara) Swami	A form of Hindu God Vishnu.

SSC	Secondary School Certificate.
Subcutaneous	Beneath the skin.
Swami	Respected Hindu guru

T

T3	Tri-Iodothyronine, is a form of thyroid hormone.
T4	Throxine, is a form of thyroid hormone.
Takleef	Trouble or pain
Taxol	A compound originally obtained from the bark of Pacific Yew tree, which has been found to inhibit the growth of some forms of cancer.
Temple	A building devoted for the worship of a God
Thamma	Grandmother.
Theek	Alright
TSH	Thyroid Stimulating Hormone.
Thyroidectomy	Surgical removal of all parts of the thyroid gland
Thyroxine	Main hormone produced by the thyroid gland.
Tirupati	Major pilgrimage in the Chittoor district of Andhra Pradesh in India.
Tumour	A swelling of a part of the body, generally without inflammation, caused by an abnormal growth of tissue, can be benign or malignant.

U

Udi	Holy ash from Baba's scared fire known as dhuni.
USG	Ultrasonography
UTI	Urinary tract infection.

V

Veda	Ancient holy scripture.
Vedic	Relating to Vedas.

W

W.B.C. Count	White blood cell count.

Y

Yagnas/Yagya	Sacrificial act or rite
Yew	A coniferous tree.
Yoga	Physical, mental and spiritual practices or disciplines which originated in ancient India to attain a state of permanent peace.